Edmund Spenser (*c*. 1552–99) conducted two careers at once: a celebrated poet, he also pursued a lifelong career as secretary to various political and ecclesiastical figures. Richard Rambuss' book explores how this latter career, usually allotted only cursory mention in accounts of Spenser's professional ambitions, informed his poetic career. Working from the fact that contemporary bureaucratic treatises defined the management of secrets as the central occupation of secretaryship, this study provides a careerist context for the attention to secrecy throughout Spenser's poetry. It takes issue with prevailing new historicist accounts which see Spenser's careerism as shaped entirely by a single-minded pursuit of laureateship along a Virgilian route from pastoral to epic. *Spenser's secret career* presents an alternative picture, arguing that for Spenser the manipulation of secrets – his own and others' – provided a strategy of self-promotion for both of his careers. In doing so, this study also considers secrecy in relation to Renaissance formations of power, gender, and subjecthood.

CAMBRIDGE STUDIES IN RENAISSANCE
LITERATURE AND CULTURE 3

Spenser's secret career

Cambridge Studies in Renaissance Literature and Culture

General Editor
STEPHEN ORGEL
Jackson Eli Reynolds Professor of Humanities, Stanford University

Editorial Board
Anne Barton, *University of Cambridge*
Jonathan Dollimore, *University of Sussex*
Marjorie Garber, *Harvard University*
Jonathan Goldberg, *The Johns Hopkins University*
Nancy Vickers, *University of Southern California*

The last twenty years have seen a broad and vital reinterpretation of the nature of literary texts, a move away from formalism to a sense of literature as an aspect of social, economic, political and cultural history. While the earliest New Historicist work was criticized for a narrow and anecdotal view of history, it also served as an important stimulus for post-structuralist, feminist, Marxist and psychoanalytic work, which in turn has increasingly informed and redirected it. Recent writing on the nature of representation, the historical construction of gender and of the concept of identity itself, on theatre as a political and economic phenomenon and on the ideologies of art generally, reveals the breadth of the field. *Cambridge Studies in Renaissance Literature and Culture* is designed to offer historically oriented studies of Renaissance literature and theatre which make use of the insights afforded by theoretical perspectives. The view of history envisioned is above all a view of our own history, a reading of the Renaissance for and from our own time.

Titles published

Drama and the market in the age of Shakespeare
DOUGLAS BRUSTER, University of Chicago

The Renaissance dialogue: literary dialogue in its social and political contexts, Castiglione to Galileo
VIRGINIA COX, University College London

Spenser's secret career
RICHARD RAMBUSS, Tulane University

Spenser's secret career

Richard Rambuss

Tulane University

CAMBRIDGE
UNIVERSITY PRESS

Published by the Press Syndicate of the University of Cambridge
The Pitt Building, Trumpington Street, Cambridge CB2 1RP
40 West 20th Street, New York, NY 10011–4211, USA
10 Stamford Road, Oakleigh, Victoria 3166, Australia

First published 1993

Printed in Great Britain at the University Press, Cambridge

A catalogue record for this book is available from the British Library

Library of Congress cataloguing in publication data
Rambuss, Richard.
Spenser's secret career / by Richard Rambuss.
     p.   cm. – (Cambridge studies in Renaissance literature and culture: 3)
Includes bibliographical references.
ISBN 0 521 41663 9 (hardback)
1. Spenser, Edmund, 1552?–1599 – Political and social views.
2. Literature and society – England – History – 16th century.
3. Poets, English – Early modern, 1500–1700 – Biography.
4. Courts and courtiers in literature. 5. Secretaries – England – Biography.
6. Secrecy in literature. I. Title. II. Series.
PR2367.P6R3 1993
821'.3 – dc20   92–8539   CIP
[B]

ISBN 0 521 41663 9 hardback

CE

For Charlie

Silence itself – the things one declines to say, or is forbidden to name, the discretion that is required between different speakers – is less the absolute limit of discourse, the other side from which it is separated by a strict boundary, than an element that functions alongside the things said, with them and in relation to them within over-all strategies. There is no binary division to be made between what one says and what one does not say; we must try to determine the different ways of not saying such things, how those who can and those who cannot speak of them are distributed, which type of discourse is authorized, or which form of discretion is required in either case. There is not one but many silences, and they are an integral part of the strategies that underlie and permeate discourses.

Michel Foucault, *The History of Sexuality*, Vol. 1

Contents

Illustrations

Acknowledgments

A number of friends and colleagues have been instrumental in the realization of *Spenser's Secret Career*. Among those who have read and
commented on it in its various stages are Julia Reinhard Lupton, Kim
Wheatley, Lindsay Kaplan, Margaret Russett, Elizabeth Mazzola, Allen
Frantzen, Jean Brink, James Carson, Marcie Frank, Elizabeth Renker,
Jennifer Clarvoe, and Orest Ranum. I found the encouragement, direction, and criticism they have provided to be invaluable. It can be no secret
that I have learned much from the galvanizing work on secrets and secret
subjects undertaken by both D. A. Miller and Eve Kosofsky Sedgwick. I
want to thank Stephen Orgel for his interest in and support of this project.
His incisive commentary guided me in determining the final shape of this
book. Special thanks to Kevin Taylor and Janet Banks of Cambridge
University Press for their care and assistance in preparing the manuscript
for publication. Many of the concerns of this book were hatched in an
exhilarating seminar on Spenser and sixteenth-century poetics conducted
by Jonathan Crewe at The Johns Hopkins University. Furthermore, he
read and commented on a number of drafts of the material presented here
with his characteristic intellectual generosity and virtuosity. To him I owe
a great deal – more than can be conveyed in any number of local citations.
But my greatest debt is to Jonathan Goldberg. First, I would like to
acknowledge the inspiration provided by the extraordinary body of
groundbreaking work on Spenser he has produced. More than that, I
want to thank him for the exacting and detailed commentary he provided
on successive versions of this project, as well as for the unstinting generosity, encouragement, and friendship he has afforded me at every turn. It
is no exaggeration to say that without him this book would not have been
written.

I am grateful for opportunities to present portions of this book to
audiences at The Johns Hopkins University, Kenyon College, Tulane
University, "Spenser at Kalamazoo" at Western Michigan University,
Rutgers University, and the 1991 Modern Language Association meeting
in San Francisco. Special thanks to William Oram. Grants from The

Johns Hopkins University and Kenyon College enabled me to complete my research. A shorter version of Chapter 2 has appeared in *ELH*, and I am grateful to The Johns Hopkins University Press for permission to reprint that material here.

Finally, I would like to thank my parents, Rosalie and Richard L. Rambuss. It gives me pleasure to acknowledge their love and support here. Charles Tonetti made the time spent writing this book a good deal more than interesting. This book is dedicated to him.

Abbreviations

EHR	*English Historical Review*
ELH	*English Literary History*
ELR	*English Literary Renaissance*
MP	*Modern Philology*
PMLA	*Publications of the Modern Language Association*
RES	*Review of English Studies*
SEL	*Studies in English Literature*
SP	*Studies in Philology*
SpStud	*Spenser Studies*
TSLL	*Texas Studies in Language and Literature*

Introduction

In *Positions* (1581), his collection of educational theorems, schoolmaster Richard Mulcaster offers this one on poetry:

For when the poetes write sadly and soberly, without counterfeating though they write in verse, yet they be no poetes in that kinde of their writing: *but where they couer a truth with a fabulous veele*, and resemble with alteration.[1]

Curiously, Mulcaster seems to be claiming here that what is most essentially poetic about poetry is neither its form nor its matter, but rather its production of a "fabulous veele," a mystified operation of covering up and secreting that privileges the latent over the manifest, the allegorical over the straightforwardly didactic. More than postulating a poetics of secrecy (in the sense that any number of other poetics could be imagined, such as, say, a poetics of power or a poetics of desire), Mulcaster insists that poetry is not poetry unless it constitutes – and is itself constituted by – a secret.

Mulcaster's dictum that secrecy, particularly in the discursive form of allegory, inheres in all poetry is fairly conventional in Elizabethan discussions of poesie. Thomas Nashe, for instance, conceives of poetry in the preface to *The Anatomie of Absurditie* (1589) as "the very same with Philosophy," except that the poet's practice is inherently "a more hidden & diuine kinde of Philosophy, enwrapped in blinde Fables and darke stories."[2] Similarly, George Chapman at the beginning of *Andromeda Liberata* (1614) contends that "Learning hath delighted from her Cradle to hide her selfe," and that the "misteries and allegorical fictions of Poesie" have always served Learning as a sort of "Hieroglyphickes" to "conceale, within the vtter barke ... some sappe of hidden Truth."[3] Chapman's remarks point beyond the seductiveness and aesthetic appeal of mystification (what is hidden appears to be both more desirable and more important) to its elitist social function. The operations of poetic hermeticism, that is, also function to close out an entire set of readers – those whom Chapman names "the base and prophane *Vulgare*, [Truth's] ancient enemies." Philip Sidney, though more wry in his endorsement of

1

this kind of Neo-Platonism, likewise builds a principle of social and intellectual exclusiveness (and exclusion) into his conception of poetic hermeticism. In his *Apology for Poetry* (published 1595), he declares that "there are many mysteries contained in Poetry, which of purpose were written darkly, lest by prophane wits it should be abused."[4]

These, too, are the terms used by Edmund Spenser, Mulcaster's best-known pupil, to describe *The Faerie Queene*. That poem, Spenser discloses in his "Letter of the Authors," is presented as "a continued Allegory, or darke conceit," which has "clowdily enwrapped" its moral and political precepts in "Allegoricall deuises."[5] Like his contemporaries, Spenser uses these veiling "deuices" as a decorous adornment for his poem. And also like them, no doubt his "darke conceits" serve at times (though Spenser doesn't say this) as a protective measure against possible censorship, as part of a cover of what Stephen Greenblatt has termed "deniability."[6]

Without desiring to neglect either of these two functions, however, my study looks to expand the context of Spenserian secrecy. I do so by considering Spenser's deployment of secrets and secrecy (not, as we shall see, necessarily the same thing) in relation to the poet's *other* career. For, in addition to his career as a national poet, Spenser also managed a relatively high-profile career as a secretary, his two-year tenure with Lord Grey in Ireland being only the best known in a succession of similar employments. I explore the ways Spenser's secretarial and bureaucratic career, which is usually allotted only cursory mention in accounts of his professional and social ambitions, coincides with and even informs his poetic career. In tracing the various ligatures between Spenser's two careers, I situate his poetic texts in relation to a developing Renaissance discourse on secretaryship, articulated in a variety of secretarial manuals, letterwriters, and bureaucratic treatises. Focusing in particular on Angel Day's *The English Secretary* (1586), a letterwriter that doubles as both a poetics and a proto-professional training manual for those who wanted to become secretaries, I show how contemporary discussions of the social and discursive practices of secretaryship, as well as the various subjectivity and power effects that accrue around it, intersect in identifiable and important ways with Spenser's poetic project.[7]

Secrecy is among the chief points of contact between those two careers. The *management* of secrets – protecting them, discovering them, even creating them – is closely bound up with Renaissance conceptions of the secretary's office. Angel Day, we shall see, points to a generative etymological linkage between *secretary* and *secret*. This derivation, I suggest, provides a professional context for the attention to secrets that is maintained throughout nearly all of Spenser's poetic texts and self-presentations – from the various ways he "secretly shadoweth himself" in the anonymously published *Shepheardes Calender*, to his circulation of exorbitant lists of texts he claims to have written but is withholding from publication, to the intimations in his published letters to Gabriel Harvey of secret meetings with the queen and covert commissions from the Earl of Leicester, to the extended "darke conceit" of *The Faerie Queene*. I examine how the various secret circuits of these texts – as well as the several *kinds* of secrets and secrecies Spenser manipulates in them, some of which are meant to be deciphered, while others are not – collude and compete with each other in his bids for patronage and employment both as a secretary (that is, as Day puts it, a repository for secrets), and as a poet whose texts are deliberately, theatrically, invested with the power of secrets known and sometimes uncovered.

D. A. Miller has suggested in *The Novel and the Police* that an analysis of the kinds of knowledge it is felt needful to veil in secrecy would tell us much about a given culture or historical period.[8] If, then, Spenser seems always to be intimating that he is covering a secret in (of? about? beside?) his text, *what is that secret*? Does it have to do with ambition, work, sex – the usual content of bourgeois concealings? Or is "the secret" something else?

As a way of approaching this question, let us return to Mulcaster's "position" on poetry and the hermeneutical problem it raises: "they be no poets in that kinde of their writing: but where they couer a truth with a fabulous veele." What is given priority in this formulation? Is it the actual *what* of the secret, its content? Or is it the allegorical veil that covers it?[9] In other words, do we first have a secret, a hidden signified that requires, as it enters into writing, a cover in order to protect it from penetration? Or does the veil itself, the operations of secrecy, come first? Is it that which is used to *make* a secret out of something that might otherwise be easily known? For Mulcaster, as well as for Spenser, I suggest that the latter expression comes closest to the mark. The unspecified "truths" Mulcaster refers to are not *a priori* secrets; they become such, become "secreted," in the text of the poet. What is inlayed in the text – and what Spenser's poetry insists on displaying at every turn – is not so much secrets, but *secrecy* itself.

Secrecy circulates through and traverses nearly all of Spenser's texts, and it provides the deep structure of those texts. It is the veil that hides (and makes) secrets – whether that veil actually covers knowledge of something, or whether it serves merely as a hollow shell – which creates the tableau for writing. There are, to be sure, "real" secrets veiled and on occasion revealed in the works and the career maneuverings I will discuss in the following pages: unspeakable aspirations for professional advancement; hidden desires; an unnamed (unnameable) beloved; a powerful patron's secret marriage; and so forth. But in addition to particular "secrets," this book is equally concerned with investigating the *forms* of secrecy and their interplay in Spenser's careerist negotiations, as well as in conceptions of subjecthood, gender, power, and writing in Spenser's texts and his culture.

Turning as it does on structures of concealment and disclosure, this book attempts, in short, to reopen the question of Spenser's career, to tell another story about that career. It does so by taking issue with prevailing new historicist accounts that regard Spenser's careerism as being shaped entirely by service to the court, and concurrent with this, as being dictated by a singleminded pursuit of laureateship along a Virgilian career trajectory from pastoral to epic. I show instead that Spenser's career goals are far more various and never strictly Virgilian. Moreover, I aim to show that his other career, the open secret of his secretaryship, signals a sustained engagement with forms of service and advancement other than the poetic. *Spenser's Secret Career* also takes issue with traditional conceptions of Spenserian secrecy as simply in the service of the higher knowledge of an hermetic poet.[10] Spenser's regular reliance on tropes of veiling and withholding, which an older school of criticism rightly identified as a central way in which meaning is deployed in his poetry, acquires a careerist resonance when read against the fact that Renaissance secretaries were thought of as repositories of secrets. The secrecy of Spenser's poems is thus redeployed both as an ever available strategy for self-promotion, as well as the way in which Spenser measures his distance from aristocratic and royal power.

1 Professional secrets

I believe I undertook amongst other things not to disclose any trade
secrets. Well, I am not going to.

Joseph Conrad, *Heart of Darkness*

In his important and influential book *Self-Crowned Laureates*, Richard
Helgerson contends that Spenser, and following him Jonson and Milton,
constituted themselves as poets laureate by programmatically, virtuosically, differing from the prevailing models for a literary career.[1] For
Spenser, this effort involved distinguishing himself from the poses of
amateurism and literary depreciation routinely struck by his contemporaries. Aristocrats such as Sidney and Harington, as well as writers of
humbler birth like Chapman and Greene, all routinely dismissed their
own verses as insignificant trifles and youthful distractions from the more
serious affairs of life. But Spenser, Helgerson argues, set out "to redefine
the limits of poetry, making it once again (if in England it ever had been) a
profession that might justifiably claim a man's life and not merely the
idleness or excess of his youth."[2] The price of such an ambitious agenda
was steep, however. In order to erect a platform of national importance
for his poetry and forge a claim on laureateship, Spenser, as Helgerson
sees it, had "publicly ... [to] abandon all social identity except that
conferred by his elected vocation." That is, only when he "ceased to be
Master Edmund Spenser of Merchant Taylors' School and Pembroke
College, Cambridge, and became Immeritô, Colin Cloute, the New
Poete" could Spenser garner the mantle of England's Virgil.[3]

Working from a dual perspective that takes into account the place of
the poems in a conspicuously managed literary career, as well as the
prevailing cultural conditions that shaped Renaissance literary production, Helgerson has provided one of the most fully developed
treatments of Spenser's major poems. Helgerson rightly emphasizes both
that the poet is always presenting and promoting himself along with his
text, and that literary authorship is itself a shiftingly delineated cultural
construct. Nonetheless, the influential narrative of the Spenserian career
that gets produced in *Self-Crowned Laureates* raises some serious

5

questions about the shape and the aims of Spenser's poetic production, questions which I will use as the launching point for advancing a rather different account of Spenser's career – or, more precisely, careers.

To begin with, it is not always apparent that there exists such a marked break between Spenser and his contemporaries in terms of how they publicly represented their literary endeavors. As late as the dedication to *Fowre Hymnes* (1596), to cite a single instance, we too find Spenser deprecating the first two hymns as trifles composed "in the greener times of my youth" (p. 586), and thus speaking in the same idiom of "prodigality" that Helgerson attributes to the Elizabethan amateurs from whom he wants to set his laureate apart. Nor does it now seem especially productive to take at face value (as Helgerson apparently does) the reiterative, mannered dismissals by Elizabethan writers of their literary efforts as no more than leisurely "toys." Critics such as Stephen Greenblatt, Louis Adrian Montrose, and Frank Whigham, who have taught us to ask not only what texts mean but also what they do – that is, by what operations they perform their cultural work – show convincingly that Renaissance *otium* was regularly *negotium* of the most serious proportions.[4]

Apart from these objections, one might still wonder exactly what it could mean for Spenser to have abandoned, as Helgerson maintains, any social identity apart from the laureate persona he is seen to be single-mindedly fashioning for himself. Not unlike the still prevailing cliché that Spenser is no less than – but also no more than – the "poet's poet,"[5] Helgerson's claim sounds like an endorsement of some version of poetic transcendency, of the belief that the greatest writers somehow must, or even can, detach themselves from their determining social and historical circumstances. Indeed, Helgerson approvingly cites Robert Durling's ecstatic verdict in *The Figure of the Poet in Renaissance Epic* that Spenser's poetic ambitions are justified by "the transcendency which spoke through him."[6] The uncritical echo of Durling aside, it may be that all Helgerson intends to do here is to signal that with Spenser we have an originative attempt by a Renaissance author to reshape his cultural conditions in such a way that they would allow for a separation of the literary as a domain apart: a version of poetic transcendency more akin to Ben Jonson's (ultimately deeply self-interested) proclamation in 1623 that Shakespeare is not of an age but for all time.[7] Yet even if we again hold at bay due skepticism about any poet's ability to achieve this kind of transhistorical ascendancy by insulating the literary from the impingements of other, more this-worldly interests and constraints, we still must ask whether or not this is in fact what Edmund Spenser did. To put it more simply: did Spenser maintain a public identity in addition to that of his self-presentation as "Englands Arch-Poet"?[8] Or was Spenser's poetic career his only career?

The answer, of course, is no. Spenser may have lived by his pen, but what he wrote wasn't always dictated by the muses of poetry. Practically from the time of his Cambridge graduation in 1576 to his death in 1599, Spenser made a living by means of a succession of administrative appointments and secretaryships, both private and civic. This is to say that he managed at once *two* public careers: one as a self-declared national poet, and the other as a relatively successful secretary and professional bureaucrat. The possibility of a singular career as a poet may never have occurred to him, and, given his social and financial ambitions, could hardly have had much appeal for him.[9] Yet nearly every critical account of Spenser's career has either absolutely privileged the poetic career over the secretarial one, or, as is most often the case, essentially ignored the latter career altogether.[10] By focusing primarily on *The Shepheardes Calender* and the initial framing of Spenser's career around his relations with the Earl of Leicester, I argue in this chapter and the next one for a resituation of Spenser and his various public self-presentations within the more complicated terrains of the "double career" in order to consider first how his literary performances give access to the ways his other career as a secretary was being pursued, and second how being a secretary informs the kinds of poems Spenser writes. Central to both of these questions, we shall see, is the matter of secrecy – of how and why Spenser recurrently deploys secrets, and how that secret deployment underwrites each of his careers.

Before we turn to the *Calender*, however, it might be useful to review Spenser's various secretaryships and bureaucratic offices.[11] According to Edward Phillips and Thomas Blount, two of his seventeenth-century biographers, Spenser first traveled to Ireland not in 1580 in the retinue of Lord Grey, but in 1577 as a secretary to Sir Henry Sidney, Philip's father and then Lord Deputy of Ireland.[12] Although some more recent biographical accounts have questioned the likelihood of this early Irish assignment, others have pointed to the purported eyewitness account in *A View of the Present State of Ireland* of a grisly 1577 scene of execution and cannibalism as corroboration that Spenser was indeed in Ireland at this time. If this first secretarial assignment in Ireland remains open to question, however, we do know that in 1578 Spenser secured the position of personal secretary to John Young, the Bishop of Rochester. This is an appointment that Spenser the poet publicizes in the "September" eclogue of *The Shepheardes Calender* when Colin Cloute is designated Roffy's (Rochester's) servingman, his "selfe boye" (176). Moreover, Spenser presented his friend Gabriel Harvey with a copy of *The Trauailer of James*

Turler (1575) bearing the inscription "*Ex dono Edmundi Spenseri, Episcopi Roffensis Secretarii. 1578.*"[13] The post was a good beginning for Spenser, and it should come as no surprise that he would want to publicize the position he had landed. Young's own career had been on the rise, and he had gained a promising succession of preferments, as well as a measure of fame from the opportunity to preach before the queen. Yet sometime during the next year, perhaps in search of an even better position, Spenser left Young's employment. His 1579–80 letters to Gabriel Harvey, published as "Three Proper and wittie, familiar Letters" and "Two Other very commendable Letters," place him at this time within the Leicester–Sidney circle and mention his attendance at court. One of these letters, ostentatiously addressed from "Leycester House. This 5 of October, 1579" (p. 638), suggests that Spenser had been able to secure some important place in the service of this powerful earl. That is certainly the impression Spenser intended to create when he refers in the same letter to his impending mission to France on confidential business for Leicester. Exactly what place Spenser occupied in Leicester House at this time is unknown, but a likely possibility is that he again held some kind of secretaryship, and in *The Ruines of Time* he renames himself Leicester's Colin Cloute, echoing and superseding Colin's nomination in *The Shepheardes Calender* as Roffy's boy.[14]

Spenser's next appointment came in the summer of 1580, when he left for Ireland to take up a new position as secretary to Lord Grey, the recently appointed Lord Deputy. Spenser held this post for two years, until Grey was recalled in September of 1582. His secretary did not accompany him back to England, however; instead, Spenser remained in Ireland, where he continued to acquire medium-level administrative positions and as much expropriate Irish land as he could. Ever watchful of opportunities for advancement, he had gained, even before Grey's departure, the additional office of Clerk in Chancery for Faculties. As holder of this fairly lucrative post, Spenser was responsible for the registration of licenses, dispensations, and grants under the authority of the Archbishop of Dublin.[15] Records show that Spenser was later appointed Commissioner of Musters in County Kildare in 1583 and 1584, prebendary of Effin in 1585, and, most importantly, Clerk of the Council of Munster in 1584. The latter office, which Spenser first held as deputy to his friend Lodowick Bryskett, entailed his attendance as secretary to both Sir John Norris, president of the Council, and to his brother Thomas, the Council's vice-president. Sometime in 1593 or 1594 Spenser sold his Munster clerkship. In 1598 he was nominated Sheriff of County Cork, "being a man endowed with good knowledge in learning, and not unskillful or without experience in the service of the wars."[16] Letters reported in the

Irish Calendars of State Papers indicate, however, that Spenser continued
in some capacity his service as secretary for the Norris brothers up until at
least a month before his death in January 1599.[17]

I have surveyed here what might be termed Spenser's "professional"
biography in order to challenge the view, explicit in Helgerson's account
and implicit in most others, that the only career Spenser had worth
considering was his poetic one, and that his administrative employment
was simply of (to use Helgerson's term) "minor" significance.[18]
Moreover, among Spenser's various bureaucratic appointments I have
emphasized his secretaryships and secretarial services for several reasons.
First, because Spenser began his career as a secretary, and from that point
on secretaryship constituted for him a relatively sustained profession to
be pursued alongside, and even in tandem with, his poetic endeavors.
Secondly, because it was a secretaryship that brought Spenser to Ireland,
his home for the last two decades of his life, and, once there, that
secretaryship which opened the doors for his accumulation of additional
offices and other marks of favor. And finally I have foregrounded Spenser
as secretary because, as I will discuss at length in Chapter 2, there are
significant points of contact to be mapped between the socio-rhetorical
formulations of Renaissance secretaryship, especially in its relation to the
handling of secrets, and the unfolding of Spenser's poetics as a constant
trafficking in secrets and structures of secrecy. Indeed, one of the principal claims of this study is that Spenser's vocational aspirations and
agendas as a poet are never cordoned off from his professional pursuit as
a secretary of office, status, and political influence.

"Ouerture" and "Couerture"

As a starting point let us consider the companion eclogues "June" and
"Julye" of *The Shepheardes Calender*, a work largely composed during
Spenser's employment as John Young's secretary. Both eclogues are
overtly careerist in topic and aim. "June" reflects chiefly on literary
vocation and the staging of Colin Cloute's poetic career: what kind of
poet should he set out to be? "Julye," on the other hand, attends to more
"professional" affairs, recounting in the form of a fable the advancement
in office and subsequent downfall of Edmund Grindal, Archbishop of
Canterbury and patron of Spenser's own employer at the time, John
Young. That "June" and "Julye" are to be read in tandem is suggested by
their parallel structuring around the topoi of hill and dale as allegories of
social position and positioning. These eclogues give us access to how
Spenser, at the beginning of his career, was negotiating his own place in
the world. Moreover, I want to suggest that the pairing of "June," with its

focus on poetic vocation, and "Julye," with its focus on professional place, exemplifies Spenser's own parallel pursuit of two careers.

Spenser's association with Young (and perhaps Grindal too) predates his secretaryship. Young had been master of Pembroke Hall during the poet's years at Cambridge, and he received his preferment as Bishop of Rochester shortly after Spenser took his degrees. Prior both to this appointment and to his term at Cambridge, Young served in London as a chaplain under Grindal, who was then Bishop of London and would in 1576 become Archbishop of Canterbury. Since 1577, however, Grindal had been suspended from his duties for his refusal to levy an across the board ban on the practice of "prophesying," a sort of *ex tempore* exegesis of biblical texts by common members of the congregation. Elizabeth wanted these unauthorized interpretive sessions suppressed on the grounds that they would open a forum for religious novelty and subversive political opinions among the "vulgar sort."[19] Though himself no radical religious reformer, the archbishop took a contrary position, and as a result, he was stripped of his civil jurisdiction in 1577 and sequestered. With the eclipse of Grindal's power and status, Young's own career seems to have stalled as well, and he never advanced beyond the Rochester bishopric. This incident would turn out to be only the first of several in which Spenser's employers, patrons, and means of access to the court were each in turn to suffer the loss of royal favor.

The account of the archbishop's career Spenser offers in "Julye" is sympathetic, but cautionary. Transparently veiling Grindal's name with the anagram "Algrin," the poem relates his sudden downfall as a fable about the dangers of prominence:

> He is a shepheard great in gree,
>   but hath bene long ypent.
> One daye he sat vpon a hyll,
>   (as now thou wouldest me:
> But I am taught by *Algrins* ill,
>   to loue the lowe degree.)
> For sitting so with bared scalpe,
>   an Eagle sored hye,
> That weening hys whyte head was chalke,
>   a shell fish downe let flye:
> She weend the shell fishe to haue broake,
>   but therewith bruzd his brayne,
> So now astonied with the stroke,
>   he lyes in lingring payne.

(215–228)

This fable is put in the mouth of the (too?) insistently humble shepherd Thomalin, who wields its violent conclusion as the clincher in his argument

IVNE.

1 "June" woodcut from *The Shepheardes Calender*, in Edmund Spenser, *Workes* (1611), p. 26.

IVLY.

2 "Julye" woodcut from *The Shepheardes Calender*, in Edmund Spenser, *Workes* (1611), p. 29.

with the eclogue's other speaker, the "proude and ambitious" Morrell. The woodcut situates Morrell atop a hill, and at the beginning of the eclogue he invites Thomalin to climb up with him "and learne to looke alofte" (see Plate 2). Citing the precariousness of the position, however, the wary Thomalin refuses:

> Ah God shield, man, that I should clime,
>   and learne to looke alofte,
> The reede is ryfe, that oftentime
>   great clymbers fall vnsoft.
> In the humble dales is footing fast,
>   the trode is not so tickle:
> And although one fall through heedlesse haste,
>   yet is his misse not mickle.
>
> (9–16)

Thomalin's response both inverts and complicates the conventional pastoral high/low topos the poem borrows from Mantuan and reapplies to social positioning. In his seventh and eighth eclogues Mantuan designates the mountains as the holiest of all places because they approach nearest to heaven. Spenser's "Julye," however, associates the hills not with godliness but with worldly advancement: "clymbe) spoken of Ambition," in E.K's laconic gloss (p. 446). Nonetheless, it is not a matter of the moral rectitude of ambitious "climbing" that disturbs Thomalin; it is the danger. The "humble dales" offer surer footing, Thomalin insists, though he admits that lowlanders are no less likely to fall on account of "heedlesse haste." It would seem then that no place in the social order, however high or low, is completely secure. But being toppled from a high place, Thomalin maintains, is far more disastrous than slipping on level ground. The "great clymbers" are the ones more liable to end up, like Algrin, "in lingring payne."

Rather quickly it becomes apparent that the debate staged between the two shepherds in "Julye" has little to do with lowliness and humility as commendable virtues for their own sake, or as attributes especially suited to those who would be pastors in an ecclesiastical capacity. Morrell indicates as much when he charges that Thomalin's real investment in lowliness has little to do with virtuousness; rather, it involves the maintenance of the ease and security of his present position: "Syker, thous but a laesie loord, / and rekes much of thy swinck" (33–34).[20] It is only fear, charges Morrell, that keeps Thomalin in the lowly dales: "For thy I wene thou be affrayd, / to climbe this hilles height" (70–71). And surprisingly Thomalin denies none of it, though his rejection of ambition is articulated in terms that go beyond acrophobia:

The rampant Lyon hunts he fast,
  with Dogge of noysome breath,
Whose balefull barking bringes in hast
  pyne, plagues, and dreery death.
Agaynst his cruell scorching heate
  where hast thou couerture?
The wastefull hylls vnto his threate
  is a playne ouerture.

(21–28)

Again the eclogue makes it clear that Thomalin's prediliction for the low-lands is not a sounding of pastoral humility. Ultimately, Thomalin refuses Morrell's "ouerture" only because it lacks "couerture" or cover – cover ·not only from the sun's scorching heat, but also, we may surmise, from its powers of unremitting scrutiny.[21] Social prominence, in short, entails a lack of good hiding places. For, to take the force of the pun here, being protected or covered also means knowing how to be *covert*, secretive.

"Julye" never quite delivers the straightforward ecclesiastical satire – "made in the honour and commendation of good shepheardes, and to the shame and disprayse of proude and ambitious Pastours" (p. 444) – promised by the "Argument" that prefaces the eclogue. This shortcoming is no doubt due to the poem's refusal to abide by that simplistic distinction between those who are "good" and those who are ambitious. While it is true that the highly-placed Algrin has been "shamed," even the lowly-minded Thomalin avoids condemning him for his careerist aspirations. Instead, Thomalin's fable boldly, outrageously, hints that the blame for this tragic downfall might be assigned as much to the misprision of a (female) eagle – who turns out to be anything but eagle-eyed in mistaking Algrin's head for chalk – as to the shepherd's prominent and vulnerable position. While reworking the familiar pastoral topos of high/low as ambivalence about *social* positioning, Spenser addresses in these terms what might be called the occupational hazards of professional ambition. Pastoral place becomes a figure in *The Shepheardes Calender* for real place in the social order. The "Julye" eclogue, though itself "covered" by the form of an ecclesiastical satire, is actually a complicated rehearsal and evaluation of the relative merits and perils associated with social promi-nence on one hand, and relative obscurity on the other. Lowland humility, though more secure, can mask laziness or passivity; climbing upwards is hazardous, but it also brings the greater rewards.[22]

This debate is brought no closer to a resolution by the end of the eclogue when both shepherds are assigned concluding mottos. Thoma-lin's motto "*In medio virtus*" is approvingly glossed by E.K. to mean that this shepherd has hymselfe sequestred from all ambition and also abhorring it in others of hys cote, he taketh occasion to prayse the meane and the lowly state, as that wherein there is safetie without feare, and quiet without danger, according to the saying of olde Philosophers, that vertue dwelleth in the middest. (p. 448)

Morrell, on the other hand, is given the motto "*In summo faelicitas*," which E.K. glosses this way:

[Whereto] Morrell replieth with continuance of the same Philosophers opinion, that albeit all bountye dwelleth in mediocritie, yet perfect felicitye dwelleth in supremacie. For they say, *and most true it is*, that happinesse is placed in the highest degree, so if any thing be higher or better, then that streight way ceaseth to be perfect happines. (ibid.; emphasis added)

The conflicting counsel of the two mottos is never reconciled, nor is one motto finally valorized over the other. The first advocates learning to be content with a social position that is "mean" (is this the Aristotelian middle, or the lowly?). The "safetie" of even this virtuous "mean" is compromised, however, by the eclogue's implicit, homophonic associ- ation of Thomalin's position in the "middest" with his dangerous "med- dling" in matters above his purview. "Harme may come of melling," he is warned while on the verge of relating his fable about Algrin: "Thou medlest more, then shall haue thanke" (208–209). The "olde Philoso- phers'" route from the mean to "felicitye" is distorted even further when we get to Morrell's motto in the recognition that such "felicitye" is related to virtue not at all; instead, "felicitye" is ultimately a function of one's standing in a hierarchy. The philosophers' "highest degree" is thus rendered inescapably social and competitive.

I want to suggest that the text's refusal to resolve the discrepancy between these mottos, the fact that it leaves their conflicting career counsel as an interpretive crux, signals an uncertainty on Spenser's part at the onset of his own career as a suitor for place and preferment. What place should *he* aim for? "Perfect happiness" seems to be available only to those who have managed to install themselves at this competitive "highest degree." At the same time, those in prominent positions, those who have put themselves forward, are more exposed, more vulnerable to censure. These aspirers are like the easily targetable Algrin, whose dramat- ic fall from royal favor taught the cautious Thomalin "to loue [the cover of] the lowe degree" (220). If the "Julye" eclogue ever does resolve itself into some kind of career lesson, that lesson would have to be – returning to the eclogue's structuring thematics of "ouerture" and "couerture" – that any overture, any opening for advancement, is to be pursued only insofar as it still affords the "climber" some kind of coverture. Accordingly, we shall find that in his own bids for preferment and patronage Spenser himself looked to perform nearly every career maneuver, and especially the most ambitious, under fairly deep cover. Often it was under the cover of secretaryship.

The terms of (c)overture apply no less forcefully to Spenser's poetic career. For another peculiarity of the presentation of "Julye" as an ecclesiastical satire is its strange conflation of the episcopal Algrin's demise with the legendary account of the death of the poet Aeschylus. Accorded the position of the founder of Greek drama, Aeschylus was, E.K. is there to remind us, likewise "brayned with a shellfishe" (p. 448). The mortal coincidence the eclogue stages between Algrin and Aeschylus may be indicative of an implicit rejection on Spenser's part of the vocation of dramatist as an "overexposed" career. The theatre would then constitute an overture consciously not pursued, one "too much in the sun." For unlike his contemporaries Gascoigne, Lodge, Lyly, Greene, Daniel, and even Sidney, Spenser apparently never wrote for the public or private stage.[23]

The question of just what *kind* of literary career Spenser then should choose is explicitly raised in "June," an eclogue which is charted with the same topography of hill and dale we find in "Julye." In "June" we hear that Colin Cloute is already an anxious climber of hills (see 1–19), as well as an "vnhappy man, whom cruell fate, / And angry Gods pursue from coste to coste" (14–15). The allusion in this eclogue to Aeneas and his epical search for the new Troy positions Colin within the trajectory of the Virgilian poetic career – a model, it is worth stressing from the onset, selected from a cultural repertoire of potential literary "careers," and one that Spenser will by no means unequivocally adhere to.[24] Even so, throughout *The Shepheardes Calender* Colin Cloute seems to be always already aiming beyond pastoral to epic, despite Hobbinol's urging in "June" that the poet forsake the hills and "to the dales resort" (21). The eclogue's woodcut depicts Colin's aspirations by showing him gesturing towards a palace located on a hilltop: a scene of looking away, that is, from the humble pastoral valleys and towards the court and the ostensible locus of career advancement (see Plate 1).

But just how far in the open is Colin Cloute, named by E.K. as the "Authour selfe" (p. 455), really willing to come? For along with his ambitious overture, we find him in "June" still seeking coverture by "pyping lowe in shade of lowly grove" (71), and thereby appearing to disavow public prominence and fame. Piping low and in the shade may indeed be the (hidden) master trope of *The Shepheardes Calender*. Yet even in this lowly and secret place Colin's ambitions are not wholly covered over. For he has assumed this station, we are told, in imitation of "The God of shepheards *Tityrus*" (81), a poet who managed from his place in the shade to be the "the soueraigne head / Of shepheards all" (83–84).

That this Tityrus is identified in E.K.'s gloss as Chaucer, *not* Virgil as we might have expected, complicates the question of models for Spenser's poetic career from the beginning of that career. Although I will take up that matter more fully in Chapter 3, it seems pertinent at this point to register two of the implications of Chaucer being brought forward in "June" as the primary model for "the new Poete." The first is that Chaucer, like Spenser, was a career bureaucrat in addition to being a poet – the father of English poetry himself thus being available as an exemplar for Spenser's own double career. The second is that the repeated invocations of Chaucer in *The Shepheardes Calender* remind us (against the overly streamlined accounts of Spenser's laureateship which currently hold the field) that he was not inaugurating his poetic career, despite the pastoral inception and the continual premonitions of an epic to come, with just a strictly Virgilian/imperial model. Hence, we find a regular reliance on doggerel (of which both Sidney and Jonson disapproved) in *The Shepheardes Calender* for the new poet's glorious entrance on the literary scene, and its evocation of Chaucer's own "Tale of Sir Thopas." The sense of a multiple poetic lineage is likewise pointed up both in Spenser's choice of the name Colin Cloute and in the *Calender*'s moral and satiric dimensions; together they signal a further opening up of poetic models and pedigrees for the inaugural shaping of Spenser's career, in this case in the direction of a Skeltonic complaint tradition.

We might begin to speculate, then, whether Spenser is drawn to the pastoral form at the beginning of his career less because it constitutes the proper Virgilian opening and more because it provides a suitable form of (c)overture for his incipient ambitions. In his letter to Harvey from Leicester House we find Spenser voicing related concerns about pastoral overture and coverture. There he worries about being too forward in his patronage maneuverings within the Leicester–Sidney circle: "I was minded for a while," he writes to his likewise place-hunting friend, "to haue intermitted the vttering of my writings: leaste by ouer-much cloying their noble eares, I should gather a contempt of my self, or else seeme rather for gaine and commoditie to doe it, for some sweetnesse that I haue already tasted" (p. 635). In particular, Spenser wonders aloud and in public whether he should take the bold step of dedicating *The Shepheardes Calender* to the Earl of Leicester (whose importance for that poem has been underplayed in readings of the *Calender* with a focus that is too narrowly regiocentric), or whether the work was "too base for his excellent Lordship ... or the matter not so weightie, that it should be offered to so weightie a Personage: or the like" (p. 635). Literary dedications in the Renaissance could indeed be touchy social matters, and in the same letter Spenser cites Stephen Gosson's presumptuous dedication of *The School of Abuse* to Philip Sidney as an embarrassing example of failing "to regarde aforehande the inclination and qualitie of him, to whome wee dedicate oure Bookes" (ibid.). Gosson, Spenser reports flatly, "was for hys labour scorned." At the same time, the letter reveals Spenser's reluctance *not* to make an overture "when occasion is so fairely offered of Estimation and Preferment." "For, whiles the yron is hote," he notes acting in the capacity of his own career counselor, "it is good striking." Spenser's solution, we may surmise, was indeed to offer the *Calender* to Leicester – or at least a fair amount of encomium to him in it, along with the evident display of Leicester's coat of arms in "October" and the suggestion in that eclogue of a forthcoming epic dedicated, not to Queen Elizabeth, but to this "worthy whome shee loueth best" (47) – yet to do so under the coverture of the title page's more modestly aimed dedication to Leicester's nephew, Philip Sidney.

But even if he sidestepped directly laying claim to Leicester's favors and patronage by means of a literary dedication, Spenser was never shy about publicizing his ties with the earl. Thus he uses his published letter to Harvey to herald his favored position, declaring – boasting – that "some sweetnesse . . . I haue already tasted" at the hands of this powerful patron. Similarly, looking back on this period in *The Ruines of Time* (1591), Spenser recalls how he "did goodnes by him [i.e., the earl] gaine" and how Leicester's "bounteous minde [he] did trie" (232, 233). The tone of these assertions in *The Ruines of Time* is disappointed and elegaic (Leicester had died some years before), but in 1579 Spenser was still full of hopes. Indeed, the letter to Harvey strikes its highest pitch of self-importance, of a career on the make, when Spenser informs Harvey (and the reading public) that he has been charged by Leicester with some continental mission and is "*mox in Gallias nauigaturi*" ("ready to sail for France") (p. 637). He expects to leave "the next weeke, if I can be dispatched of my Lorde. I goe thither, as sent by him, and maintained most what of him: and there am to employ my time, my body, my minde, to his Honours seruice" (p. 638).

The ostensible purpose of this planned trip to France most likely involved carrying letters, another duty regularly linked to secretaryship. But Spenser's grandly enunciated claims of placing "my time, my body, my minde" at his master's disposal seem designed to suggest that something more is at issue than a routine courier assignment. One possibility would be intelligence work, and it was not at all uncommon in the period for letter carriers, messengers, and, once again, secretaries to double as spies.[25] Philip Sidney, for example, was sent to the continent on an informal intelligence mission by the queen. As Elizabeth's ambassador, his official duties were to convey her grief on the death of the late emperor to the new Emperor Rudolf and his mother. On his way, Sidney was also to visit the Count Palatines Lewis and Casimir to "condole the death" of their father. However, Sidney's "Instructions" were quite clear, Malcolm William Wallace reports in his biography of Sidney, in indicating that the young envoy's chief responsibility was covertly to gather as much information as possible regarding current political affairs in the Empire and among the princes of Germany.[26]

No record exists of Spenser ever having been similarly commissioned by Elizabeth, though he does make a rather startling allusion to a possible meeting with her in his letter to Harvey. Apparently addressing his correspondent's desire to hear all details of this audience, Spenser dismisses out of hand Harvey's curiosity, enjoining that, "Your desire to hear of my late beeing with hir Maiestie, must dye in it selfe" (p. 635). Since gaining access to Elizabeth was, Robert Naunton tells us in *Fragmenta Regalia*, difficult if not virtually impossible to those who were "neither very well known nor a sworn servant to the Queen,"[27] most commentators have taken this as an admission on Spenser's part of some disappointed prospect. But he never actually admits as much, his disclaimer being framed in far more ambiguous, even enticing terms. Here we need to bear in mind that the Spenser–Harvey correspondence was not, despite the insistence of the volume's prefatory note to the contrary, an exchange of private letters between friends which serendipitously happened to find their way into the hands of an interested publisher. The appearance in print in 1580 of the "Three Proper, and wittie, familiar Letters," as well as the "Two Other very commendable Letters," was very much a career overture on the part of Harvey and Spenser, a purposeful venture of public advertisement to display the rhetorical facilities of the writers – their "ingenious deuising" in the volume's own terms (p. 610) – and to declare their rising fortunes. Read in this context, it is possible to see Spenser's absolute refusal to discuss a purported meeting with the queen – dismissed from the letter only after he has himself broached the topic – as a hint tantalizingly dropped that he really did have some business with her, and confidential business at that. That is, Spenser's stentorian silence on the subject has the quality of a self-promotional ploy, designed to create the impression that he knows something that is concealed, that he has a secret, and hence the importance of one who has a secret. As Eve Kosofsky Sedgwick (following Foucault) remarks in another, but not wholly unrelated context, a refusal to disclose can be as pointed and as performative as any outright revelation.[28] Here I want to suggest, in anticipation of the argument of Chapter 2, that Spenser's refusal to disclose can be read as a public assurance that he can keep secrets (like a trustworthy secretary), even when it entails withholding them in a friendship that would normatively operate as one in which secrets would be shared.

It is the pronounced display of secrecy, more than the historical fact of whether or not Spenser actually had an audience with the queen in 1579, that concerns me here. Apart from the account he provides in his letters to Harvey, we know little about Spenser's actual activities during the year before he left for Ireland. What does emerge from this period, however, are repeated intimations that Spenser had something to conceal, that he was involved in some secret intrigue or other. Harvey discloses as much in an unaddressed letter (another secret?) that appears in his *Letter-Book*:

And heare I will take the occasion to shewe you a peece of a letter that I lately receyvid from the Courte written by a frende of mine, that since a certain chaunce befallen unto him, *a secrett not to be revealid*, calleth himself Immeritô.[29]

The concurrence Harvey's letter posits here between this unspoken secret and the generation of the pseudonym "Immeritô" suggests that the scenario around Spenser's cover names may be more involved than the status Helgerson grants them as simply denoting the effacement of the poet's extra-poetic social or professional identity. Moreover, Harvey's intimation is followed up by a quotation from the very letter in which Spenser cryptically alludes to a meeting with the queen. Is, then, this "secrett not to be revealid" related to whether or not Spenser had an audience with Elizabeth, and, if he did, what was then said? That is, is Harvey referring to some secret which passed from Spenser to the queen?

Leicester's gnat

In order to carry my speculations further about this admittedly extravagant proposition, I want now to turn to *Virgils Gnat*, a poem Spenser included in his 1591 *Complaints* but probably wrote between 1579 and 1580 while he was still in Leicester's employment. A consideration of this poem in its context of Spenser's relations to Leicester, and of Leicester's relations to the court, can give more texture to Spenserian secrecy and its structures of coverture and overture. What we will find in *Virgils Gnat* (as we find throughout Spenser's career) is a constant transitivity between on the one hand maintaining the secrecy of a secret, and on the other inviting the secret's penetration by signalling its existence. For Spenser, that is, there never appears to be an absolutely binary opposition between keeping secrets and the many ways of giving them away. In *Virgils Gnat*, the result is a cover of secrecy that has become increasingly labile.

A close translation of the *Culex*, a poem thought to be written by Virgil in his youth (a beginning before the beginning of the *Eclogues*), *Virgils Gnat* is a fable about a well-meaning insect who stings a sleeping shepherd in the eyelid to wake and warn him about the approach of a menacing snake. The unlucky gnat is rewarded for its efforts by being swatted and killed. That night it appears to the shepherd in a dream, lamenting its confinement to the peripheries of Elysium, a place represented – in contrast to the gnat's own "arrested career"[30] – as one of satisfaction and completed destinies. The shepherd is moved by the gnat's "iust complaint" (629), and compensates it by providing a lavish burial and memorialization, thus, one supposes, entitling the gnat to his Elysian rewards.

The poem's headnote declares that it was "long since dedicated" to the now deceased Earl of Leicester, and Spenser, in the prefatory sonnet he attaches to *Virgils Gnat*, forthrightly names this "great Lord" as "the causer of my care" (2). But while this opening declaration suggests that Leicester should be identified with the negligent shepherd, the allegory of the poem that follows is far from transparent. Accordingly, Spenser refuses to specify what his "care" is, revealing only that it "may not be showen" (13), that it must remain secret. Moreover, he insists that the poem itself is for the earl's eyes only: "In clowdie teares my case I thus complaine / Vnto your selfe, that onely priuie are" (3–4). If Spenser really meant to exclude all readers from the poem apart from Leicester, however, what are we to make of his decision to publicize his private – indeed "secret" – complaint by publishing it even at this late date? For he certainly recognized the possibility that publication would open up the hermetic interpretive community of which he is now the only living member:

> But if that any *Oedipus* vnaware
> Shall chaunce through power of some diuining spright,
> To reade the secrete of this riddle rare,
> And knowe the purporte of my euill plight,
>   Let him rest pleased with his owne insight,
> Ne further seeke to glose vpon the text:
> For griefe enough it is to grieued wight
> To feele his fault, and not be further vext.

(5–12)

No place here for the likes of an E.K. But while Spenser plays the sphinx who would close us out of his text with a riddle, he is in the same gesture inviting us to become Oedipus and solve it. What is remarkable about these lines, in fact, is Spenser's implicit assumption that the "secrete of this riddle rare" can be known – is actually "easily knowen" (14), as he says several lines later; but also that the inevitable penetration of his secret must not, paradoxically, interfere with the business of keeping the secret a secret. In this way, Spenser fashions a privileged interpretive community around himself and his secret, all of which is predicated upon a logic of secrecy which recognizes that you do not have a secret if no one else knows you have it. The only way to constitute such a group of "secret-sharers" is to give away one's secret – or at least give away the secret that one has a secret, that one knows secrets.

What, then, is Spenser's open secret, the secret, he intimates, that was somehow responsible for his loss of favor with Leicester?[31] Many critics seem disposed to defer respectfully to the (at least ostensible) wish of the text *not* "to [be] glose[d] upon," including Harold Stein, who dismisses the question in no uncertain terms in *Studies in Spenser's Complaints*: "Spenser fell from grace in the years 1579–1580. Let us be satisfied with that."[32] But I propose, despite Stein's dismissal, to take up the invitation that is always the flipside of Spenser's ostentatious hermeticism by "glosing" this "riddle rare" in terms of the intrigue surrounding Leicester's own infamous secret. I am referring, of course, to the earl's 1578 marriage to Lettice Knollys, the widow of the first Earl of Essex and second cousin to Elizabeth. Their marriage was kept hidden (at least from the queen) for more than a year, though court gossip had linked them as lovers as far back as 1565, when she and the soon-to-be Earl of Essex were still newlyweds. It was even alleged that the countess had two children by Leicester during the years her husband was away serving in Ireland as Lord Deputy. These rumors may have been unfounded, but Leicester stirred up talk again in 1575 when, upon Essex's recall to England, he too vehemently urged that his lover's husband immediately be returned to Ireland. Essex was sent back in 1576, only to be taken ill by a violent case of dysentery and thereafter die. It was whispered about that Leicester had Essex poisoned, but a post-mortem uncovered no evidence of foul play. (Whether it helped matters that the inquest was conducted by Sir Henry Sidney, Leicester's brother-in-law, we do not know.) With Essex gone, Leicester and the countess, despite the murmurs of adultery and murder, could now indulge their mutual desires legally, if no less covertly.

Where does Spenser fit in all this? Perhaps nowhere. But is it possible that he may have been the means by which Leicester's own "cover" was undone, allowing the queen to learn that the man she once loved (or at least may have married) had long since given himself to a cousin she was well known to have disliked? In posing these questions, I want to stress my intention to keep a metadiscursive distance while pursuing this line of speculation. That is, I am less intent upon finally determining the factuality of Spenser's involvement in these affairs than I am in indicating the scope of potentialities that arises from his and Harvey's complementary deployment of secrecy and court intrigue in 1579.

Implicating Spenser in the disclosure of Leicester's secret is only a conjecture, but there does seem to be some circumstantial evidence to place him around the court when the secret was uncovered. The context is the proposed match between Elizabeth and the French (and Catholic) Duc d'Alençon. In the summer of 1579 Alençon sent a special ambassador, Jean de Simier, to England to further the marriage negotiations. Leicester was, not unexpectedly, at the fore of the opposition to the marriage, and the earl was taken on by Simier as something of a personal enemy. For a time, it appeared that Simier was succeeding and that England would indeed have a king at last. Given the high stakes involved, the French match was the subject of constant, anxious debate in the Privy Council, particularly between the days of October 2 and 8. Sometime during this period the queen was informed of Leicester's marriage.[33] She is reported to have been furious at the thought of the earl openly opposing her marriage all the while secretly enjoying his own. The result was Leicester's temporary banishment from the court and very nearly a trip to the Tower as well. It has been widely surmised that Simier was the whistle-blower, using Leicester's "secret" as a means to disgrace the earl and thus possibly minimize the effects of his opposition to Simier's attempted royal matchmaking.

Assuming that this account is right, how did Simier come to learn Leicester's secret? Curiously, the portion of the letter to Harvey in which Spenser broaches the subject of his meeting with the queen was penned from Westminster on October 15, within days of Elizabeth's discovery of Leicester's secret marriage. Could Spenser have played some part in this disclosure? Was he called into court in order to tell Elizabeth the secret? Or, perhaps more feasible, was he the means by which Simier, who then in turn informed the queen, first became acquainted with Leicester's private affairs? Is Spenser's secret – which he claims in *Virgils Gnat* "may not be showen" – the secret that he disclosed Leicester's secret?

The exorbitant scenario I have been suggesting makes Spenser something of a double agent: on the one hand, packed and ready to be sent by Leicester on a confidential mission to France, and, on the other hand, giving away his master's secrets to either a disapproving queen or an adversarial Simier. While such a possibility is not unthinkable, it does not seem very likely. It *is* thinkable only insofar as Spenser's theatrical manipulations of secrecy, which are designed both to cover up and to call attention to his (secret) relations with these powerful figures, open a blank space within which all sorts of dissimulative schemes might be inscribed. At the same time, the double agent plot is unlikely for the reason that Spenser probably would not have done anything, at least purposefully, to jeopardize his own advancement by disgracing or crossing the powerful earl he had just claimed as his new patron. It is also most unlikely inasmuch as it makes the twenty-seven-year-old Spenser seem a more important player in the affairs of the court than he probably was – a ploy which may of course have been the very point to all his and Harvey's secret intimations all along.

Yet even if Spenser did not double-cross Leicester by giving away the earl's secret to the queen in October, he did give it away in March – that is, in the "March" eclogue of *The Shepheardes Calender*, which was entered for publication in 1579, but probably circulated in manuscript sometime before that. In this eclogue two shepherds, Willye and Thomalin, wonder what is responsible for arousing "lustie Love" after his long hibernation. Thomalin, by whom is meant according to the eclogue's Argument "some secrete freend" (p. 428), inquires:

> How kenst thou, that he is awoke?
> Or hast thy selfe his slomber broke?
> Or made preuie to the same?

> (28–30)

Rephrased in less (but not much less) guarded terms, Thomalin appears to be asking if his friend has lately heard of any secret love affairs – a patent invitation to gossip. Ironically, Thomalin himself had already answered this question with his proposal to

> sporten in delight,
> And learne with Lettice to wexe light,
> That scornefully lookes askaunce.

> (19–21)

This is, of course, precisely what Leicester was doing with his own Lettice, though it is hardly likely that he would have wanted his doings publicized in this way.

E.K. is there to provide a screen for this potentially scandalous disclosure, however, and his abbreviated, single-line gloss on the name "Lettice" offers an instructive example of how one version of encryptment operates in Spenser's poetry. By indicating that "Lettice" is "the name of some country lasse" (p. 430), E.K. is able to address two audiences at once. Those "insiders" who already know the "secret" would be able to discern in his gloss a further reference to the former Countess of Essex and now Countess of Leicester. She had indeed become something of a "country lasse," then being in hiding in the country and afraid to show her face at court.[34] But to those on the "outside," to those who do not know the secret, E.K.'s non-committal gloss seems designed to deflect any interpretive impulse towards decoding a real person behind this a little too uncommon pastoral name: Lettice is any country girl, or none at all. The gloss would thus let Spenser have it both ways: the allusion to the secret is easily decipherable by the "right" readers and opaque to everyone else. In this way, to adapt the terms of Jonathan Crewe's provocative discussion in *Hidden Designs* of Sidney's sonnets as encrypted poems, secrecy functions to affirm the hermetic solidarity of a particular community (whether an extended family, a court, or a political faction), while further excluding the excluded, who may not even know they are being excluded.[35] Spenser's brash revealing and reveiling of his master's secret could be seen, then, as an attempt to enlist himself more securely in the Leicester party. He is one of them: he shows he knows – and "keeps" – the secret.

Still another way of reading Spenser's too bold naming of Leicester's new bride in "March" – a way that would allow us to link this moment more closely to *Virgils Gnat* and the sting in that poem which warns the careless shepherd of approaching danger – is to take that eclogue as another of the *Calender*'s cautionary fables. One of the concluding emblems in "March" registers the difficulty of loving wisely: "To be wise and eke to loue, / Is graunted scarce to God aboue" (119–120). Loving wisely, as we have noted, did not appear to be something the earl had been doing. And loving wisely in this eclogue means, among other things, being aware that inquisitive "shepherds" are always following Cupid around, "spying" on him (31) and "peeping close" (73) into his doings. The "preuie" marks of love (30) hardly ever remain privy. Furthermore, the gossipy exchange between the shepherds is a reminder that people do talk and do name names – in this case, the name of "Lettice." The public naming of Lettice may thus be Spenser's means of cautioning Leicester, under the cover of doggerel and bucolic frivolity to be sure, about the impossibility of keeping his private "sporting" a secret. Is this the warning sting in the eyelid which Spenser gave his master? Is Spenser telling Leicester that the secret is in danger of being found out, or that it has already been found out?

However we construe Spenser's intentions in deploying Leicester's secret in this fashion – that is, whether as a means to enroll himself in the company of privileged insiders, or as a means to alert the earl about the dangers of outsiders uncovering the secret, or, most likely, as a combination of both these motives – the danger of such open trafficking in secrets has to be acknowledged. For the handling of someone else's secrets always entails the possibility that the attempt to show oneself to be an insider can come across more as a threat, or as at least an unwelcome reminder, that as an assertion of complicity. And furthermore what kind of secretary is it that ever reveals, even if in an obscured form, his master's secrets?

Profession and vocation

These problems no doubt bear on the fact that by the summer of 1580 Spenser was out of Leicester House and on his way to Ireland as the new Lord Deputy's secretary – an appointment that has been variously interpreted as rebuke and as reward. Thus were answered the grand hopes of being sent overseas which Spenser had expressed in the previous year to Harvey. Instead of touring France, he found himself commissioned to a country that fiercely resisted the colonial government of which he was now a bureaucratic representative. Even so, Ireland did afford Spenser with opportunities for career advancement he never seems to have found in England. The Calendar of Irish State Papers and other records indicate that during the two years he spent as Grey's secretary, Spenser collected, in addition to other local administrative posts, a substantial amount of real estate, expropriated from Irish rebels and distributed by Grey to his servants and supporters. Spenser's university degree had already earned him the status of gentleman, but he became a member of the landed gentry by virtue of the property he acquired in Ireland. In 1590 he gained the patent to New Abbey, a former monastery in County Kildare, along with a plantation of 3,000 acres in the Munster resettlement scheme. Spenser may always have hoped for a corresponding degree of advancement back in England but it never came. Although the Munster plantation scheme failed disastrously in the end, Spenser's Irish career as a secretary and public official was successful enough for him to make the island his permanent home. Ruth Mohr speculates that, had Spenser lived long enough to be installed in the office of Sheriff of County Cork to which he had been nominated, and had he continued to rise in the government of Ireland, he may very well have gained a knighthood.[36]

But what about his other career, the literary one? Although we know that Spenser was working on The Faerie Queene, a project begun even before he left for Ireland, he published nothing for more than a decade. In the Envoy to The Shepheardes Calender he promised to "send more after thee" (p. 416), but this pledge was answered only by the issuings of the second (1581) and the third (1586) editions of his inaugural volume of poetry. England's "new Poete" seemed to have vanished from the public literary scene almost as soon as he was introduced. This disappearing act may be related to the anxiety Spenser expressed in The Shepheardes Calender about finding a place for his "pierlesse Poesye" ("October," 79), as well as to Colin's repeated breaking of his pipes – a gesture that looks as if it signals the frustrated conclusion of a poetic career rather than its inception. But Spenser's absence from the literary scene may also be an indication that his poetic vocation was for a time subordinated to his duties as a bureaucrat. That he was willing to align his priorities this way is indicated in the letter to Harvey:

I was minded also to haue sent you some English verses: or Rhymes, for a farewell: but by my Troth, I haue no spare time in the world, to thinke upon such Toyes, that you knowe will demaund a freer head, than mine is presently. (p. 638)

Such a prioritization of administrative duties over poetic aspirations may have been the case once again during Spenser's demanding secretaryship under Lord Grey.

As if in compensation for his lack of literary publication in the 1580s, numerous letters written during these years in Spenser's distinctive secretary hand have been found, as well as others not penned by him, but which he addressed. The general substance of these letters is fairly consistent. Many are responses to the discouraging complaints of Burghley and the queen that Grey's Irish policies were excessively brutal – and too expensive to boot. The letters also make regular requests for still more troops, and for more victual and pay to sustain them. As Grey's tenure in Ireland drew on, the letters express increasingly urgent petitions for his recall to England and his discharge from the seemingly impossible state of affairs that was Ireland under English rule in the 1580s and 1590s.

Also worth mention are the letters turned up by H. R. Plomer in the Irish Public Records Office signed, "*copia vera, Exr. Ed. Spenser, Secretary to the L. Grey, L. Deputy here.*"[37] Plomer's findings confirm that Spenser was Grey's *chief* secretary, responsible for writing many of the most important communiqués himself, as well as for examining and endorsing those transcribed by other clerks. We also know from contemporary bureaucratic records that, in addition to writing, copying, and dispatching letters, the task of paying spies was numbered among Spenser's duties. The picture that comes into focus here from these records, and from Spenser's *A View of the Present State of Ireland*, is in decided contrast to our notion of a secretary as someone who stays back at the office behind a desk. Spenser seems to be constantly at his master's side, both in Dublin at parliamentary sessions and in the field on military expeditions. And he managed to keep himself in the thick of Irish politics after Grey's recall by seeking out and gaining further appointments.

In sum, we have seen that Spenser never relinquished his secretarial career for an exclusively literary one. Even after he received a handsome pension of fifty pounds from Elizabeth in 1591 for the first installment of *The Faerie Queene*, Spenser did not (or could not) forgo his professional pursuits in Ireland for the life of a patronized court poet, single-mindedly dedicated to the fulfillment of his poetic ambitions. Nor, despite the claim of Helgerson that he "publicly ... abandon[ed] all social identity except that conferred by his elected [poetic] vocation," is there any evidence to suggest that Spenser ever attempted to conceal or to downplay his highly visible career as a secretary. On the contrary, such matters as Spenser's self-signing in his gift book to Gabriel Harvey as "*Edmundi Spenseri, Episcopi Roffensis Secretarii.* 1578," or the even more public designation of Colin Cloute as Rochester's "selfe boye" in *The Shepheardes Calender* signal his pride in his appointment as the bishop's personal secretary. The name Colin Cloute, coincident with its literary pedigree going back to poet laureate Skelton, thus seems to double as the title for Spenser in his capacity as secretary/poet. He similarly uses it in *The Ruines of Time*, again as we have seen, to publicize his employment by Leicester. Moreover, Spenser advances *A View of the Present State of Ireland*, his insider account of the "Irish problem" and his ruthless solutions to it, from his position and experience as an administrator and planter, not as a poet. Claims about Spenser's programmatic effacement of his "social identity" become even more unsupportable when one recognizes that, beginning with Camden, nearly every Renaissance account of his life mentions (often in the same breath as Spenser's poetic achievements) his tenure in Ireland as the Lord Deputy's personal secretary.[38]

My own account of Spenser's multiple careers is presented with the further intention of working towards a finer sense of the terms "career," "profession," and "vocation" as they apply to him. Often these designations are too readily conflated or made synonymous.[39] Spenser does indeed publicize himself in *The Shepheardes Calender* as an emerging national and nationalistic poet. Having begun with a pastoral apprenticeship of "Oaten reeds," as he declares in the proem to Book 1 of *The Faerie Queene*, his poetic career will culminate in the "trumpets sterne" of epic. This trajectory follows one fairly well-established model for a poetic career, and it is evidence of Spenser's ambitious *vocation* to be known as England's Virgil (though we have also seen that Spenser was concurrently promoting himself as both Chaucer's and Skelton's heir as well). But all his public professions as an aspiring laureate poet did not make him a *professional* poet. In Ben Jonson's *Epicoene* Sir John Daw declares: "Every man that writes in verse is not a poet ... they are poets that live by it, the poor fellows that live by it."[40] And if Spenser had hoped to "live by it," hoped to be a professional poet, he probably would have earned a better living writing either for the stage he avoided, or, even more lucrative at the time, writing orthodox theological tracts and pamphlets.[41] It should come as no surprise, however, that the man who claimed family ties with the aristocratic Spencers of Althorp would not have settled for the uncertain social position of the regularly maligned professional writer. Rather, if we are to speak of Spenser having a "profession," that profession would have to be his career as a secretary – a career he maintained throughout most of his adult life. It is also, as I have shown, a career that he knowingly and publicly pursued in his poems and published letters.

Yet while I have been arguing for a distinction between Spenser's "vocation" and Spenser's "profession," I am most concerned with the interstices of his two careers. Writing and the various routes of the rhetorical from "scholarship" to courtly service is obviously one. The management of secrets is another, equally important ligature. But more than indicating the points of contact between these careers, I will suggest in what follows that Spenser's career as a secretary provided him with a discursive practice and professional model that had a shaping effect both on his poetry and on the role he envisioned for himself as a poet. In short, even as a poet, Spenser writes as a secretary – as one, we shall see, who not only takes what appears to be a form of poetic dictation from his muse, but who also is busily employed in the management of secrets. In order to specify further what it means in the sixteenth and seventeenth centuries to write and work as a secretary – what I should like to call, adapting a famous phrase of Foucault's, the secretary function – let us now turn to some of the letterwriters and bureaucratic treatises of the time, and especially to Angel Day's *The English Secretary*.[42] By bringing together secretaryship, secrecy, and literary production, Day's text, along with *The Shepheardes Calender* which it parallels in significant respects, delivers a linkage, a kind of "secret-sharing," between Spenser's secretarial and poetic careers.

2   The secretary's study: the secret designs of
    The Shepheardes Calender

> – till when I lock these projects in the closet of Your secrecy.
>   Thomas Blount, *The Academie of Eloquence* (1654)

The structuring force of secrecy for *The Shepheardes Calender* is attested
to by E.K., whose identity is itself constructed as one of that text's
cardinal undisclosed secrets, in the "December" gloss on Colin Cloute's
"f[r]agraunt flowres" as his "sundry studies and laudable partes of learning, wherein how our Poete is seene, *be they witnesse which are priuie to his
study*" (p. 466; emphasis added). In one sense, what E.K. supplies here is
the expected gloss, since flowers are a conventional Renaissance figure for
the display of eloquence and learning. No doubt then, as Annabel Patterson remarks in her important discussion of this eclogue, E.K. is promoting "the *Calender* and its glosses [as] the record of a considerable
education."[1] In doing so, however, E.K.'s gloss establishes a principle of
intellectual and social exclusiveness (and exclusion) that solicits us to
think about something more than Spenser's humanist credentials. That
"something more" is registered in the gloss's punning move from
"studies" to *a* "study," from Spenser's endeavors as a scholar to his study
as a particular *place*.

What kind of space then is Spenser's study, and what does it mean to be
privy to it? His study is certainly, again as Patterson notes, "the space
filled with books, the place pastoral as he understood it could be written."[2] But E.K.'s tantalizing note suggests that Spenser's study is not only
a library, not only a kind of literary echo chamber in which the lexicon of
pastoral topoi may be invoked and reworked. For Spenser's study is also,
E.K. intimates, a "priuie" place, a place where secrets are being kept.[3]
Chief among the secrets to be read there, I will argue in this chapter, is the
secret of the secretariat, the open secret of Spenser's careerism, revealed
here under the dissimulative cover of pastoral humility.[4] Spenser wrote
The Shepheardes Calender, it will be remembered from Chapter 1, while
he was employed as secretary to John Young, Bishop of Rochester. The
poem shows him looking to continue and advance that career by attach-
ing himself in a similar capacity to some more highly-placed employer and

patron. In my view, *The Shepheardes Calender* thus not only marks Spenser's auspicious poetic debut; it also serves through its display of his (secret) study as an advertisement of Spenser's qualifications for secretaryship.

The link between secretaryship and secrecy was regularly asserted in the period, but perhaps never more saliently than in Angel Day's letter-writing manual *The English Secretary*. There we are informed repeatedly that a secretary is foremost "a keeper or conseruer of the secret unto him committed."[5] Day substantiates this claim by uncovering *secret* at the root of the word *secretary*, so that "by the verie etimologie of the worde it selfe, both Name and Office in one, doe conclude uppon secrecie" (Pt. 2, p. 103). Day thus fashions a secretary who literally has become his office, has become the privy place where his master withdraws to store secrets. Just as "we do call the most secrete place in the house, appropriate unto *our owne private studies* ... a Closet," he notes, " ... the partie serving in such place may be called a Secretorie, ... as hee is a keeper and conseruer of secrets" (emphasis added). Such is, I propose, the very place where Spenser has positioned himself in *The Shepheardes Calender*: his privy study (in both senses of the term) can be named, to borrow the title of another Renaissance letterwriter, "the secretary's study."[6] Spenser is the poet, that is, who pursues privy study (his education, his "f[r]agraunt flowres," his secretaryship) and *is himself a privy study* – an available and trustworthy secretary.

In the first part of this chapter I discuss the social and discursive formations of secretaryship, including the erotics and the diffuse subjectivity effects that accrue around the office, as they are figured in Day's *English Secretary* and other related Renaissance letterwriters and bureaucratic treatises. In the second part of the chapter, I use that discussion as a key to unlock, to help make us "priuie" to the secret study of "this our new Poete." This chapter thus continues and specifies the argument begun in Chapter 1 by tracing the various, and often competing, even conflicting, secret circuits along which Spenser is at once bidding in *The Shepheardes Calender* for employment as a reliable secretary and manager of secrets, and at the same time disclosing that he is already in on – and has his own – secrets.

The English secretary

Angel Day's *The English Secretary* was not only among the most popular letterwriting manuals of its time, it was also the most ambitious.[7] To begin with, Day's was the first English letterwriter declaring itself to be comprised almost entirely of original letters.[8] This claim alone distinguishes

The English Secretary from the precedent established by its principal forerunners. *The Enimie of Idlenesse* (1568), the earliest printed English letterwriter, for instance, gathers exemplary letters copied mostly from Cicero, and announces itself as a translation on its title page: "Set forth in English by William Fulwood, Marchant, &c." Similarly, Abraham Fleming stakes no claim to having composed the model letters collected in his voluminous *A Panoplie of Epistles* (1576). On the contrary, Fleming establishes the authority of his manual on the very fact that he has *not* authored it. The letters that make up his book, he assures us, were *"not broched in the seller of myne owne braine, but* [were] *drawne out of the most pure and cleare founteines of the finest and eloquentest Rhetoricians, that have liued and flourished in all ages"* (5ᵛ). The book's table of contents makes good on this boast, listing examples selected from Cicero, Plato, Socrates, Aristotle, Cato, Seneca, Erasmus, and even a letter of Ascham's to the queen. Fleming seems especially proud of the exotic flair brought to his letterwriter by the number of foreign writers to be found in its pages, including epistles culled from the likes of Darius, Cyrus, Diogenes, Alexander, and Macropedius. Such letters, he writes, were "hastily gathered out of outlandish gardens (for, *the most part of these flowers ... grewe in forreigne countries: ... from farre were they fet, and therefore the more deintie)*" (6ᵛ).

In contrast, Angel Day does take credit for authoring the models that comprise his letterwriter, which first appeared in 1586. "Almost all of which Epistles before set downe," he declares at the end of the book's table of contents, "were nowe sodenly *by the Author* ordered and inuented to their severall examples" (edition of 1586; emphasis added). No doubt Day's eschewal of foreign illustrations relates to the nationalism of his project, which is clearly signalled by the manual's title: Day's letterwriter is an *English* "Secretary." Having been produced by one "greatlie affecting the benefite of his cou[n]trie" (edition of 1586; q1ʳ), *The English Secretary* promotes English, and it promotes the ability of the English to write proper letters. To this end, Day fills his letterwriter with examples that conceivably would more closely correspond to the needs of its perceived audience. Unlike the compendiums of Cicero's essayistic civic epistles, or the even less practical examples of such letters as "wherein the Pope forbiddeth King Ferrand the building of a Castell," or "wherein the Emperor maketh pece with the King of Hungary," offered in Fleming's and early editions of Fulwood's manuals, Day provides his own "Example of an Epistle expostulatorie touching certaine iniuries betweene two friends" (Pt. 2, p. 19) and "An Example of an Epistle Accusatorie ... from a marchant to the father of his servant" (Pt. 2, p. 5).[9] Day's model letters, that is, are more the sort one might imagine those needing a letterwriter in the first place – those of the "middle," not noble class; those who wrote in the vernacular, not the Latin of diplomatic affairs – would be exchanging. Presumably it was examples such as these, in addition to its surely well-thumbed collection "Of Epistles Amatorie," that secured the popularity of Day's manual and established a precedent for the letterwriters that followed it.

There is, however, another trajectory running through *The English Secretary* that travels alongside, but also cuts across, Day's innovative attempt to produce more utilitarian epistolary models. That trajectory is the one that points past the route from letters to literacy and towards the route from letters to what we call the literary, or what Sidney calls the "poetical" in his *Apology*.[10] For, along with Day's (at that time) unprecedented claim to have himself authored the model letters on display in his manual, the way he emphatically calls attention to his own powers of composition begins to suggest a kind of literary inventiveness not apparent in the works of his English predecessors. It isn't that Fulwood and Fleming did not regard their letterwriters as possessing some sort of value in terms of what we have come to think of as literary. They did. But these letterwriters were meant to be valued only inasmuch as they were anthologies of the finest examples selected from other, mostly foreign, authors writing in Latin. While Fulwood and Fleming were satisfied with the roles of compiler and translator, however, Day nominates himself an author: his letters are "by the Author ordered and inuented." More than this, Day accords his letters, as we shall see, a status comparable to that allotted by Fulwood and Fleming to the letters of Cicero, Erasmus, and the others. Like them, he too will contribute to a poetics of letterwriting.

Day's aspirations toward the literary can also be read in his directions on how the model letters in *The English Secretary* are to be employed. For he discourages the practice of users simply copying out the letter (making whatever slight emendations necessary to personalize it) which most nearly addresses their concerns. Such slavish imitation, Day remarks in an analogy that emphasizes individuation and artistry over workmanlike craftsmanship, rarely brings good results no matter how fine the model:

in this matter of writing Epistles, nothing is more disordered, fonde, or vaine, then for anye one, of a thinge well done, to take forth a president, and thinke to make vnto him selfe thereof, a common platforme for euery other accident . . . (much like vnto a foolish Shoemaker, that making his shoes after one fashion, quantitye and proportion: supposeth the same forthwith of abilitie fitte to serue euery mans foot) (edition of 1586; p. 4)

The letters in *The English Secretary* are offered, then, not so much as form letters, but as models of good form. And to show exactly in what their good form consists, Day's letters come complete with their own system of

annotation. Day glosses nearly all of his letters – "To the greater ornament whereof" (edition of 1586; q2^r) – with a fairly extensive scheme of
marginal notes. Day's glosses signal both the individual parts of his model
letters and his exemplary employment of numerous rhetorical tropes
throughout those letters. In the lengthy "example of an Epistle Accusatorie in the state Juridiciall and Coniecturall" (Pt. 2, pp. 9–14), for instance,
Day marks the occurrence of such figures as exordium, emphasis, allegoria, synonymia, metalepsis, metanoia, sententia, climax, and a few dozen
more. After this fashion, Day's text comes to look less like a humble
vernacular letterwriter and begins to approximate the thoroughly glossed
humanist editions of classical texts that were so popular in the sixteenth
century. This is to say that *The English Secretary* is published, not unlike
Spenser's ready-glossed *Shepheardes Calender* of the previous decade, as a
kind of exemplary humanist pedagogical text.[11]

Yet Day's ambitions for *The English Secretary* were not entirely
realized until the book's reedition in 1592. Its first edition, which Day
calls the "vntimelie fruite by occasion of the hastie gatheryng of the same"
(edition of 1586; q3^r), presents only about half of the matter he would
eventually include in his expansive and expanding manual. Day pledges
here that, to complement its marginal annotations, the next edition of *The
English Secretary* would include full "descriptio[n]s of the FIGURES,
SCHEMES, and TROPES, as before I haue noted" (ibid.). He made good
on this promise in 1592 by appending, along with some forty new letters,
what no other vernacular letterwriter had: a twenty-five page dictionary
of rhetorical forms and uses.[12] This compact "Declaration of all such
Tropes, Figures or Schemes," which is allotted its own title page in the
design of Day's book, is offered to help readers "ornifie" their own
writings. Such embellishment is necessary, Day is convinced, because "no
speech [is] to be accounted valuable or of weight, that is not graced with
these parts" (Pt. 2, p. 76). The absoluteness of the claim "no speech" is
significant inasmuch as it points up Day's aspiration not to be merely
another epistolographer. For with the addition of the "Declaration," the
scope of Day's manual opens beyond the presentation of model letters
to the larger province of the rhetorical. The expanded edition of *The
English Secretary* is thus now able to double as a kind of rhetorical
handbook – a poetics, not just of letterwriting, but of *letters* in the sense of
the literary.

It is hardly surprising that the reedition of *The English Secretary*
would take shape along such axes, given that Angel Day was himself a
poet. He published a poem entitled "Wonderfull Strange Sightes seene in
the Element over the Citie of London and other places" (?1585), and in
1586, more importantly, an elegy in six-line stanzas "Upon the Life and

Death of the most worthy and thrice renow[n]ed knight, Sir Phillip Sidney" (dedicated to Sir Francis Walsingham, who, in addition to being Sidney's father-in-law and the one who received the bill for his extravagant funeral, was the most powerful secretary in England at the time). Following the vogue for pastoral established by Spenser's own *Shepheardes Calender*, Day also published a pastoral romance, *Daphnis and Chloe* (1587), whose title page advertises its own artistry for "Excellently describing the weight of affection, the simplicitie of loue, the purport of honest meaning, the resolution of men, and disposition of Fate." This prose narrative in four books (with songs interspersed) is essentially a translation of Longus by way of Amyot's French version. Day adds to it, however, his own interpolation, "The shepeards Hollidae," which advances, the title page continues, "the praises of a most peerlesse Princesse, wonderfull in Maiestie, and rare in perfection." The genres and topics of these works, particularly the pastoral encomium in honor of Elizabeth and the elegy for Sidney, are just the sort with which an aspirant might look to inaugurate a literary career in late Elizabethan England. Another poetic effort of Day's worth mentioning in this context is the commendatory poem he contributes to William Jones' *Nennio* (1595), a translation of the Italian treatise on the qualities of true nobility. Interestingly, a like set of verses from the pen of Spenser can be found next to Day's poem at the beginning of Jones' book.[13]

Despite Day's poetic endeavors and what they might indicate about his literary aspirations, nearly all of the critical and historical attention directed to Angel Day has concerned itself with *The English Secretary* in its capacity either as a collection of model letters or as a rhetoric. But the completed version of Day's manual does not end with the "Declaration of al such Tropes." It includes a third major section, a lengthy treatise "Of the partes, place and Office *of a Secretorie*."[14] Much of this treatise is derived from Francesco Sansovino's *Del Secretario* (1565). But Day, the son of a parish clerk, was apprenticed for twelve years to a stationer, Thomas Duxwell, and he claims to have himself served for some time as a secretary as well – and thus to be discoursing on this office with the authority of his own professional experience.[15]

Numerous Renaissance letterwriters titled themselves "Secretaries," including Thomas Gainsford's *The Secretaries Studie* (1616), John Massinger's translation of Jean Puget de la Serre's *The Secretary in Fashion* (1640) (see Plate 3), John Hill's *The Young Secretary's Guide* (1687), and even Henry Care's *The Female Secretary* (1671). Yet for the most part, these handbooks were presented as anthologies of more or less useful, and sometimes edifying or amusing, epistles. They were "Secretaries" only insofar as they generated (pre-written) letters to meet, and no doubt to

3   Title page *The Secretary in Fashion: or a compendious and refined way of expression in all manner of letters* by Jean Puget de la Serre, trans. John Massinger. Many Renaissance letterwriters called themselves "Secretaries." They served as such by producing pre-written letters to meet, but also to form, the correspondence requirements of their users.

form, the correspondence needs of their readers.[16] In contrast, the completed version of Day's *English Secretary*, along with its usefulness as a letterwriter, also functions as a kind of proto-professional training manual for those who actually wanted to become secretaries themselves, for those – and here we may think of Spenser once again – who sought to attach themselves professionally to their social superiors.

Day's subsequent additions to his handbook suggest that he conceived a somewhat different audience (or audiences) for his *English Secretary* from the one envisioned by the writers of other "Secretaries." Generally speaking, the earlier letterwriters were addressed to those who were able to read and write English, but did not necessarily have the benefit of a grammar school and university education. This is how Fulwood, for example, designates in some prefatory verses the class which he expects his letterwriter to serve:

> For know you sure, I meane not I
> the cunning clerkes to teach:
> But rather to the vnlearned sort
> a fewe precepts to preach.
>
> (Aiiiᵛ)

His "onely intent," he writes in the preface to the 1578 edition of his manual, "is to place downe such precepts, and set foorth such instructions, as may (in mine opinion) best serue to edifie the ignorant." Fulwood is here thinking primarily of the merchant class to which, according to his manual's title page, he himself belongs. In the introductory epistle to a 1607 edition, Fulwood directs those who would "clime of high *Parnassus* hill," those who aspire to high literacy, to "surview" "*Googe*, or *Golding*, *Gascoyne* else . . . / Or twentie worthy writers moe, / that drawe by learnd lyne" (A2ʳ). In a more aggressive vein, Abraham Fleming's letterwriter – the full title of which is *A Panoplie of Epistles, Or, a Looking Glasse for the Unlearned* – is offered as a weapon to be deployed by "the vnlearned . . . as sufficient furniture to arme and enable them against ignoraunce" (5ʳ).

The first edition of *The English Secretary* was similarly addressed to "the unlearned . . . to whom the want hereof [i.e., of a guide to letterwriting] breedeth so diuers imperfections, as with many wishes they could desire to be amended, knowing how greeuous it is to participate *their moste secreat causes to an other*, and laye their chiefest trust in the affiaunce of an others credite" (edition of 1586; pp. 2–3; emphasis added). Note that even when his book is "only" a collection of letters, we find Day registering an essential relation between secretaryship and secrecy.[17] More will be said on this account later in the chapter; at this point in the discussion I am chiefly concerned with Day's reconception of his intended audience in later editions of *The English Secretary*. Revising the first edition's address to the unlearned, Day determines in the 1592 edition that his book is appropriate for "any Learners capacitie whereout the Scholler or any other that is unfurnished of the knowledge thereof, may gather ayde and furtherance" (B2^v). Perhaps even more telling is the occurrence of this remark in a substantially rewritten introductory essay, originally called "The Epistle to the courteous Reader," but now retitled by Day as "To the *learned* and curteous *Readers*" (B1^r).

The addition of the essay on "the partes, place and Office *of a Secretorie*" is in keeping with Day's look upwards, and he conceives a more exclusive audience for this last section of his manual. That audience would be young men who did have the benefit of schooling, young men from the rising classes who hoped to secure places *as secretaries*. The administrative duties of a nobleman's secretary presuppose both a formal education and a measure of courtly finesse.[18] Thus, rather than being aimed indiscriminately at the unlearned and the learned, Day addresses the "Office" in particular "to those that bee greatest learned, best advised, discreetest gouerned, and most worthiest ruled" (Pt. 2, p. 101) – exemplars of humanist enculturation. Such qualities will be elaborated over the course of Day's discussion as the prerequisites for secretaryship, which is, he insists, of "great[er] consequence ... and more circumstance, than by everie one is considered" (Pt. 2, p. 102).

Robert Cecil, himself principal secretary (following in the footsteps of his father William) during the latter years of Elizabeth's reign, advises in his treatise on "The State and Dignity of a Secretary of State's Place" (published in 1642) that even the highest ranking secretary nonetheless "be created by himself, and of his own raising."[19] Just so, many of the most successful secretaries of his day were ambitious self-made men, *novi homines* as they were called, who rose to posts at court in an expanding secretarial corps or to places of intimacy and influence as the functionary of some noble. For as a career, secretaryship offered promising, and sometimes even spectacular, opportunities for advancement. The position of principal secretary, to take the most illustrious example, was for a long time little more than any number of minor appointments in the royal household. But under the Tudors it gradually developed into one of the most powerful executive offices in the realm, bringing along with the appointment a position on the Privy Council, the supreme governing body under the crown.[20] Stephen Gardiner, Thomas Cromwell, William and Robert Cecil, Francis Walsingham: these men were among the most powerful politicians in Tudor England, each one operating from and aiming to expand the office of principal secretary.

When the will of the sovereign was declared in council or in parliament,

the responsibility of seeing it implemented most often lay with the secretary. As chief representative of the crown, no facet of the administration
fell entirely outside his purview. In addition, the office of the principal
secretary was the headquarters for foreign affairs. To it diplomatic
reports were made, and from it orders were communicated to ambassa-
dors. And to spies. For, as I noted in the preceding chapter, the Elizabethan secretariat (and Walsingham in particular) can be credited with
the development of the first national secret service.[21] The cornerstone of
the secretary's office, however, was his position as the keeper of the
crown's signet: he drafted the monarch's letters and he wielded the
monarch's signature. It is not difficult to imagine the considerable opportunities of influence – and sometimes shading beyond influence to control
– such a position could afford. Gervase Markham declares in his *Conceyted Letters, Newly Layde Open* (1618) that it is by letters

which even the whole state of the world is sustained ... For ... how shall Kings
know and communicate their great actions, enlarge their bounds, redresse their
peoples iniuries, how shal the noble, know intelligence to serve his Countrie, the
Merchant trade ... or any or all sorts of people speake at a farre distance, but by
the helpe of Letters only[?] (A3)

As the machinery of authority, government, and business became increasingly dependent upon letters, the secretary's status and powers were
enhanced proportionately.[22] He styled the written voice of the monarch;
he wrote the words that articulated royal will. It is conceivable that the
letters, commissions, and declarations he scripted at the monarch's
(verbal) command seldom passed from the secretary's hands without
bearing something of his own imprint.[23]

"It was on account of such duties as these," Florence M. Grier Evans
notes in *The Principal Secretary of State: A Survey of the Office from
1558–1689*, " ... that the idea evolved of the secretary as the channel of
communication between crown and subjects."[24] The road to the
monarch, especially during the tenure of Thomas Cromwell and then
again during that of William Cecil, traveled directly through the office of
the secretary. Even so, few explicit powers seem to have been attached
ipso facto to his position. Thus we find Nicholas Faunt, who worked in
Walsingham's secretarial corps, reporting the impossibility of defining the
precise scope of the secretary's prerogatives in his "Discourse touching
the Office of Principal Secretary of Estate" (1592):

Nowe amoungst all particuler offices and places of charge in this state, there is
none of more necessarie vse, nor subiect to more cumber and variableness; then is
the office of principall Secretarie, by reason of the varietie, and uncertaintie of his
imployment, and therefore with more difficultie to be prescribed by spetiall
methadd and order.[25]

Secretary of State Robert Cecil concurs: "All officers and counsellors of princes have a prescribed authority by patent, by custom, or by oath, the secretary only excepted."[26] Because of the elasticity of his commission, the secretary stands out from – and often above – all the other officers and councillors of the prince. Their authority, however great, is prescribed and thus fixed. The secretary's powers and privileges are not similarly predetermined, and in this sense they appear to be functionally unlimited.[27] Consequently, it regularly lay with the individual secretary to fashion of his position what he could. "To a large extent," Evans reports, "the man made the office."[28] The Renaissance secretariat was open for a spectacular degree of individual virtuosity.

Much of what the secretary did was performed on the authority of the monarch, who of course embodied the chief limitation on the secretary's power. Here is Cecil again:

All servants of princes deal upon strong and wary authority and warrant in disbursements as Treasurers, in conference with enemies as Generals, in commissions in executing offices by patent and instructions, and so in whatever else; only a secretary hath no warrant or commission, no, not in matters of his own greatest particulars, but the virtue and word of his sovereign.[29]

What the secretary possesses, instead of a specific warrant or commission, is the "virtue and word of his sovereign." He speaks in the (ventriloquized) voice of the monarch; he acts under the aegis of royal "virtue" or power. The secretary's duties are whatever his sovereign happens to assign in any given instance, and his authority is, Cecil contends, as capacious as the circumstances might dictate: "For such is the multiplicity of actions, and variable motions and intents of foreign princes, and their daily practices, and in so many parts and places, as secretaries can never have any commission, so long and universal as to secure them."[30] Curtailing the secretary's power, it is implied here with surely no little self-interestedness on Cecil's part, would be tantamount to limiting the sovereign. The unfixed, variegated powers of the secretary necessarily mirror the "variable motions and intents" of the sovereign. As Cecil's treatise unfolds, it traces the path along a series of parallelisms by which secretary and sovereign are situated in a mutually dependent, even mimetic relation to each other:

So as a secretary must either conceive the very thought of a king, which is only proper to God, or a king must exercise the painful office of a secretary, which is contrary to majesty, and liberty; or else a prince must make choice of such a servant of such a prince, as the prince's assurance must be his confidence in the secretary, and the secretary's life his trust in the prince.

Cecil begins with a clear distinction between the prince and the secretary, as well as between the thoughts and actions appropriate to each. But such distinctions are no sooner in place than they are effectively elided. And what is offered in their place are the mirror effects of reciprocal dependence in which each is the guarantor of the other: the secretary depends upon the prince for his life; but in turn the prince himself, Cecil notes, is only as secure as the confidence he is able to place in his secretary.

Of course, few aspiring secretaries could have hoped to rise, like Walsingham and the Cecils, to the position of principal secretary. Nonetheless, as Day's "Office of a Secretory" shows, the paradigm for the idealized relations between any secretary and his employer is remarkably very much the same. Day observes that the secretary, being "at the pleasure and appointment of another to be commanded" (Pt. 2, p. 104), is in the first order a servant. But his discussion quickly moves past this initial recognition in its impetus to reconfigure the secretary more as an appendage or an extension of his employer's will than as simply another household servant subject to that will. In fact, the bonds that comprise this master–servingman relation are, according to Day, closer than those derived from blood. "There is also by that very name of servant a kind of fidelitie and trust required," he insists, "more especiall then that betweene the sonne and the father" (ibid.). Parent and child happen to be linked by nature, Day continues; but a secretary and his master have entered into a mutual contract of trust, a bond he sees as far more compelling. Consequently, the "disposition of goods, estate, principall affaires," usually the charge of the eldest son and heir upon his father's death, is better left, as Day sees it, in the secretary's more dependable hands. He thus recommends the example of those who, unlike, say, Shakespeare's imprudent Lear, "have refused to commit themselves in times of hazard to their Children, but rather haue relied themselves wholie on the assurance of their seruants" (Pt. 2, p. 105). Day's secretary is more trustworthy than a son, and hence more deserving of a uniquely privileged position in the master's confidence and affections.

More profoundly indentured than a slave and more deeply trusted than a son, the secretary is best described, Day insists, not as a servant, but with the privileged name of friend:

By this measure nowe of Fidelitie, trust or loyall credit of a servant, in which place our Secretorie, as you see standeth bounden by first degree of his seruice, it maie secondlie be coniectured, in what respectiue estate, he ought for the residue of that which to his attendance appertaineth, bee accounted a Friend. (Pt. 2, p. 111).

Bound to his master in what Day calls "this friendlie knot of loue," the secretary's constant "conuersing, his neerenesse and attendance" generates between the two "a coniunction, which ... groweth in the end to a simpathie unseparable, and therby all intendment concludeth a most perfect vniting" (Pt. 2, p. 113). Nicholas Faunt likewise invokes the "reciprocall love" this master and servingman bear for each other, while Robert Cecil even more forthrightly inscribes these bonds within an erotic register, comparing the private counsels of master and secretary to "the mutual affections of two lovers, undiscovered to their friends."[31] The inviolability of such intimations, Cecil continues, is analogous to the "solemnization of marriage." Such terms may strike us as particularly resonant when the secretary's master happens to be, as Cecil's was, an unmarried female sovereign who actively solicited the courtship of her male subjects and ministers.[32] Nonetheless, almost always the affectively charged intimacy of the master–secretary "coupling" was a relation *between men.* And it is, as Cecil intimates, the ostensible secrecy ("undiscovered to their friends") of that relation – in contrast to the public nature of marriage – that invisibly and indivisibly joins the secretary to his master. The tie that binds is the secret one.

At this point it is worth pausing to observe that despite the significant devaluation of secretaryship in the twentieth century (owing in part, no doubt, to its relatively recent but widespread re-engendering as a "woman's place"), many of the terms generated in these Renaissance treatises have endured to characterize contemporary master–secretary pairings at their highest levels – that is, at levels where the master–secretary pairing remains a male homosocial relation. For example, a fairly recent *New York Times Magazine* article, "The Fabulous Bush and Baker Boys" by Maureen Dowd and Thomas L. Friedman, reports on the exceptional *friendship* (their term) of President George Bush and his Secretary of State, James Baker.[33] President Bush's "very ideology," Dowd and Friedman report, "is friendship."[34] They then go on to provide evidence at every turn to demonstrate, despite Baker's occupation of a position in the governmental hierarchy structurally lower than Bush's, that this is a political marriage among equals: "their partnership ... began three decades ago [with the two men] as peers and, to a remarkable degree, they still are."[35] In the service of sustaining the always precarious male parity the article constructs, Dowd and Friedman show us "the two most powerful friends in the world" exchanging ribald jokes, "play[ing] out an earthy good ol' boy ritual," "teas[ing] each other about everything under the sun," and engaging in the circumscribed rivalry of weekend athletics.[36]

As friends and political soulmates, the President and his Secretary "think so much alike," we are told, that they can "communicate with half-sentences and glances."[37] Fostering this "unbelievable" flow of communication is the kind of all-hours male intimacy that the Renaissance discourse on secretaryship establishes as the very grounds of the office:

The two call back and forth as many as a dozen times a day, and the President often wakes Baker on weekend mornings for a phone chat. When the President and the Secretary travel abroad together on Air Force One, and Barbara Bush stays home, the President gives Baker the First Lady's berth for the night.

The Air Force One anecdote opens onto another way to hear Dowd's and Friedman's contention that "Now the two pragmatists are out of the closet."[38] More than that, the authors of this article proffer such intimacy, carried even to the point of the secretary taking the place of the wife in bed, as unique to this particular "master" and his secretary. However, after reading Day, Cecil, and Faunt we know otherwise, recognizing that bureaucratized – literally closeted – male affectional relations of just this sort historically have structured secretaryship in its most idealized form.

The terms of intimacy and endearment between men that echo in the treatises of Day, Cecil, and Faunt (as well as the *New York Times* article on Bush and Baker) accord wholly with the conventions of Elizabethan male friendship between master and servingman discussed in an important essay by Alan Bray.[39] Yet, as Bray shows, the signs of socially sanctioned male friendship – embraces, protestations of love, even sharing the same bed – might also, in other circumstances, be produced as corroborating evidence of unnatural kinds of male intimacy. The valences of Renaissance sodomy, we must remember, were not simply sexual; sodomy was a signifier – in its commonplace affiliation with treason, heresy, and sorcery – of wholesale social, even cosmic, disruption.[40] Consequently, what preserves the socially productive and desirable intimacy between master and servant from any association with what is "unnatural" is not necessarily the sort or degree of physical and emotional closeness involved. Rather it is, Bray argues, a kind of "class" compatibility – the operative assumption being that both masters and their close servingmen would be gentle, men "made of their own metal, even a loaf of their own dough, which being done ... the gentleman received even a gentleman into his service," as it is quaintly put in *Health to the Gentlemanly Profession of Seruingmen* (1598).[41] Thus, as Bray points out, Simonds D'Ewes' charges in his autobiography that Francis Bacon was a sodomite pivot as much on the too lowly social status of the menial servant he had made his regular bedfellow as they do on the fact that Bacon had in the first place deserted his wife's bed to sleep with a man.[42]

We can thus see why Day is so insistent in *The English Secretary* that, despite the subordinate standing of a secretary, no unequal union is being proposed between this servingman and his master. Like the *New York Times Magazine* article on Bush and Baker, which contends that the longstanding friendship of these two men belies the hierarchy implied in the relation of President to his Secretary, Day consistently mobilizes the tropes of friendship to posit an egalitarianism that would cover over the subordination implicit in secretaryship: "The limits of Friendship (as it might be obiected) are streight," he writes, "and there can bee no Friend where an inequalitie remaineth" (Pt. 2, p. 111). Day thus suggests that the "simpathie of affections" which exists between his model secretary and master goes a long way in effacing social inequality: the secretary is "himselfe in reputation a Gentleman" (ibid.) if the man he serves is one, Day declares. (An especially Spenserian way of reading Day's "Office of a Secretorie," with its catalogs of requisite virtues, is to see the treatise as another attempt at the familiar Renaissance project of "fashioning a gentleman.")

It is the secretary's duty, Day continues, scrupulously to observe his master's habits so that he can be "a zealous imitator in all thinges, to the intent that knowing the effects of his Lord, with what ends and purposes they are carried, and unto what forme and manner of writing he is speciallie addicted" (Pt. 2, p. 130). As imitator in all things, one of the things the secretary must imitate is the master's hand, even to the extent of being able to replicate his signature – the sign(ing) we have come to privilege as the authenticating discursive mark of individual subjectivity.[43] Concurrently, the secretary should know how to read his master's mind as well as his hand, being able to anticipate his master's "ends and purposes." We can see that Day's agenda thus goes well beyond the notion that the secretary's skills and social station need to be commensurate with the status of the man he serves. More than this, Day articulates the process by which a secretary comes to don his master's self. Secretaryship thus does not simply mean transcribing, copying down the words of the master; rather it entails becoming the simulacrum of the master himself. That is how the secretary, in Day's term, is "accomplished" (Pt. 2, p. 132).

The result of Day's "accomplishment" enacts a symbiosis of master and secretary so complete it becomes difficult to determine where the thoughts of one let off and the other begin:

Much is the felicitie that the master or Lord receiueth evermore of such a servant, in the chary affection and regard of whom affying himselfe assuredlie, he findeth *he is not alone a commander of his outward actions, but the disposer of his uerie thoughts, yea he is the Soueraigne of all his desires*, in whose bosome hee holdeth the repose of his safety to be far more precious, then either estate, liuing, or advancement, whereof men earthly minded are for the most part desirious. (Pt. 2, p. 115; emphasis added)

Who is being nominated with the title of "Soueraigne" here? Given the secretary's status as a servant, that title must belong to his master. Yet this proper social ordering is troubled by Day's proposition that the master recognizes "he is not alone a commander of his outward actions," that the secretary has some stake in the power of command. (But what stake is that?) Day's declaration of powersharing between master and secretary is a startling one, but the grammar of the passage seems clear on at least this much. Accordingly, it would appear that the next clause – "the disposer of his uerie thought" – would be a further modification of the secretary's office. Yet this clause is ambiguous in meaning and in grammatical assignment. Is Day asserting that "the *secretary* is the disposer of the master's thoughts," implying that the secretary's task is to enact the wishes of his master, to turn the master's thoughts into deeds? Or does he mean "the *master* is the disposer of the secretary's thoughts," suggesting perhaps that the secretary is so thoroughly indentured to his master that his very thoughts are disposed, controlled by the master? The clause might also be construed, in an even more pronounced unravelling of social station, as an assertion that the secretary is the real prime mover here, that the "master" merely disposes, merely enacts the will of the secretary. If this is so, the secretary, having already displaced son and spouse, now looms to stand in place of the master himself, whom he imitates in all things.

A similar displacement is spectacularly observed by Jacques Derrida in his own letterwriter of sorts, *The Post Card: From Socrates to Freud and Beyond.* In the book's "Envois" – which is actually a collection of letters, or as Derrida names them, "the remainders of a recently destroyed correspondence"[44] – he describes his discovery of a postcard reproduction of the frontispiece of Matthew Paris' *Prognostica Socratis basilei* (see Plate 4):

I stopped dead, with a feeling of hallucination (is he crazy or what? he has the names mixed up!) and of revelation at the same time, an apocalyptic revelation: Socrates writing, writing in front of Plato, I always knew it, it had remained like the negative of a photograph to be developed for twenty-five centuries – in me of course. Sufficient to write it in broad daylight. The revelation is there, unless I can't yet decipher anything in this picture, which is what is most probable in effect. Socrates, the one who writes – seated, bent over, a scribe or docile copyist, Plato's secretary, no?[45]

Thus is staged an inversion of what is perhaps Western culture's most famous master–secretary affiliation. Everyone, Derrida points out, has always believed that Socrates did not write, that he came before Plato, who more or less wrote according to his dictation.[46] But Matthew Paris' engraving reverses all that. We see that it was Plato who dictated to Socrates. He reaches around the older philosopher, and with his outstretched finger he gives an order; he tells Socrates what to write. Here,

4 *Prognostica Socratis basilei,* frontispiece (detail), the work of Matthew Paris (thirteenth century). Matthew Paris' engraving, which depicts Plato dictating to Socrates, inverts the chain of command in what is probably our culture's most famous master-secretary affiliation.

according to Derrida, we uncover "the secret of reproduction" (a secret, I might add, that we have known all along): Plato is the real author of the Socratic voice.[47] Reproduction *is* production. The secretary thus lays claim to the position of primacy and power; it is really he who dictates what is to be written, and then signs his master's name to it.

At the same time, by directing attention to the odd way in which the subordinate Socrates physically dominates the engraving, Derrida suggests that the matter of authority and authorship figured here is still more complicated than any straight reversal of power. Moreover, Socrates' name is signed, unlike Plato's, with a capital letter: "Socrates/plato." So who dominates whom? "The one in the other, the one in front of the other, the one after the other, the one behind the other?" Derrida speculates in terms which echo against the undertones of bureaucratized (that is, closeted) homoeroticism sounded in the treatises of Day, Cecil, and Faunt.[48]

For Derrida, Matthew Paris' image of Socrates and Plato raises the question of control between master and secretary in unanswerable terms. That problematic also underwrites Angel Day's *The English Secretary*. It is impossible to determine, we have already seen, the disposer and the disposed in the puzzling nomination "the disposer of his uerie thoughts." And Day's elliptical grammar makes it just as impossible to specify the subject of the crucial appositive clause which follows it: "yea he is the Soueraigne of all his desires." Is the antecedent of "he" the master, making the antecedent of "his" the secretary? Or is it just the opposite? Day does not allow the possibility of grammatically distinguishing between the master and the secretary, thus undoing the familiar and socially grounding distinctions between commander and commanded, disposer and disposed, sovereign and servant. Such oppositions, Day's text implies, have no purchase in the extraordinary case of the secretary.

"How can it otherwise be thought," Day answers those who might contest his claims about secretarial "accomplishment," "but that our Secretorie being one euerie waie so waightilie to be imployed as he is, partaking as he doeth with so manie causes of importance, *and undiscouered secrets and counsels* . . . [must be] by a great deale to be beloued?" (Pt. 2, p. 113; emphasis added). Day begins his discussion of secretaryship by inviting his readers to "run . . . into the nature of things secret" (Pt. 2, p. 103), and here the "secret" of the intimate position into which this exceptional servingman has been able to insinuate himself is uncovered. The secretary is so near his master (both in terms of proximity and likeness), Day affirms, because he is the respository for all the master's secrets. Secrecy, Elias Canetti reminds us, is at the very core of power, so often measured by what is known and withheld – and known to be withheld.[49] As Milton's Samson learns upon exposing his "capital secret" to Dalila, to tell one's secret is to place oneself under another's power.[50] (Though one can also imagine situations where the powerplay is enacted in the opposite direction, in which the confiding of one's secret to another empowers the discloser. The secret-sharing that occurs in the secretary's closet seems to be transacted along both these axes.) Thus Montaigne cautions in his essay "Of friendship" that "neither can all the secret thoughts of fathers be communicated to children," while suggesting that it is the sharing of secrets which constitutes friendship, a relation more intimate than any family ties.[51] For Angel Day, secrets define, even name the secretary's office: he is the "keeper and conseruer of the secret vnto him committed" (Pt. 2, pp. 102–103). Similarly, Faunt construes the secretary as his master's "owne penne, his mouth, his eye, his eare and keeper of his most secrett Cabinett."[52] The management of secrets – and not, as we might expect, taking dictation or conducting the master's business affairs – is revealed to be the secretary's principal office.

Although Day seems to have expected that his elaboration of secretaryship in terms of the handling of secrets would provoke some controversy ("albeit there happily maie be opinions some waie contrarying unto my present deliuerie, touching the originall of this title" [Pt. 2, p. 102]), his claims were hardly idiosyncratic. Indeed, it is a commonplace of Renaissance discussions of secretaryship to establish secrets as its primary business. We have already noted the private and markedly affective terms Robert Cecil uses in his treatise to describe what is transacted between the sovereign and the secretary: their counsels are like "the mutual affections of two lovers," which necessarily remain secret, "undiscovered to their friends." Nicholas Faunt's "Discourse touching the Office of Principal Secretary" likewise insists that "secrecie and faithfulnes bee chiefly required" in any secretary.[53] Such stipulations compel him to advise against the principal secretary employing many subordinates: a "multitude of servantes in this kinde," he warns, "is hurtfull and of late yeares hath bredde much confusion with want of secrecie."[54] But beyond a concern with the preservation of the secrets already entrusted, Faunt also charges the secretary with the responsibility of discovering new ones. To this end, the secretary must regularly "conferre with secrett intelligencers both strangers and others."[55] No doubt Faunt's interest in espionage followed from his service as secretary to Walsingham, whom Elizabeth is reported to have nicknamed her "moon," and whom William Camden praised as "a diligent searcher out of hidden secrets."[56]

Once a secretary has found out such "hidden secrets," he must be careful to lock them away, advises Robert Beale, Walsingham's brother-in-law and Clerk to the Privy Council, within

a speciall Cabinett, whereof he is himselfe to keepe the Keye, for his signetts, Ciphers and secrett intelligences, distinguishing the boxes or tills rather by letters than by the names of the Countryes or places, keepinge that only unto himselfe, for the names may inflame a desire to come by such thinges.[57]

Beale's "Treatise of the Office of a Councellor and Principall Secretarie to her Majestie" (1592) thus discloses secrets inlayed with secrets: a secret agent concealing his secrets in a locked cabinet inscribed with ciphers.

The figure of the locked and hidden cabinet (or its synonym in these discussions, the closet) recurs throughout Faunt's and Day's treatises as well, but Day goes further by troping on this trope and making the secretary himself that locked cabinet or closet in which the master's secrets are stored, and to which only the master holds the key. The closet is the place for the "reposement of secrets," "the most secret place in the house," Day reminds us, and then concludes that "in respect of the couertnes, safetie and assurance in him reposed, and not otherwise, the partie seruing in such a place may be called a Secretorie" (Pt. 2, p. 103). Day carries the correlation between this servant and his office so far as to metaphorize the secretary's body as ideally itself a closet. "To a closet," he notes, "there belongeth properlie a *doore*, a *locke*, and a *key*" (Pt. 2, p. 103). Similarly, since the secretary is in Day's phrase "but the closet, whereof another hath both the key, use and commandment," he ought to be "as a thick plated doore, where no man may enter, but by the locke which is the tongue, and that to be of such efficacie, as whereof no counterfeite key should bee able to make a breache" (Pt. 2, p. 124). The secretary is his office.

Day goes on to describe this closet – and, metonymically, the secretary – as the place "where our dealings of importance are shut vp, a roome proper and peculiar to our selves" (Pt. 2, p. 103). It is the place for writing, the place "appropriate vnto our owne priuate studies," for which "we keepe the key our selues, and the vse thereof alone doe onelie appropriate vnto our selues." This secret room – and again by extension this secretive servant – is, in Day's striking formulation, the space in which we "doe solitarie and alone shut up our selues." One cannot help noticing Day's repeated invocation of the language of the self here, as well as his registration of a formative relation between writing, secrecy, and subjectivity: in the secretary's closet (among other places in early modern culture) an interior, private subjectivity begins to speak, begins to be scripted. Here the self is coming to be formed in and as its secrets: *we are our secrets*. Fittingly, secretaries were called "inward men" in the Renaissance.[58] And no wonder Day's secretary – a closet in which is closed up his master's secrets, his master's self (that is, his master's secret self) – is able to simulate his master, to be both his servant and his imitator "in all thinges."

E.K.'s cabinet of secrets

The cabinet is likewise a figure of determinative significance in *The Shepheardes Calender*, another text penned by a secretary. Colin Cloute, having sequestered himself "in secreate shade alone" (5), and thus calling from one hiding place to another, summons Pan in "December" to

"Hearken awhile from thy greene cabinet, / The rurall song of carefull Colinet" (17–18). Like the troping of Angel Day which turns the body of the secretary into a closet, these lines homophonically conjoin the shepherd and the cabinet in the renaming of Colin as "Colinet" – so that the poet himself becomes a kind of cabinet. At the same time, the lines recall the *vert cabinet* of Pan in Marot's *Eclogue au Roy* (1539). In Marot's poem, the god stands for Francis I. In Spenser's eclogues, however, the function of Pan (like much else in the *Calender*) is disseminated, and he alternately names Henry VIII, a pagan nature god, the Good Shepherd (Christ himself), and a muse-like source of inspiration for pastoral poetry. The placement of Pan, the "God of shepheards all" (7), inside the green cabinet – thereby making the cabinet the enclosed place where pastoral songs are inspired, composed, performed, and heard – in effect resituates the entire *Calender* inside this privy space.

The cabinet of Spenser's inaugural volume of poetry holds an impressive array of secrets. Its first is the secret of authorship. The name of the *Calender*'s author is never uncovered in its pages, prompting the book's envoy to figure the poem in the first of its many Chaucerian locutions as an orphaned text, a "child whose parent is vnkent" ("To His Booke," 2). In the sixteenth century, anonymous publication was a standard practice among writers of gentle birth, as well as among aspirants to gentility; in *The Shepheardes Calender*, however, the withholding of the author's name has the quality of the deliberate management of a secret. This unknown poet does sign himself "Immeritô" (i.e., unworthy – to be named?) at the end of the envoy, though we are told that it is a different name, the name of Colin Cloute, "vnder whose person the Author selfe is shadowed" (p. 418). Even so, the figure of the multiply nominated but still anonymous "Author selfe" behind these shadow names is never revealed to be Spenser. Instead, his aliases keep opening up like Chinese boxes, as in this gloss from the "Januarye" eclogue, to uncover still other names:

COLIN CLOVTE) is a name not greatly vsed, and yet haue I sene a Poesie of M. Skeltons vnder that title. But indeede the word Colin is Frenche, and vsed of the French Poete Marot (if he be worthy of the name of a Poete) in a certain Aeglogue. Vnder which name this Poete secretly shadoweth himself, as sometime did Virgil vnder the name of Tityrus. (p. 422)

From Immeritô to Colin Cloute to Skelton to Marot to Virgil to Tityrus. This recovery (and recovering) of names continues on through to the next eclogue, where the name Tityrus again appears, though now it is decoded as a reference not to Virgil but to Chaucer, "whose prayse for pleasaunt tales cannot dye, so long as the memorie of *hys name* shal liue, and the name of Poetrie shal endure" (p. 426; emphasis added).

"Colin Cloute" thus comes to represent not a singular "Author selfe," but rather a dispersal of authorial signings, identities, and agendas.[59] "Colin Cloute" is the ghost signature of a poet who is also a secretary, writing – not unlike one taking dictation at his master's hand – under the cover of a name (or names) other than his own. And no doubt still another name to be added to this list is that of Philip Sidney, who, according to the envoy, is meant to provide cover for the book by hiding it "Vnder the shadow of his wing" ("To His Booke," 7). In fact, the name of Sidney, *most worthy of all titles*" the dedication proclaims, is the only name inscribed on the *Calender*'s title page: an indication that this text, sent out like a letter, has been written for him – "for him" surely in the sense of being dedicated to him, but perhaps also for him in the secretarial sense of being drafted by another and "signed" with his name.

It may always have been easy enough, notwithstanding the author's multiple acts of discovery and recovering, to attach the name of Edmund Spenser to *The Shepheardes Calender*. That assignation is certainly one of the intentions of the Spenser–Harvey correspondence, which publicly identifies Spenser as Immeritô. However, the "real identity" behind the initials "E.K." – the other(?) hand responsible for more than half of the written text that comprises the *Calender* – has never been deciphered. Moreover, E.K.'s typically curious, when not outrightly cryptic, commentary is responsible for much of the volume's shadings of secrecy. His prefatory epistle provides a good example. It poses as a platform for introducing the new poet and thus rectifying the circumstances of his being, as E.K. taking a phrase from Chaucer's Pandarus puts it, "Vncouthe vnkiste" (p. 416); for "so soone as [but not now, we might interject] his name shall come into the knowledg of men . . . he shall be not onely kiste," Spenser's own Pandarus boasts, "but also beloued of all, embraced of the most, and wondred at of the best" (ibid.). Yet E.K.'s epistle is addressed neither to the general reader, nor even to Sidney, as we might expect from the name inscribed on the title page, but to Gabriel Harvey, who is depicted in the same letter as the poet's "most special good frend" (p. 418) and thus the one person least likely to need such an introduction to the new poet.[60] The social enfoldedness of this kind of coterie secrecy introduces the *Calender* as a book intended only for "friends."

Even more remarkable is how much less than expected E.K. ever reveals about such matters as the identity of the poet he is supposed to be publicizing, the meaning of specific eclogues, or of (in his own phrase) "*The generall argument of* the whole booke" (p. 419). E.K.'s epistle reads at times less like the letter of introduction it purports to be and more like a catalog of the concealments that lie in store in the poems that follow. For instance, despite his claim that Spenser's adopted idiom in the *Calender* is "both English, and also vsed of most excellent Authors and most famous Poetes" (p. 416), E.K. soon recasts these quaint archaisms and rusticisms as ciphers in a kind of hermetic language that, without his gloss as a key for decoding them, would remain for us "either as vnknowen, or as not marked" (p. 418). E.K. describes the poet's intentions and true subject matter as similarly occluded, though he insists at some length that Spenser is merely exhibiting good pastoral form in choosing "rather to vnfold great matter of argument couertly." For "So flew Theocritus . . . Virgile . . . Mantuane . . . Petraque . . . Boccace . . . Marot, [and] Sanazarus," E.K. declares in another exfoliating chain of names, and "So finally flyeth this our new Poete, as a bird . . . [who] in time shall be hable to keepe wing with the best," covered as he is under the name of Sidney.

In this instance we can take E.K.'s notoriously unreliable commentary as reliable, but only up to a point. Anonymity, cover names, covert agendas, and dissimulation can all be numbered among the principal clichés of Renaissance pastoral, as well as of other Renaissance courtly maneuverings. As Puttenham's *The Arte of English Poesie* (1589), another anonymously published text, indicates – in a formulation that sounds as if it could have been lifted right out of E.K.'s epistle – pastoral operates by "glaunc[ing] at greater matters" under "the vaile of homely persons."[61] William Webbe's *A Discourse of English Poetrie* (1586) likewise refers to the genre's "cloake of simplicitie" as the means by which pastoral poets can "eyther sette foorth the prayses of theyr freendes, without the note of flattery, or enueigh grievously against abuses, without any token of bitternesse."[62] These citations register the extent to which a reliance upon the mechanisms of concealment and dissimulation is built into the Renaissance conception of pastoral. What I am claiming is striking about *The Shepheardes Calender* is not its frequent, almost constant, dependence upon the conventions of pastoral veiling and occlusion; rather it is the ostentation with which the text announces the fact every time such conventions are employed – the flagrance of its secrecy.

That secrets are being stored within is constantly intimated to the reader of *The Shepheardes Calender*, even when what is hidden is no secret:

Hobbinol) is a fained country name, whereby, it being so commune and vsuall, seemeth to be hidden the person of some his very speciall and most familiar freend, whom he entirely and extraordinarily beloued, as peraduenture shall be more largely declared hereafter. (p. 422)

This is E.K.'s less than opaque gloss on the first appearance of the shepherd Hobbinol in "Januarye." "[S]eemeth to be hidden" is exactly to the point, since Gabriel Harvey has already been commended as the poet's "most speciall good frend" in the prefatory epistle. He is again similarly named, though this time as E.K.'s own "verye singular good freend," in another note from the "Januarye" gloss just before the one on Hobbinol's name. Yet in case these secret signposts have gone unmarked, the "hidden" identity of Hobbinol is fully divulged (Colin's of course continues to be withheld) in the midst of the gloss on the "September" eclogue:

Colin cloute) Nowe I thinke no man doubteth but by Colin is euer meante the Authour selfe. Whose especiall good freend Hobbinoll sayth he is, *or more rightly Mayster Gabriel Haruey*: of whose speciall commendation, aswell in Poetrye as Rhetorike and other choyce learning, we haue lately had a sufficient tryall in diuerse [of] his workes (p. 455; emphasis added)

E.K. makes it no secret that Hobbinol secretly names Harvey. (Why this particular "secret" is so forthrightly exposed when so much else remains obscured in the *Calender* is a question I will take up later in the discussion.) There are a few other identifications disclosed by E.K., such as the revelation that the "white beare" of "October" (48) is "the most honorable and renow[n]ed the Erle of Leycester" (p. 458), though this could hardly be much of a secret given that the bear is taken from Leicester's quite public coat of arms; or that Pan in the "Aprill" eclogue names the queen's father, which is, unlike the Leicester allusion, an identification that might go unknown without the gloss. Many of the secrets stored in *The Shepheardes Calender*, however, are neither open secrets nor opened secrets, and in most instances E.K.'s annotations are less forthcoming. Thus, while boasting that "by meanes of some familiar acquaintaunce I was made priuie to his counsell and secret meaning in [the eclogues], as also in sundry other works of his," E.K. concurrently declares his reticence to share any insider information that might admit a reader into the poet's "priuie" (cabinet) counsels: "Now as touching the general dryft and purpose of his AEglogues, I mind not to say much, him selfe labouring to conceale it" (p. 418). On the other hand, E.K. is always ready to point out, in a manner similar to the instructively glossed model letters of Angel Day, "a pretty Epanorthosis ... and ... Paronomasia" (p. 423) or "a patheticall parenthesis" (p. 440) as they occur in the eclogues. Pages of his regularly mystifying headnotes and endnotes confirm E.K.'s reluctance to give away much in the way of meaning or intention. From the gloss to "Februarie": "Phyllis) the name of some mayde vnknowen, whom Cuddie, whose person is *secrete*, loued" (p. 426; emphases added throughout). From the Argument of "March": "But more particularlye I thinke, in the person of Thomalin is meant some *secrete* freend" (p. 428). From the "Aprill" gloss: "The Widowes) He calleth Rosalinde the Widowes daughter of the glenne ... which I think is rather sayde to *coloure and concele* the person, then simply spoken" (p. 433). From the "June" gloss: "Menaclas) the name of a shephearde in Virgile; but here is meant a person *vnknowne and secrete*, agaynst whome he often bitterly inuayeth" (p. 443). From the gloss to "August": "By Perigot who is meant, I can not vprightly say" (p. 451). From the gloss of "September": "As also by the names of other shepheardes, he *couereth* the persons of diuers other his familiar freendes and best acquayntaunce" (p. 455), and "This tale of Roffy seemeth to coloure some particular Action of his. But what, I certeinlye know not" (ibid.). From "November": "The personage is *secrete*, and to me altogether vnknowne" (p. 460), as well as "The person both of the shephearde and of Dido is vnknowen and *closely buried* in the Authors conceipt" (p. 463). And so on and on. Unflaggingly playing his part in maintaining the *Calender*'s cover of secrecy, E.K. – either by pleading ignorance of the poet's designs or by simply refusing to disclose them – habitually provides glosses that fail to gloss the text they are supposed to illuminate. Rather than drawing back the pastoral veil and uncovering what has been secreted in these deeply encrypted poems, E.K.'s annotations veil more than they ever reveal. *It is thus not secrets that E.K. discloses but rather secrecy itself.* Even in the rare instance where we find him denying any hidden agenda on the part of the poet – as in the Argument to "Februarie" when he declares that the eclogue is rather "morall and generall, then bent to any secrete or particular purpose" (p. 423) – E.K.'s disavowal has the opposite effect of consequently raising the stakes and calling attention to what then must be concealed in the ecclesiastical and political satire it prefaces.

E.K.'s function, then, is to encode the text as full of secrets. But what of these secrets? What content is there to them? Could each secret be deciphered in the way that the Hobbinol/Harvey identification is? My suspicion is that they cannot, that much of what is on display in the *Calender* as a secret is constituted as an empty secret.[63] As an epistemological category, the secret remains elastic in form inasmuch as it is able to receive and release its contents continuously. "What originally was manifest becomes secret," Georg Simmel observes in the course of his valuable study of the structures of secrecy and secret societies, "and what once was hidden later sheds its concealment."[64] Theorized this way, the chief investment in a secret may not lie in the actual content of the secret – which may or may not be disclosed at any given moment, or may even have been known all along; rather that investment could be simply in the employment of the apparatus of secrecy. Sometimes that is all there is: the form of a secret, hollowed out, concealing nothing except its own emptiness. This is the empty secret, in which we look for something to be stored, some hidden piece of information, and instead discover (or do not) that there is nothing there except for secrecy. Such is often the case, I suspect, in *The Shepheardes Calender*. This is not to claim, however, that all the secrets in Spenser's text are of the same order. Indeed, one could speak meaningfully here of a plethora of secrecies. Yet even when there does appear to be a real content to some secret stored in the poem – some special referent (like Leicester's secret marriage in "March") that is concealed or goes unsignified except as a secret – it is arguable nonetheless that what is secreted is less significant to the designs of the *Calender* than the fact of and insistence upon secrecy, than secrecy as a trope.

But why the constant display of secrecy? Once again, Simmel can be of help here. Secrets, he shows, regularly function as a form of adornment, and, like other forms of adornment, their aim is "to lead the eyes of others upon the adorned."[65] In order to do so, the secret depends, Simmel maintains, upon the essential contradiction that "what recedes before the consciousness of others and is hidden from them is to be emphasized in their consciousness," so that "one should appear as a particularly noteworthy person precisely through what one conceals."[66] The ostentatious staging of secrets in *The Shepheardes Calender* can similarly be seen as a tactic of self-promotion, as a form of adornment – along with the text's rhetorical flowers, as well as its emblems, woodcuts, and scholarly gloss – designed to focus interest on the new poet's work and enhance its cultural status. We are encouraged, in short, to measure the importance of the *Calender* in terms of the amount of secrecy that adheres to it and is invested in it.

Similarly, there is an element of self-promotion in the *Calender*'s recurring references to a storehouse of works its author is supposed to have written but has yet to uncover in print. Spenser opens the volume with the promise – in terms which again suggest that he regards his texts as letters to be sent and received – that he is ready "to send more after thee" ("To His Booke," 18), but only if this first installment finds an approving audience of "friends." The titles of some of these withheld (and in that sense secret) texts appear in the prefatory epistle to Harvey, who, like his friend Immeritô, is also said to have written "so many excellent English poemes ... which lye hid" (p. 419). What is ascribed there to "our new Poete" is an extensive, markedly Chaucerian, canon that includes "his Dreames, his Legendes, his Court of Cupide, and sondry others," all of which are reported to "slepe in silence" (p. 418). This inventory, in effect, publicizes Spenser as having nearly matched, even before his debut in print, the figure he himself helps canonize as the father of English poetry. The gloss for "June" further adds to the store of the new poet's undisclosed *copia* by referring to and citing from a collection of "his

Pageaunts" (p. 443). Moreover, in the Argument to "October" we are told that Spenser has also completed a rhetorical handbook, *The English Poete*, which E.K. promises to have published shortly.

Of course none of these works as such were ever brought forth in print, although several of the titles continue to be disseminated in later publications by Spenser as items in increasingly exorbitant advertisements of withheld texts. In one of the "Three proper and wittie familiar Letters," Spenser boasts to Harvey that

> my *Dreames* shoulde come forth alone, being growen by meanes of the Glosse ... full as great as my *Calendar*. Therein be some things excellently, and many things wittily discoursed of *E.K.* and the Pictures so singularly set forth, and purtrayed, as if *Michael Angelo* were there, he could (I think) nor amende the best, nor reprehende the worst. I know you woulde lyke them passing wel. (p. 612)

Advertising the excellence of this text while continuing to withhold it, Spenser represents himself as a writer who reserves more than he ever displays, who always has something important, something one would very much want to see, hidden away. That is, like the namesake of Angel Day's manual, the poet/secretary Spenser is always storing secrets.

Harvey responds to this display of withholding with a mock complaint about being denied a look at either the highly-touted "Dreames," or yet another unpublished poem entitled the "dying Pellicane." Harvey also gestures playfully towards unmasking the reservist strategy (he has used it too) behind his friend's enticing advertisements of what he never seems quite ready to unveil in public: "I imagine," he writes, "your *Magnificenza*, will holde vs in suspense as long for your nine Englishe *Commoedies*, and your Latin *Stemmata Dudleiana*" (p. 620). Keeping the reader in suspense, keeping the text a secret – here is yet another Spenserian signature: the poet's "Magnificenza" is signed "Suspense(r)." A further index of texts held in reserve is recorded in the printer's preface to Spenser's volume of *Complaints* (1591). Although nothing is now said about the existence of any dramatic works, the preface does provide Spenser with yet another extensive unpublished corpus, in this case one of predominantly devotional works, including translations of *Ecclesiastes* and the *Canticum canticorum*, a work called *The Sacrifice of a Sinner*, a book of hours, and *"The seuen Psalmes"* (p. 470).

The appearance of rushing into print was shunned by Elizabethan writers with gentlemanly aspirations, as J. W. Saunders' classic essay "The Stigma of Print" demonstrates.[67] It seems probable, though, that something more than decorous delay is involved in the continued circulation in print of these extravagant inventories of withheld texts. Religious writer, dramatist, Latin elegist, rhetorician, translator, Chaucerian poet of dream visions and legends: Spenser's phantom canons – always hidden in plain sight – continually refashion and extend his literary achievements, promoting him as an even more prodigious writer than he is known to be from his already considerable publications. It will probably never be determined how many, if any, of these "lost works" existed as nothing more than titles, or whether some were indeed written and have subsequently disappeared because Spenser never chose to publish them, and hence really were secret. But even *The Faerie Queene*, a poem he did in fact write (if not complete) and unveil in print, existed at least for a time as another withheld and secret text, deposited, according to Lodowick Bryskett, Spenser's good friend and fellow English civil servant in Ireland, in "a goodly cabinet, in which this excellent treasure of vertue lieth locked vp from the vulgar sort."[68]

Spenser's closet

A cabinet is precisely where one, having read Angel Day's handbook or any other Renaissance treatise on the subject, would expect a secretary to have stored secrets. In *The Shepheardes Calender* Spenser, we have seen, stores many of his secrets – or more precisely stores secrecy – in the "cabinet" provided by E.K.'s editorial apparatus. This recognition leads to a further one: in the "person" of E.K., Spenser has written the secretary function into the structure of his own text. The repository for the secrets of another; employing his pen in the interests of another; possessing no independent existence apart from his relation of service to another (who knows E.K. as anything but Spenser's glossator?); having no real name of his own except the one that Day likewise bestows on the secretary – the name of "verie special and singular good frend" (p. 416): E.K. can be said to occupy the position of a secretary. The very "selflessness" of E.K. exemplifies the intimacy, the secret-sharing, of the master–secretary coupling, remarked by Day and others, in which the two men have been elided into one subject position. For behind E.K.'s hand – whether those obscure initials are the signature mark of an Edward Kirke, or of Fulke Greville, or of Gabriel Harvey, or even more likely of the poet himself – is surely the hand of Spenser. E.K.'s prefatory epistle, full of hardly subtle assertions of Spenser's claim to the mantles of Chaucer and Virgil, is transparently a letter drafted at the behest of the poet it is meant to promote. Nor do E.K.'s glosses, in all the elaborate ways they are made to play off the discoveries and recoverings staged within the eclogues, have the appearance of being the work of an independent commentator. Instead, what E.K. has written bears the mark of having been directed, maybe even dictated by Spenser.

It is important, then, to recognize that the deployment of secrecy in *The Shepheardes Calender* is more than a highly-wrought publicity stunt, more than a newcomer's means of garnering attention by adorning his first book with what Muriel Bradbrook has termed "delicious you-know-who's."[69] It needs to be recognized, moreover, that the *Calender*'s secreting is routinely carried beyond mere discretion, beyond the provision of a cover of deniability against censorship. My argument is rather that the secret designs of *The Shepheardes Calender* have more to do with Spenser's *employability*. That is, Spenser's manipulations of secrecy in the *Calender*, along with the evidence it provides of his humanist education and rhetorical abilities, are displayed as credentials for aristocratic service. The talent for producing poetry of a certain kind was often a means of entrance into the employment in a noble house.[70] Spenser's first volume of poetry was composed and published with just such a career aspiration. In it, we see him angling for patronage and for office, throwing out lines to Sidney, to Leicester, even to Elizabeth. The *Calender* is Spenser's bid for preferment, undoubtedly as a poet of national or laureate stature, but also – since, as I argued in Chapter 1, the professional and the vocational were never segregated for him – for preferment as a secretary.

That *The Shepheardes Calender* is a bid for career advancement is apparent in the "Aprill" eclogue, a poem that celebrates equally the glory of the monarch to whom it is dedicated and the skill of the poet who is able to style that glory into a song. At the beginning of the eclogue Colin Cloute is referred to as "the Southerne shepheardes boye" (21). E.K.'s gloss is characteristically evasive ("Seemeth hereby that Colin perteyneth to some Southern noble man, and perhaps in Surrye or Kent") (p. 433), though it would be plain to those who knew the poet that, like the designation of Colin as Roffy's "selfe boye" in "September," this is another allusion to Spenser's position as John Young's secretary. However, Colin's showy encomium in "Aprill" is a gift, not to his current employer, but to a potential employer and patron, the queen herself. E.K. informs us that Colin has left behind "all former delightes and studies" (p. 431) and has set his sights far beyond the "Kentish downes" (p. 433). In line with this proposed change in station, Colin takes for himself a new job description, replacing his title as "the Southerne shepheardes boye" with a more ambitious self-nomination: "Shee is my goddesse plaine, / And I her shepherds swayne" (97–98).

It is significant that Colin's song in "Aprill" has a frame, that it is a poem within a poem. And in this frame we are twice told that, although the lay was composed by Colin, it has been left up to Hobbinol to "recorde" it: "But if hys ditties bene so trimly dight," Thenot requests, "I

praye thee *Hobbinoll*, recorde some one" (29–30). Likewise, the eclogue's
Argument reports that Hobbinol "taketh occasion . . . to recorde a songe,
which the sayd Colin sometime made in honor of her Maiestie, whom
abruptely he termeth Elysa" (p. 431). The primary sense of "recorde" in
these instances is musical. It means to sing or play, which is exactly what
Hobbinol, taking the place of the regularly disappearing Colin Cloute,
does in the eclogue. But "recorde" also connotes transcription and the
scene of Hobbinol copying Colin's words, putting them down in writing.
Acting in such a capacity, Hobbinol occupies a position *within* the poem
analogous to the one occupied by E.K. outside or in the margins of it:
both instance the secretary function, dutifully recording words that
belong to and are dictated by another. It is thus not only the author
function that is subject to dispersal and multiplication in Spenser's text,
but the secretary function as well. The sustained diffusion of voices and
subject positions in *The Shepheardes Calender* is itself related to the
secretary function, which diffuses subjectivities (both the secretary's and
the master's) even as it secures them within the site of the bureaucratic
closet.

It is appropriate, then, that the erotics of the secretarial function are
given their fullest articulation in *The Shepheardes Calender* around the
figure of Hobbinol, who serves as "secretary" and as friend. At the
beginning of the "Aprill" eclogue Hobbinol names Colin as him "whome
long I lovd so deare" (10), and in "Januarye" we hear of Hobbinol
attempting to draw Colin's attentions away from Rosalind with gifts and
"with dayly suit" (56). E.K.'s lengthy gloss calls attention to this as a
scene of male courtship: "In thys place seemeth to be some sauour of
disorderly loue, which the learned call paederastice: but it is gathered
beside his meaning" (pp. 422–423). "Gathered beside": does this mean
gathered apart from his meaning, we might ask, or gathered next to it?
For even as E.K.'s pedantic note unfolds in the direction of a platoni-
zation of "paederastice" that appears to disavow male relations that are
sexual, it nonetheless affirms the value and primacy of male bonds that
are eroticized:

For who that hath red Plato . . . may easily perceiue, that such loue is muche to be
alowed and liked of, specially so meant, as Socrates vsed it: who sayth, that in
deede he loued Alcybiades extremely, yet not Alcybiades person, but hys soule,
which is Alcybiades owne selfe. And so is paederastice much to be preferred
before gynerastice, that is the loue whiche enflameth men with lust toward woman
kind.[71] (p. 423)

These "much preferred" relations between men are more properly
revealed (and reveiled) in the Renaissance under the name of friendship,
and earlier in the same note E.K. identifies Hobbinol – in a naming that

corresponds to Day's ultimate description of the secretary – as the author's "very speciall and most familiar freend" (p. 422). Moreover, the relations between these two friends, like those "undiscovered" affections between master and secretary in William Cecil's "The State and Dignity of a Secretary of State's Place," are, in E.K.'s word, "hidden." That is, these relations exist – to use a phrase that signifies both in the discourse of secretaryship and in the homosocial order in which the secretary has his place – as *relations of the closet*. In that space, the "love" that can speak (as friendship) may approach something more (c)overtly sexual.

The bonds between friends threatened by Rosalind in "Januarye" are mostly restored by the "June" eclogue, but she is only one of several rivals to Hobbinol to emerge over the course of the *Calender*. In the "September" eclogue, Hobbinol's claim on Colin as "my ioye" (177) is echoed and superseded by Colin's procurement of a position as Roffynn's "selfe boye" (176) or secretary. This supplantation lines up the occupational and the erotic (just as Cecil's treatise on secretaryship does) by situating Hobbinol in an analogous position with regard to Roffynn as to the one he holds in relation to Rosalind: Hobbinol is always the one left behind. Thus, Goldberg observes in "Colin to Hobbinol," "as Colin moves beyond the pastoral world, Hobbinol stays behind, representing what must be refused in order to advance."[72] I would suggest, moreover, that the dispensing with Hobbinol repeatedly staged in the eclogues relates to the fact that one of the very few secrets the *Calender* does uncover, one of the only times it satisfies our desire for referentiality, is in the disclosure that Hobbinol names Harvey. Soon to step into the role of nearly everyone's favorite whipping boy, Harvey was making a public spectacle of himself by means of his overweening careerism, his overtures without coverture. It was Harvey and not Spenser, for instance, who was singled out for ridicule by Nashe for the publicity stunt of the "Familiar Letters."

In the eclogues, Colin Cloute is always leaving behind Hobbinol and what he represents; correspondingly in the gloss, Spenser seems to be disowning Harvey by opening up the secret of Hobbinol. At the same time, however, the display made of Hobbinol is more complicated than an outright dissociation insofar as that disavowal also serves as the means to occult Colin's own career (and erotic?) ambitions by displacing them as Hobbinol's and hence not his own. For Hobbinol's/Harvey's route is also the announced route to worldly advancement, and his credentials, as well as his singular career highlight of presenting a poem to the queen during her progress, are duly recorded in the "September" gloss. Furthermore, Harvey was already a Fellow at Pembroke when Spenser entered the college as a sizar (a poor scholar assigned servant's duties in exchange for room and board) in 1569, and he surely served as something of a mentor for his similarly career-minded young friend. "The intimacy with his special friend," Goldberg continues, "writes the aspirations within the rhetorico-literary even as the name Hobbinol insists that such aspirers know their place: boys, secretaries to the great and powerful."[73]

That is just the place Colin Cloute envisions for himself in "Aprill" in relation to Eliza. We find him "recording" her – her image, her words – just as Hobbinol records Colin's pastoral lay. For at the same time that Eliza receives Colin's song as a gift, she also serves as the muse that has dictated its terms. The master–secretary dimension of the muse–poet relation is perhaps most pointedly figured by Milton (another poet who worked as a secretary) in the prologues of *Paradise Lost*, where his muse "deigns / Her nightly visitation unimplor'd / And dictates to me slumb'ring."[74] The expression is not as explicit in *The Shepheardes Calender*, but the notion that the words are ultimately the muse's (that is, the queen's), and not the poet's who records or copies them down, is likewise suggested in the Argument prefacing the "October" eclogue. In the mystified account given there, poetry is produced by means of "celestiall inspiration" and a certain *enthousiasmos* "poured into the witte" of the writer (p. 456). Thomas H. Cain notes that the root meaning of *enthousiasmos* takes us back to the scene of a god possessing and speaking through a spokesman – or when the spokesman is a writer, I add, dictating to a secretary.[75] The poet who is the privileged recipient of this *enthousiasmos* is not the originator of what he has written. He merely transcribes, puts on paper, the words "poured into" him. In the eclogue itself, the terms Cuddie uses to describe what the queen does for Colin – she "teach[es]" "lyftes," "rayse[s]" and "cause[s]" (91–93, 95) – imply, Cain asserts, that Elizabeth herself is the source of this *enthousiasmos* for her poet. She is the power inspiring and dictating her own epideictic poetry, a point dramatized in "Aprill" when she is the one who is awarded the poet's bays:

> I see *Calliope* speede her to the place,
>   where my Goddesse shines:
> And after her the other Muses trace,
>   with their Violines.
> Bene they not Bay braunches, which they doe beare
>   All for *Elisa* in her hand to weare?

> (100–105)

Not only the subject of Spenser's poem, Elizabeth is the power inspiring and dictating it. He figures her as the "voice" that has spoken what he has written, and figures himself as her amanuensis, her secretary/poet.[76]

And, unlike the "poore Muse" (9) that the impoverished pastoral poet Cuddie serves in "October," the queen can reward the hand she employs:

"Let dame *Eliza* thanke you for her song," Colin Cloute unabashedly proposes in "Aprill" (150). And what are the thanks that Spenser would hope to receive from the queen? Surely it is poetic patronage, the "price" and the "prayse" that Cuddie and Piers debate in "October," the eclogue in the *Calender* most explicitly concerned with the social and economic relations between poets and patrons. But might the desired reward from Eliza also be a position in *her* cabinet? This is not to say that the poet of *The Shepheardes Calender* was necessarily promoting himself here as the queen's secretary at the level of Cecil or Walsingham, though such an ambition is not wholly outlandish. Secretaries, we have seen, were regularly drawn from Spenser's own ranks, those of middle-class, university-trained men. Thomas Smith – author of *De Republica Anglorum*, noted Greek scholar, Regius Professor of Civil Law, and incidentally Harvey's fellow townsman – provided one enviable example of advancement through scholarly distinction to the office of Secretary of State and Privy Councillor. Another prominent model for such an ambition, and one perhaps even more germane for Spenser, comes from the French poet Marot, an acknowledged influence on *The Shepheardes Calender*. In fact, Puttenham turns the career of Marot into an ideal standard for the relation between poet and ruler. "Frauncis the Frenche kinge," Puttenham reports approvingly, "made ... Clement Marot of his privy Chamber for [his] excellent skill in vulgare ... Poesie."[77] Significantly, the measure of success here is not any poetic honor, but a bureaucratic office. And that attainment, as Annabel Patterson has argued with different emphasis, delineates the privy place for which the doubly-employed Spenser – poet and secretary – could have (secret) designs: the place of cabinet councils.[78]

3   "In sundrie hands": the 1590 *Faerie Queene* and Spenser's *Complaints*

> Note also, that in every state, of what quality soever, a secret or cabinet-council is mainly necessary.
>
> *Cabinet-Council Containing the Chief Arts of Empire and the Mysteries of State: Discabineted* (attributed to Walter Ralegh)

The ostentatious disclosure of a cabinet of secrets in *The Shepheardes Calender* points up a conflict in the logic of concealment, a logic which dictates that the only way to show that one is a reliable keeper of secrets is to reveal that one has them. This logic shuttles the secret in two directions at once, involving an endless oscillation between two questions. What must be done in order to maintain the secret as a secret? But also, what must be done in order to disclose it, to make it known insofar that the secret of keeping a secret does not remain secret?[1] The undisclosed, in other words, must continue to operate on some discursive level. Thus at every turn *The Shepheardes Calender* speaks secrecy, if not actual secrets. Even so, it is questionable to what extent Spenser's necessary display of secrecy troubles and perhaps even undermines the *Calender*'s advertisement of his fitness to serve as a secretary – that is, as a silent, dutiful repository for secrets. For surely it would be a dubious move to employ a secretary who publicizes that he knows secrets, and knows that they are one field in which power relations are conducted. Angel Day's *English Secretary* and the other Renaissance treatises on secretaryship we have examined show that the master–secretary relation is one in which the latter figure is not always strictly silent and compliant. Yet none of these accounts of secretarial empowerment would deny that such qualities are at least the necessary pretense in an employer's selection of a secretary. The question then becomes: was Spenser's open deployment of secrecy in *The Shepheardes Calender*, along with its attendant power, knowledge, and subjectivity effects, a successful promotional strategy, or could this display – did this display – rebound?

The answer depends, I think, on what we make of Spenser's appointment as secretary to Lord Grey after the publication of the *Calender*. Was this position, which required the exchange of the attractions of the court for the comparative "wilds" of Ireland, another step towards the realization of his professional aspirations, or was it the disappointment of them? Muriel Bradbrook's view in "No Room at the Top: Spenser's Pursuit of Fame," perhaps the first study of Spenser as careerist, is unequivocal. As she sees it, Spenser was sent off, dismissed to Ireland, because of the criticisms of royal dealings (criticisms, it should be added, regularly heard within the Leicester circle) that he indiscreetly gave voice to in *The Shepheardes Calender* and in *Mother Hubberds Tale* – a punishment by exile which left the poet, Bradbrook remarks, "buried in a kind of Elizabethan Siberia."[2] Maybe so; but before we settle on this conclusion, we should consider whether, if Spenser had indeed so entirely fallen out of favor at court, the largesse of any aristocratic employment would have followed, much less a position that required him to handle correspondence directed to the queen and her chief ministers. When the disclosure of John Donne's secret marriage to Ann More ruined his career at court in 1601 and occasioned the loss of his position as secretary to Thomas Egerton, Donne's bid for a lower level Irish secretaryship was turned aside, as was his next attempt to secure a similar post with the Virginia Company at an even further remove from the court in the New World. Spenser, however, not only landed the position of the Lord Deputy's chief secretary, but also managed once there to capitalize on his personal and professional ties to Grey, even after Grey was recalled to England, to garner additional offices and expropriate Irish land. Contrary to the notion of a painful, obdurate Irish exile, Spenser's first decade in Ireland was a relatively prosperous, if unglamorous, period, entailing the enhancement of his own social and economic stock. Whether he hoped to spend the rest of his career there is, of course, another matter.

The culmination of that first decade in Ireland was Spenser's publication of Books 1–3 of *The Faerie Queene*, entered by publisher William Ponsonby in the Stationers' Register on December 1, 1589. With this poem, Spenser, advancing from pastoral to epic, attained the final phase of the Virgilian career progression. Equally importantly, the poem permitted him to elaborate on a much grander scale the conceit of the *Calender*'s "Aprill" and "October" eclogues, in which he had figured his verse as a form of poetic dictation received from a monarch who is both his master and his muse. This chapter will follow the more or less hidden paths by which this idealized fiction of poetic production – what I will call Spenser's secretarial poetics – shapes the first three books of *The Faerie Queene*, as well as that conceit's rather abrupt displacement in the collection of poems which follows them. For Spenser's next publication, appearing in 1591, is not a further installment of the promised twelve books of Elizabeth's epic; it is instead a decisively non-laureate, non-imperial volume of *Complaints*, in which praise of the sovereign and celebration of national destiny is conspicuously neglected. Offered in their place is an expansive articulation of what I regard as Spenser's own professional frustration of "Still wayting to preferment vp to clime" (*Mother Hubberds Tale*, 76), frustration that his epic accomplishment did not merit further advancement and with it, presumably, a place at court. An anthology of new compositions and possibly older, recycled ones, *Complaints* is moreover prefaced by a charged reclamation of Spenser's texts as the poet's own property.[3] This assertion of authorial ownership is established in the publisher's preface to *Complaints* against unnamed literary "imbezile[rs]" (those who don't give proper payment?), and it runs counter to the ostensible premise of the first installment of *The Faerie Queene* that the epic, offered to Elizabeth as a textual "mirror" or transcription of her majesty, is literally hers, and not the poet's, who merely served as the secretary who recorded it.

The argument of this chapter is, in short, that the move from the 1590 *Faerie Queene* to *Complaints*, along with the more "personal" works that follow in its wake (*Colin Clouts Come Home Againe*; the "Marriage Poems", the appearance of Colin Cloute in the 1596 installment of *The Faerie Queene*), enacts a significant public renegotiation of both Spenser's relation to the court and his terms of literary management.[4] This renegotiation entails Spenser's staging of a suspension of his role as imperial poet – a detour *in media res* from his path along the high Virgilian career route – and, concurrent with this detour, a "revival" of the medieval forms of complaint, dream vision, estates satire, and fabliau. Spenser uses these "antique" genres as a means for unmasking certain fictions upon which patronage and courtly advancement depend. That is, whereas the impulse in his poetry up through the 1590 *Faerie Queene* was to keep secrets, the impulse in the 1591 *Complaints* is to expose them.

"Hidden still": *The Faerie Queene* 1–3

The first book of *The Faerie Queene* opens with a concatenated series of invocations which provides, as has been discussed at length in Spenser criticism, a self-reflexive account of the poem's origins and the poet's shaping of his career.[5] Less remarked on, however, is the degree to which the poetic etiology Spenser offers there is structured, as by now we should have come to expect, in terms of a manifest secrecy:

> Lo I the man, whose Muse whilome did maske,
>   As time her taught, in lowly Shepheards weeds,
>   Am now enforst a far vnfitter taske,
>   For trumpets sterne to chaunge mine Oaten reeds,

> And sing of Knights and Ladies gentle deeds;
> Whose prayses hauing slept in silence long,
> Me, all too meane, the sacred Muse areeds
> To blazon broad emongst her learned throng:
> Fierce warres and faithfull loues shall moralize my song.

This stanza speaks of unmasking, of breaking the sleep of silence, of blazoning abroad a hidden history. Yet for all the impetus towards disclosure here, much remains obscure. For if pastoral was only a mask, and if the move to epic feels uncomfortably compelled ("enforst"), what kind of poet then is really putting himself forward here, however reluctantly? The Virgilian self-identification – "Lo I the man" – of the opening line does not effect the anticipated disclosure of the author, but only an unmasking of his muse, presumably leaving the author's own cover intact. And who is his muse unmasked to be? The succeeding stanzas uncover an array of possible identifications: a pretended shepherdess (st. 1.2); Clio or Calliope, as the "holy Virgin chiefe of nine" (st. 2.1); Venus (st. 3.2); the "Goddesse heauenly bright" (st. 4.1); the "Great Lady of the greatest Isle" (st. 4.3); the poet's "dearest dred" (st. 4.9). But whether, as Jonathan Goldberg asks, these are the names of as many different figures of invocation, or whether they are alternate identifications for the same source of inspiration – thereby treating, I add, the muse to the same occluding process of dispersal continually on display in *The Shepheardes Calender* – is not at all apparent at this point in the poem.[6] What is clear, however, is that all the masking, all the secreting, has not ended with the proem's inaugural unmasking. Prefacing a book deeply invested in the successive veilings and unveilings of its central characters, the proem is perhaps best taken as the discovery of muse and poet merely altering their disguises.[7]

The familiar Spenserian trope of secrets revealed in order to be reveiled circulates as well through the second stanza and its disclosure of the muse's "euerlasting scryne":

> Helpe then, O holy Virgin chiefe of nine,
>   Thy weaker Nouice to performe thy will,
>   Lay forth out of thine euerlasting scryne
>   The antique rolles, which there lye hidden still,
>   Of Faerie knights and fairest *Tanaquill*,
>   Whom that most noble Briton Prince so long
>   Sought through the world, and suffered so much ill,
>   That I must rue his vndeserued wrong:
> O helpe thou my weake wit, and sharpen my dull tong.

Scrine, Judith H. Anderson points out in a recent study of the metaphorics of sources in *The Faerie Queene*, comes from the Latin word *scrinium*.[8] For its meaning, she directs us to Robertus Stephanus' *Thesaurus linguae latinae* (1576–1578), where *scrinium* is derived from *secernendum* ("setting apart, secreting") and defined as a shrine or sacred place for the preservation of precious objects or mysteries (*secreta*). Anderson also cites Thomas Cooper's *Thesaurus linguae romanae & britannicae* (1584), a standard scholastic dictionary in Spenser's day, which defines *scrinium* as "a coffer or other like place wherein jewels or secrete things are kept." She moreover calls attention to the citation by both Cooper and Stephanus of Catullus' phrase "librariorum ... scrinia" – the booksellers' chests of manuscripts or rolls – among their illustrations of the meanings of *scrinium*, as well as to the establishment under the later Roman emperors of several kinds of public *scrinia* to serve as archives for books and various other written records. In addition to the *thesauruses* (or "treasuries") cited by Anderson, I would like to add one more: Robert Estienne's *Dictionariolum Puerorum Tribus Linguis Latina, Anglica, and Gallica* (1552), which includes the term "cabinet" in its inventory of synonyms for *scrinium*.[9] This association allows us to establish a link between the *The Shepheardes Calender*'s "green cabinet" – taken to be, as has been argued in the previous chapter, the privy study of this poet/ secretary – and the refiguring of this secret place in *The Faerie Queene* as the scrine administered by the poet's muse.

These longstanding associations of scrines with written records bear directly on the scrine of *The Faerie Queene*, which serves as the repository for a text ("antique rolles") concealed within the text. From this hidden text the poet claims he has derived his epic: Spenser's pretext is literally a secret. More specifically, what is locked up in the muse's scrine, according to the proem, is the history of Prince Arthur's protracted quest for "fairest *Tanaquill*"; and to tell *that* story, it is intimated here, is to tell what is secret. Thus the single time Arthur narrates, in response to Una's inquiry about his "secret wound" (1.9.7.8), his visionary encounter with the "Queene of Faeries," he does so in terms of divulging a secret:

> Yet sithens silence lesseneth not my fire,
> But told it flames, and hidden it does glow,
> I will reuele, what ye so much desire.

(1.9.8.6–8)

Having first fostered an aura of secret-sharing, Arthur then relates his mysterious dream of Gloriana, as the Tanaquill of the proem (an identification which awkwardly recalls a powerful Roman *wife*) is quickly renamed. But what his dream means and what its relation is to his presence and purpose in Faery Land – that is, whether the dream was the agency responsible for bringing him there by "wayes yet neuer found" (st. 7.6), or whether it was some other "cause to me vnghest" (st. 7.2) – remains a mystery Arthur himself cannot penetrate:

Full hard it is (quoth he) to read aright
The course of heauenly cause, or vnderstand
The secret meaning of th'eternall might,
That rules mens wayes, and rules the thoughts of liuing wight.

(st. 6.6–9)

Echoing Merlin's promise concerning the disclosure of the Prince's lineage "As time in her iust terme" will reveal (st. 5.9), the departing Faery Queen implies that with her imminent return all "secret meanings" will "when iust time expired ... appeare" (st. 14.4). This pledge establishes Gloriana as the vanishing point at which the inscrutable (at least to Arthur) providential design that produces the hero on schedule in the eighth canto of each book will coalesce with his own erotic quest.[10] To Arthur, however, who has borne this promise within himself and searched for "Nine monethes ... in vaine" (st. 15.9), the now overdue revelation should already have come to term. As everyone who has read *The Faerie Queene* knows, however, the poem neither then nor ever fully makes good on this promised disclosure. No sooner does Gloriana offer her troth than she disappears forever from the poem. If, as David L. Miller suggestively remarks in *The Poem's Two Bodies*, Gloriana is to be taken as the poem's vanishing point, its synecdoche for completion, then the unobtainable, undiscoverable Faery Queen is also its synecdoche for secrecy.[11]

Thus, even though *The Faerie Queene* begins by identifying as its narrative core the quest to locate Gloriana, it is precisely this story that remains on the whole untold in the poem. Arthur's appearances over the course of the epic, while regular, are short-lived. And the poem, in a departure from its accounts of the quests of the other knights for their beloveds, or even the Prince's own hot chase after Florimell in the first canto of Book 3, never shows Arthur actually searching for Gloriana. Nor do we ever find him asking directions from those, like Una or Red Crosse or Guyon, who have just come from her court. For that matter, it is not clear what exactly it might even mean for Arthur to pursue a figure from out of his dreams. Implicit in his ecstatic praise of her beauty – "So faire a creature yet saw neuer sunny day" (st. 13.9) – is the question of whether or not she exists at all. For, as the Prince regularly reminds us, Gloriana is literally "no where" (2.9.7.8) to be found. *The Faerie Queene*, in other words, never discloses the Faery Queen.

I will return shortly to the question of the poem's investment in keeping her as its secret, in failing to produce the Faery Queen – a question which later gets refigured by Spenser in the *Amoretti* (1595) as one of not producing (i.e., not finishing) *The Faerie Queene*.[12] Let us now, however, return to the description of the records stored in the muse's "euerlasting scryne" as "hidden still" – continuing to be hidden, always hidden,

hidden silently – to observe that the request to unlock the scrine and disclose its secrets always already contains its own denial.[13] From this inaugural refusal of disclosure, it would appear that Spenser's epic, like *The Shepheardes Calender*, the deeply encrypted volume of pastoral poetry that precedes and predicts it, will unfold as an even more expansive tableau for the discovery, not of secrets, but of secrecy per se.

Similarly, the chronicle of imperial British history that Arthur reads within the chamber of Eumnestes in the House of Alma – the second instance where the poem discloses a scrine – breaks off at the very moment it would reveal his (to him) secret ancestry:

> After him *Vther*, which *Pendragon* hight,
>   Succeding There abruptly it did end,
>   Without full point, or other Cesure right,
>   As if the rest some wicked hand did rend,
>   Or th'Authour selfe could not at least attend
>   To finish it: that so vntimely breach
>   The Prince him selfe halfe seemeth to offend,
>   Yet secret pleasure did offence empeach,
> And wonder of antiquitie long stopt his speach.

(2.10.68)

Expecting to find the name of the hero in this stanza, we instead discover the poet in his place, the pun on Arthur/Author marking the space of an authorial self-inscription. The insistent assertion of the author's hand in producing the text – a rendering that becomes both a rending and a veiling – creates effects we have observed before in Spenser's poetry. One is the exhibition of his abilities as a kind of amanuensis, whose hand is poised to "record" (9.56.3) whatever is dictated by Tudor dynastic interests. Put in other terms, Eumnestes, who tirelessly labors to transcribe and lay "vp in his immortall scrine" (9.56.6) the text which would eventually produce Elizabeth, is a surrogate within the poem for the author in the Spenserian capacity as poet/secretary and now historian. At the same time, the lacuna broken open in this record through the supplantation of Arthur's name by "th'Author selfe" (a tag that recurs from *The Shepheardes Calender*) also shows up as a marker of authorial investiture – one characteristically scripted by Spenser in terms of the constant attraction of the secret (is this what the text registers as Arthur's "secret pleasure"?), of an anticipated discovery yet to be unveiled, of the poet's own secret reserve. Here, as in his flagrant exhibitions of secrecy in both the *Calender* and the "Familiar Letters" to Gabriel Harvey, Spenser "signs" himself into *The Faerie Queene* as the withholder, the repository, of a secret. And in this case it is more than Arthur's biography that is reserved by the hand of the author. Arresting the text at Uther and preventing it from reaching

Arthur's birth, the poet also withholds the Prince's final union with Gloriana. This deferred ending means, among other things, that, although the *"Briton moniments"* is advertised in the canto's opening stanzas as Tudor propaganda, this text literally ends up with no place for Elizabeth – or at least no place for her apart from one within Spenserian deferral.

What I am suggesting is that Spenser's marked resistance to ending the narrative, his refusal to allow it ever to reach Elizabeth, is a redoubling strategy that works toward mutual empowerment *and* limitation for both the poet *and* the queen. By employing the familiar (politico-)theological trope of revealing the queen as what cannot be revealed, Spenser's text preserves her beyond her representation as a transcendental figure. Coincident with this, the deferral of the queen also serves the poet's efforts to reserve a measure of control, however circumscribed, over her representation. That is, if the Faery Queen must be preserved as unrepresentable, Spenser is the one doing the preserving, the one keeping her secret. In what follows I will explore the entailments of Spenser's strategy of non-disclosure for both the poet and the subject of his poem.

Spenser's endeavor to fashion some leverage of power – here it is once again the power to withhold – is maintained in view of the increasingly marginalized position of the poet as it is represented in the proems. We have already begun to trace the course by which the queen is discovered as the secret cynosure of *The Faerie Queene*'s every story. In the proem to Book 1, this path is marked by the re-representation from stanza to stanza of the poem's announced subject until Elizabeth alone occupies that position:

> And with them eke, O Goddesse heauenly bright,
>   Mirrour of grace and Maiestie diuine,
>   Great Lady of the greatest Isle, whose light
>   Like *Phoebus* lampe throughout the world doth shine,
>   Shed thy faire beames into my feeble eyne,
>   And raise my thoughts too humble and too vile,
>   To thinke of that true glorious type of thine,
>   The argument of mine afflicted stile:
> The which to heare, vouchsafe, O dearest dred a-while.
>
> (st. 4)

The poem's depth of field has been progressively constricted from a compass of unspecified "gentle deeds" performed by a group of knights and ladies in the first stanza, to the story of one knight and one lady (Arthur and Tanaquill) in the second, to its insular focus on the solitary figure of Elizabeth in the stanza quoted above. Declared in this final stanza of the proem to be herself both the epic's form ("stile") and its substance ("argument"), she is the poem's one subject. The only multiplicity here is the multiplicity of her nominations and attributes.

By the same token, the task of the muse in the proem's second stanza of abetting the poet's "weake wit" and sharpening his "dull tong" (2.9) is also now subsumed by the queen, who "shed[s] thy faire beames" into his "feeble eyne" and "raise[s]" his "thoughts too humble and too vile." These vatic powers recall the efficacy of Eliza's "immortall mirrhor" likewise to "rayse ones mynd aboue the starry skie" in *The Shepheardes Calender*'s "October" eclogue (93–94), another text in which she doubles as both the subject of the poem and the muse who has inspired it.[14] To write (for) the queen, in short, is to accept her dictation. The most pointed expression of Spenser's secretarial poetics in *The Faerie Queene* occurs in Book 3, when Spenser gives over the poem to Elizabeth so that "Thy selfe thy prayses tell, and make them knowen farre" (2.3.9). After this fashion, *The Faerie Queene* becomes a textual mirror, reflecting back to the queen the representation of herself she has herself dictated: 'And thou, O fairest Princesse vnder sky, / In this faire mirrhour maist behold thy face."

That invitation is extended in the proem to Book 2, where the structuring conceit that the poem is a royal mirror is given its most elliptical figuration.

> Right will I wote most mighty Soueraine,
>   That all this famous antique history,
>   Of some th'aboundance of an idle braine
>   Will iudged be, and painted forgery,
>   Rather then matter of iust memory,
>   Sith none, that breatheth liuing aire, does know,
>   Where is that happy land of Faery,
>   Which I so much do vaunt, yet no where show,
> But vouch antiquities, which no body can know.
>   . . .
> Of Faerie lond yet if he more inquire,
>   By certaine signes here set in sundry place
>   He may it find; ne let him then admire,
>   But yield his sence to be too blunt and bace,
>   That no'te without an hound fine footing trace.
>   And thou, O fairest Princesse vnder sky,
>   In this faire mirrhour maist behold thy face,
>   And thine owne realmes in lond of Faery,
> And in this antique Image thy great auncestry.
>
>   (st. 1, 4)

I claim that this is the most elliptical expression of the text-as-mirror conceit because of the subtle shift effected here in the referent of the recurring figure of "this faire mirrhour." In the proem to Book 1, that mirror is the "grace and Maiestie diuine" of the queen. In the proem to Book 2, however, what is now put forward as that mirror is the poem itself, serving in the capacity of a reflective transcription of royal grace and majesty. Notwithstanding Spenser's substitution of his literary representation of the queen for the queen herself, these stanzas continue the displacement of the writer as author by Elizabeth, who appears paradoxically here as a reflection in the mirror of the text, as a product of the text, and as the absolute originator of the text. Concurrently, the proem's obsessive, preemptive rehearsal of objections to its narrative claims – that the poem is the result of idleness; that Fairy Land does not really exist; and, perhaps most suggestive with regard to Spenser's career as a secretary, that the poem is a "forged" document – makes its hermeneutical circle even more hermetic. To all readers other than Elizabeth, the text is offered, A. Leigh Deneef remarks, as a deliberately contrived riddle, the way to Faery Land being found only "By certaine signes here set in sundry place."[15] In fact, the only possibilities Spenser seems to allow here for readers of his poem apart from Elizabeth are various sorts of misreadings – of "misweening" (st. 3.4) what the poem declares yet "no where shows," so that even those who may have successfully managed to find Faery Land might still be excluded from its mysteries by being "too blunt and bace." In exempting Elizabeth alone from the perils of misprision, the proem suggests that, in addition to being its subject and source, she is also its intended and only audience. Elizabeth, in Goldberg's neat formulation in *Endlesse Worke*, "*is* the text in vital ways: its producer, its substance ... and its reader."[16] In effect, the proem asks the queen to gaze at the representation she has dictated of herself looking at herself.

But what place does Spenser allot for himself in this closed hall of mirrors? I would suggest that it is an intimate one, the place of an especially privileged servant. That is, Spenser's mediatorial act of holding up a mirror for the queen may be regarded as his self-installation in something like the position to which he had been aspiring since the "Aprill' and "October" eclogues of *The Shepheardes Calender*. For, although the admonitory looking glasses of the *Mirror for Magistrates* tradition might be what comes to mind here first, the looking glass also had its place in a far more private domain.[17] To behold oneself in a mirror, as Anne Ferry reports in *The "Inward" Language*, was regarded as a rather intimate act in the sixteenth century, one associated with introspection and most often performed in privy chambers.[18] Moreover, until some time after glassmaking technology had crossed over the channel from the continent at the beginning of the seventeenth century, real glass mirrors (in contrast to those made of various metals) were highly prized possessions. Along with other valuables ranging from jewels to financial records, looking glasses were regularly stored in private rooms, closets, cabinets – and scrines. The private nature of the act of looking into a mirror is exemplified in the second canto of Book 3 of *The Faerie Queene* when Britomart "Into her fathers closet" retires in order to view herself in a looking glass, and thus to reflect upon affairs "that mote to her selfe pertaine" (st. 22).

In Puttenham's *Arte of English Poesie*, the most career-minded of all sixteenth-century poetic treatises, success is consistently measured not as much by laurels, nor by financial reward, as it is by a poet's gaining access to the privy chambers of lords and rulers. Chief among the examples Puttenham cites on this account is that of Virgil, who is named "friend" by Augustus and permitted to "solace" with the emperor in his "chambers, and gardins when none other could be admitted."[19] Similarly, Thomas Sternhold was rewarded for his poetic achievement by Henry VIII with an appointment as "groome of his priuy chamber."[20] Such was also the case with the French poet Alain Chartier, whose verses, Puttenham reports, earned him a place at the king's table, as well as kisses from the queen. Poetry thus constitutes one means of gaining entrance to privy chambers and being able there to solace with lords. Another path to such intimacy, we have seen, is that of the secretary, the uniquely privileged servant whose particular domain is the privy chamber, and who is the simulacrum or mirror of the master he serves in that place. Those two routes – the poetic and the secretarial – coalesce in exemplary fashion in *The Arte*'s account of poets who have "made it" when Puttenham goes on to suggest that the chief reward garnered by Chartier for his verses was the bestowal of a royal secretaryship.[21] Those same two routes to privy chambers are also made to coalesce in Spenser's own secretarial poetics as they shape the 1590 *Faerie Queene*. By putting himself forward here as the privileged functionary of the queen who holds up to her the poem as a private mirror, a mirror that reflects back what she has herself dictated, Spenser contrives – if only (for now at least) in the symbolic scheme of his poem – a fulfillment of the aspiration to install himself in the queen's private cabinet.

We have been examining how the master trope of Elizabeth as mirror/mirrored "authorizes" (in the related senses of both authority and authorship) the entire continuum of production, reception, and imagined reward in *The Faerie Queene*. Yet the image that mirror reflects, as Louis Adrian Montrose cogently observes in "The Elizabethan Subject and the Spenserian Text," is broken up, and methodically refracted throughout the poem.[22] In an often cited passage from "A Letter of the Authors,"

Spenser signals his intention to divide, in his own take on the familiar political doctrine of the monarch's two bodies, the already doubled Elizabeth:

In that Faery Queene I meane glory in my generall intention, but in my particular I conceiue the most excellent and glorious person of our soueraine the Queene, and her kingdome in Faery land. And yet in some places els, I do otherwise shadow her. For considering she beareth two persons, the one of a most royall Queene or Empresse, the other of a most vertuous and beautifull Lady, this latter part in some places I doe expresse in Belphoebe, fashioning her name acording to your owne excellent conceipt of Cynthia (Phoebe and Cynthia being both names of Diana). (p. 407)

The Faery Queen and Belphoebe are, Spenser reports, only split "shadows" of Elizabeth, who is always hidden "some places els." And as shadows, they veil more than they ever reveal, much like the mirror the queen is presented with in Book 2's proem, now oddly shrouded and "enfold[ed] / in couert vele, and wrap[ped] in shadowes light" (st. 5.1–2). These divided shadows, the Letter continues, are then to be further bifurcated inasmuch as Gloriana doubles both as the abstract quality of glory in the allegory's "generall intention" and as the person of Queen Elizabeth in its "particular." Even the supremely solitary and aloof Belphoebe likewise bears the marks of doubleness. Not only does she have a twin sister in Amoret, but her own name is, we are told, compounded from the already multiply-named Diana ("Phoebe and Cynthia being both names of Diana"). What Spenser expresses in the letter to Ralegh is a kind of inverse metonymy, in which the parts (these multiply divided and shadowed figurations of the queen) are the means by which the whole is *concealed* rather than expressed.

The notion that the queen is not to be written as a unitary representation is played out over the course of the narrative sprawl of Book 3, the book that purports to "Contayn" or pen – to hold, but also "pen" as in the "life-resembling pencill" of Zeuxis or Praxiteles (pro. 2.2–3), or the poet's own "humble quill' (st. 3.3)[23] – chastity, the virtue "farre aboue the rest" because it is Elizabeth's own:

> It falls me here to write of Chastity,
> That fairest vertue, farre aboue the rest;
> For which what needs me fetch from *Faery*
> Forreine ensamples, it to haue exprest?
> Sith it is shrined in my Soueraines brest,
> And form'd so liuely in each perfect part,
> That to all Ladies, which haue it profest,
> Need but behold the pourtraict of her hart,
> If pourtrayed it might be by any liuing art.

(st. 1)

Let us take seriously the question Spenser proposes in this stanza. Why indeed does the poet need to "fetch ... / Forreine ensamples" (it is always a plurality of examples) when the queen herself, the examplar of chastity, is available as a model? Or why offer a representation at all when the real thing is at hand? The answer given in the proem, according to Montrose, is that "because the queen's virtue and beauty are so perfect they are unrepresentable by painters and poets, except by a series of accommodations and displacements."[24] This fiction, however, must have been an increasingly difficult one to maintain in 1590. Elizabeth was then 57, and praising her as a beautiful young virgin must have seemed like a hopelessly belated gesture, though one no doubt dictated by the queen's own well-known attempts to appear agelessly youthful. Indeed, the stanza implicitly questions, even as it defers to the queen's unfigurable perfection, the assumption that her virtues and beauty exist apart from their portrayal by painters and poets. For what is being "shrined" (and *scrined* – for *scrine* also means shrine), what we would see if we were granted access to this sacred/secret space of the sovereign's breast, is, as Montrose notes, neither the queen nor a vision of chastity itself. What we would find hidden there is instead a "pourtraict of her hart," another representation.

We are informed, in fact, that the image we see mirrored in Book 3 is actually another poet's portrait of Queen Elizabeth:

> But if in liuing colours, and right hew,
>   Your selfe you couet to see pictured,
>   Who can it doe more liuely, or more trew,
>   Then that sweet verse, with *Nectar* sprinckeled,
>   In which a gracious seruant pictured
>   His *Cynthia*, his heauens fairest light?
>   That with his melting sweetnesse rauished,
>   And with wonder of her beames bright,
> My senses lulled are in slomber of delight.
>
> But let that same delitious Poet lend
>   A little leaue vnto a rusticke Muse
>   To sing his mistresse prayse, and let him mend,
>   If ought amis her liking may abuse:
>   Ne let his fairest *Cynthia* refuse,
>   In mirrours more then one her selfe to see,
>   But either *Gloriana* let her chuse,
>   Or in *Belphoebe* fashioned to bee:
> In th'one her rule, in th'other her rare chastitee.

(st. 4–5)

The "sweet verse" invoked here is, of course, Walter Ralegh's "The Ocean's Love to Cynthia," which proffers another fragmented and unfinished figuration of the queen. Almost imperceptibly, these stanzas delineate the poem's traversal, not only from Elizabeth to proliferating representations of her, but also from "referentiality to intertextuality."[25] It is Ralegh's "fairest *Cynthia*" – his poem, not the queen – that is reflected and refracted in *The Faerie Queene*'s "mirrours more than one" (st. 5.5–6). Spenser moreover accords a remarkable seductive and generative power to Ralegh's poem, making his *Cynthia* (again the text, not the "real" Cynthia) the female intermediary through which the "ravishment" of one male poet by another is accomplished. The resultingly fertile scene of male accouplement, *cum* insemination and reproduction, anticipates the account offered later in the same book of Chrysogenee's solarized conception of Belphoebe and Amoret. Spenser finds that, like the "slombring swowne" (6.7.3) Chrysogenee slips into after bathing in a fountain of "all the sweetest flowres" (6.6.9), his own "senses lulled are in slomber of delight" by Ralegh's "*Nectar* sprinckeled" poem. And in this state of poetic enravishment, he too is penetrated by "beames bright," just as Chrysogenee is "pierst into her wombe" with "sun-beames bright" (6.7.5–7). Whereas Chrysogenee gives birth to twins, however, it could be said that Spenser's "impregnation" by Ralegh results in the generation of the array of virgins – Britomart, Florimell (and her false double), as well as Belphoebe and Amoret – that populate Book 3, occasioning the ecstatic response of John Upton, Spenser's eighteenth-century commentator: "What a variety of chaste females!"[26]

The poem also shadows the queen with the more disruptive versions of her virtue embodied by the likes of the predatory but unmarried Malecasta, and possibly even by Marinell – in which case chastity is no longer an attribute of singularly female innocence, but rather a maternal law enforced on an unwilling son.[27] What it means that Elizabeth is shadowed and veiled in a proliferation of images and texts in *The Faerie Queene* – images and texts which no longer speak of singularity or fullness – has been variously interpreted. For Montrose, who regards the poem as the site of an "interplay between submission and resistance to the project of royal celebration which ostensibly defines it," the continual fragmentation and refiguration of the queen's image calls into question any claim of hers "to shape herself and her subjects, to personify the principle and power of form."[28] Elizabeth J. Bellamy, on the other hand, contrives a high poststructuralist reading of the dissemination of the queen into mere approximations of her name and power. The poem and its unsuccessful efforts to nominate Elizabeth "as unmediated Pure Name" represents, in Bellamy's Demanian account, a vocative *and* vocational "crisis": "Even as Arthur's search for Gloriana informs the structure of *The Faerie Queene*, we may surely go one step further and claim Spenser's parallel, and equally futile, search for Elizabeth as the epic's ultimate quest."[29] The poem is hence a "failure" because the poet is never able "to call forth her image from behind her 'couert vele' (2 proem 5.2) as the ultimate sanctioner of his epic task."[30]

I am, however, advancing an opposing paradigm for the 1590 *Faerie Queene*. Rather than seeking to "name" Elizabeth, or to lift the "couert vele" that always obscures her, the poem's investment, I suggest, lies precisely in maintaining that veil, in keeping her (as its) secret. And rather than occasioning the vocational crisis Bellamy describes, Spenser's secreting of Elizabeth serves as the poetic substantiation of his vocation as a poet who is also a secretary – who is, to recall Angel Day's formulation, "a keeper or conseruer of the secret unto him committed."

In this instance, that secret is the "couert vele" which covers Elizabeth throughout the first three books of *The Faerie Queene*. Spenser's reluctance to divest Elizabeth completely of her veil is a matter of propriety, a propriety that is political as well as personal. For here we might pause to consider just what this tautologically designated "couert" or *hidden* veil is. In "The Double Session," Derrida figures the veil that is hidden as the hymen.[31] If this too is the case with the queen's hidden veil in Spenser's epic, her hidden veil can also be glossed in terms of some sort of "Secret of Secrets" – another tautology which also happens to name a fifteenth-century handbook on rulership. The "couert vele" the poem demarcates but refuses to penetrate is thus both the virgin queen's hymen and the "secret" of her rule. This is to say that Elizabeth's unique leverage of monarchal power was constructed, as is well known, specifically in terms of her virginity. As Elizabeth declared in her first parliament, she would be pleased to be assigned the epitaph "that a Queen, having reigned such a time, lived and died a virgin."[32]

At the same time, it is apparent that the deployment of secrecy in *The Faerie Queene* extends beyond decorousness, as well as beyond what Montrose discusses as a self-censoring reluctance to penetrate and demystify the secrets of power (a self-censoring, incidentally, that does not seem to last through the 1596 installment of the poem).[33] For if, as a career secretary, Spenser is routinely required to keep the secrets of others, he has shown that he is also able to keep them on his own behalf, and the non-arrival of the fully unveiled queen serves her poet's interests as well as her own. Consequently, we have noted how *The Faerie Queene* produces, but is also itself produced by, multiple instances of resistance and even refusal to uncover what it keeps sealed within the muse's scrine. It is the blank of the veil(ed), the keeping of a secret – whether it covers a hidden signified, a key to something, or whether it is merely a hollow structure – that here, just as in *The Shepheardes Calender*, opens up the space of writing.

I would further suggest that the economy at work in *The Faerie Queene* dictating what can and cannot be revealed is homologous to that of *The Shepheardes Calender*. In the previous chapter we saw that the homoerotic, contrary to what might be expected, is one of the few matters the *Calender* is not at pains to veil. Hobbinol is an open and pronounced suitor for the affections of his friend Colin Cloute, and at stake in his suit is the prospect of restricting Colin within the confines of an edenic, all-male pastoral world. More importantly, the Hobbinol/Gabriel Harvey identification is, again as we saw in Chapter 2, one of very few secrets that is positively opened in the *Calender*'s cabinet of secrets. Whereas the name of the male friend is disclosed, however, the identity of Rosalind, the disruptive female figure in these triangulated affairs, is not and never has been deciphered. The essential "secret" of *The Faerie Queene*, as we have seen from its always multiply veiled figurations of Elizabeth, is likewise gendered female, while the position of the similarly career-minded male friend (once again openly named in a prefatory letter attached to the poem) is this time occupied by Ralegh.

A further correspondence between the two texts is suggested by E.K.'s treatment of Rosalind's name as a sort of anagram, "which being wel ordered, will bewray the very name of hys loue and mistresse" (p. 423) – "as if," Goldberg wryly comments, "the name were itself disordered (or the name of disorderly love)."[34] Jean Starobinski, summing up Ferdinand Saussure's voluminous work on anagrams, suggests that anagrams are signposts to a hidden discourse within a discourse.[35] One clue for discerning the "discourse" concealed in the anagrammatic disordering of the woman's name in Spenser's poetry might be gathered from Puttenham's transposition of Elizabeth's name in *The Arte of English Poesie*. In his hand, the phrase "*Eliss[z]abet Anglorum Regina*" is reordered as "*Multa regnabis ense gloria*" ("By the sword shalt thou raigne in great renowne"), which in turn is reconfigured as "*Multa regnabis sene gloria*" ("Aged and in much glorie shall ye raigne").[36] These plays on the letter and their prediction of a long reign are ostensibly offered as a gift to the queen, who, Puttenham reports, "took pleasure sometimes in the deciphering of names." Yet the anagrams and their transformation of the sword into old age are also, in Saussure's terms, a secret discourse on how to deface the queen's name. In this secret discourse, Elizabeth is rendered – represented, but also divided, as she regularly is in Spenser's *Faerie Queene* – at the level of the cryptogram, so that altering the order of a letter changes everything. One transposition endows her with a (phallic) sword, while the next leaves her aged and "castrated." The space between *ense* and *sene* marks, as I will discuss in Chapter 4, the gap or divide between the first three books of *The Faerie Queene* and the final three.

Spenser's *Complaints*: "Into each secrete part"

The proems to the 1590 *Faerie Queene* tell one story about the origins of the poem and the career of its poet, who seems to have proceeded directly, if uneasily, from his pastoral pipes to the higher strains of epic. Another story is suggested, however, by the seventeen dedicatory sonnets to various nobles (though, significantly, *not* to the queen) Spenser appends to his epic.[37] The recurring allusions in these sonnets to labor and husbandry repoint the economies of poetic production and consumption in *The Faerie Queene* by supplanting the court, the ostensible locus of the proems and their insistent regiocentricity, with a rural scene of agrarian industry that is more pertinent to the domain of georgic than epic. To the Earl of Oxford, Spenser offers his poem as "the vnripe fruit of an vnready wit" (2); to the Earl of Essex as "these first labours" (14); to the Earl of Ormond as "the fruit of barren field" (14); and so on. These tokens of premature harvesting – terms which Milton's *Lycidas* will apply so violently to pastoral, the usual genre of beginnings – imply both Spenser's familiar seeming reluctance about publication, as well as an alternative view of his epic as a continuation of poetic apprenticeship rather than its culmination – a move, once again, which presages Milton's repositioning of *Paradise Lost* as a prefatory work in the opening lines of *Paradise Regained*, the poem which comes after his epic.

As Jane Tylus has shown, in this period the language of husbandry speaks patronage, and Spenser's object in these georgically-inflected dedications of maintaining his circle of patrons (and perhaps even expanding it) is apparent enough.[38] But the terms of Spenser's patronizing agrarianism are further loaded in this context by the way he repeatedly calls attention to the laborious cultivation of his epic in a "sauadge soyle" ("To Grey," 12; "To Ormond," 2), too far removed from the established centers of cultural production, where there is "Not one *Parnassus*, nor one *Helicone* / Left for sweete Muses to be harboured" ("To Ormond," 6–7). Moreover, the qualities attributed to the produce of this savage (Irish) soil hint at something potentially more disruptive than a callow harvest or an untimely prolongation of poetic apprenticeship. For the fruit that is merely "vnripe" in the sonnet addressed to Oxford turns "wilde" in the sonnet to Ormond, only to be become positively noxious in the sonnet to Ralegh, the sequence's final dedication to a male patron. There Spenser recharacterizes his poetic offering as menacingly "vnsauory and sowre" (8).

If such declarations, which manage to strike at once registers of humility, compliance, and complaint, can be said to anticipate the volume of poems Spenser would publish next, they also turn back to the first book of *The Faerie Queene* and the career of its hero, the Redcrosse Knight. In his letter to Ralegh, Spenser relates the awkward episode of this same "tall clownishe younge man" putting himself forward at Gloriana's court to demand his first chivalric adventure, and "that being graunted, *he rested him on the floore*, vnfitte through his rusticity for a better place" (p. 408; emphasis added). The clownishness and "rusticity" of this emblematically named Redcrosse Knight might bring to mind any of the various country naifs of *The Shepheardes Calender*. But the same qualities also link him to that poem's author, who likewise makes a nameless debut as Immeritô, as well as to the narrator of *The Faerie Queene*, another "rustick" ("To Grey," 11), who represents himself as similarly green in the chivalric arena.[39] Of course everything changes for the Redcrosse Knight when his career is reconstructed at a climactic moment near the end of Book 1. There the lowborn knight, seemingly hatched out of the earth itself "in an heaped furrow" (10.66.2) is renamed, not once, but twice – progressing from Georgos (*geos*, earth, but also georgic) to "Saint *George* of mery England" (st. 61.9), from one "brought ... vp in ploughmans state to byde" (st. 66.5) to a national hero of apocalyptic stature.

The careerist fantasy that is conceived here is, I suggest, a particularly charged one for Spenser. It is the fantasy of being able to change places in the social order, of the outsider moving inside, of the lowborn gaining entrance to the Faery Queen's court and subsequently being reinvested there as a figure of cultural authority. Thus it hardly seems coincidental that in *The Faerie Queene*'s dedicatory sonnet to the Countess of Pembroke Spenser describes the inaugural gesture of his poetic career as being "*lift[ed] out of the flore*" (6), just as Redcrosse sits on the floor waiting for the boon that will initiate his advancement from plowman to patron of England. That the romance narrative adumbrated in the career of Redcrosse may be understood as one about the position of the poet in the culture is further suggested by its epiphany on canto 10 atop Mount Contemplation:

> That done, he leads him to the highest Mount;
>   Such one, as that same mighty man of God,
> That bloud-red billowes like a walled front
>   On either side disparted with his rod,
>   Till that his army dry-foot through them yod,
> Dwelt fortie dayes vpon; where writ in stone
>   With bloudy letters by the hand of God,
>   The bitter doome of death and balefull mone
> He did receiue, while flashing fire about him shone.
>
> Or like that sacred hill, whose head full hie,
>   Adornd with fruitfull Oliues all arownd,
>   Is, as it were for endlesse memory

> Of that deare Lord, who oft thereon was fownd,
> For euer with a flowring girlond crownd:
> Or like that pleasaunt Mount, that is for ay
> Through famous Poets verse each where renownd,
> On which the thrise three learned Ladies play
> Their heauenly notes, and make full many a louely lay.
>
> (10.53–54)

Through the sort of topographical and tropological condensation figured here, the site of poetic inspiration can be analogized to other loci of legal and religious authority: Mount Contemplation is like the poet's Parnassus, *and* it is like Sinai (itself a scene of writing, where divine law was "writ in stone / With bloudy letters"), *and* it is like Olivet (where Christ himself wears a flowering crown that resembles the poet's laurel). The elision of this trio of peaks in Mount Contemplation is of a piece with Spenser's larger project – one which he shared with the likes of Sidney, Gascoigne, Puttenham, Jonson, and others, whatever varying investments and conceptions of poetry differentiate their individual agendas – of attempting to resituate poetry from a marginal position where it exists only as "ydle rimes" ("To Burleigh," 7) to a place of high cultural importance.

Spenser may have hoped to see just such an ambition realized when he returned to England in 1590, the first three books of *The Faerie Queene* in hand, after nearly a decade of civil service toil in Ireland. Accompanying Walter Ralegh, his new-found patron and Irish neighbor, he traveled to London in order to oversee the publication of the opening installment of his epic, but also, as the poem's mass of dedicatory sonnets testify, to renew in person and in print his court connections. And under the sponsorship of Ralegh, Spenser, one of the lowest born of all the major Elizabethan poets, was indeed received at court. There, like a few privileged poets before him, he was able to present the queen with his *Faerie Queene*. According to *Colin Clouts Come Home Againe* (1595), Spenser's regressively pastoralized account of his reception at court as "a simple silly Elfe" (371), Elizabeth was pleased with the gift, "And it desir'd at timely houres to heare" (362). Even so, no preferment, no courtly office, was directly forthcoming, and after about a year's waiting Spenser returned to Ireland and his interests there. Once back in Ireland, he was granted a royal pension of fifty pounds, a reward which he seems to have felt was too hardfought and too long deferred.[40] Moreover, while fifty pounds made at the time an enviable stipend *for a poet*, it was a trifle compared to the wealth accrued by many courtly entrepreneurs.[41] And Spenser, I have argued, never seems to have set his sights on being "only" a poet.

Probably before he left England for what must have looked more and more like a permanent station in Ireland, Spenser's *Complaints* was

entered on the Stationers' Register. *Mother Hubberds Tale*, one of the
poems in this collection, is also in large part a story about a pilgrimage to
court – though in this account the court no longer functions as the
cynosure of potential reward and approbation, but rather as the site of
institutionalized self-abasement and humiliation:

> Most miserable man, whom wicked fate
> Hath brought to Court, to sue for had ywist,
> That few haue found, and manie one hath mist;
> Full little knowest thou that hast not tride,
> What hell it is, in suing long to bide:
> To loose good dayes, that might be better spent;
> To wast long nights in pensiue discontent;
> To speed to day, to be put back to morrow;
> To feed on hope, to pine with feare and sorrow;
> To haue thy Princes grace, yet want her Peeres;
> To haue thy asking, yet waite manie yeeres;
> To fret thy soule with crosses and with cares;
> To eate thy heart through comfortlesse dispaires;
> To fawne, to crowche, to waite, to ride, to ronne,
> To spend, to giue, to want, to be vndonne.
> Vnhappie wight, borne to desastrous end,
> That doth his life in so long tendance spend.
>
> (892–908)

In this self-perpetuating, ever more wildly excessive economy of disappointment, each hopeful sign of reward is instantaneously transvalued
as its own negation – so that, for instance, "To feed on hope" actually
means "to pine with feare and sorrow." And even when this seemingly
interminable system of frustration at last does give way, it is only to be
replaced by a potentially endless paratactic cataloging of unabated, and
ultimately ruinous, postures of abjection: "To fawne, to crowche, to waite
... / To spend, to giue, to want, to be vndonne."

Notwithstanding the bile of this complaint, which is nowhere answered
or mitigated in the poem or elsewhere in the volume, *Mother Hubberds
Tale* resembles in some other important respects the journey-to-court
narratives we have been examining. Its central characters, the Fox and the
Ape, fit the pattern of lowborn laborers, who (not unlike the aspiring
Redcrosse Knight) are cavaliers in search of adventures that will improve
their station:

> Wide is the world I wote and euerie streete
> Is full of fortunes, and aduentures straunge,
> Continuallie subiect vnto chaunge.
> ...
> Abroad where change is, good may gotten bee.
>
> (90–92, 101)

Despite, or perhaps because of, contemporary anxieties about the stability of class structures when families were moving up and down in the social and economic scale more rapidly than at any time before the nineteenth and twentieth centuries, the mutable world of *Mother Hubberd* allows for nearly boundless social mobility and self-improvisation.[42] Moreover, changing one's place in this world appears to be no more difficult than changing one's clothing.[43] By donning the appropriate garb, the Fox and the Ape trade occupations upwards from near the bottom of the social hierarchy all the way to the top, progressing from vagrants to shepherds to clerks to courtiers to minister and monarch. The implication here is that if one knows how to strike the right poses, every position in the social order, even the highest, can be impersonated. The alternate title of the poem, *Prosopopoia*, in fact means impersonation.

Correspondingly in *The Faerie Queene*, Redcrosse's "taking on him knighthood" ("A Letter of the Authors," p. 408) is originally effected at the level of taking on a change of attire. Putting on the spiritual armor St. Paul details in Ephesians 6 transforms him from a clownish upstart into a Protestant warrior. Redcrosse becomes what he wears. Of course, one would want to distinguish the knight from the similarly upwardly mobile Fox and Ape inasmuch as the latter are a pair of rogues, given to deceit, thievery, and even murder. But what is not usually registered in discussions of *Mother Hubberds Tale* is that the poem gives little indication that the enterprising pair have always been unredeemably corrupt.[44] Rather, it opens with an account of their dutiful, though ultimately unrewarded, service in what we are given no reason to question are legitimate occupations. Thus the Ape complains of years of being passed over for a deserved promotion:

> For I likewise haue wasted much good time,
> Still wayting to preferment vp to clime,
> Whilest others alwayes haue before me stept,
> And from my beard the fat away haue swept.
> That now vnto despaire I gin to growe,
> And meane for better winde aboute to throwe.

(75–80)

The story is much the same for the Fox. Unlike his aristocratic predecessor Renard, who is an important nobleman in the various medieval story cycles which provide a central source for *Mother Hubberds Tale*, Spenser's Fox has been toiling in an unfulfilling track as what appears to be a career civil servant:

> Thus manie yeares I now haue spent and worne,
> In meane regard, and basest fortunes scorne,
> Dooing my Countrey seruice as I might,

No lesse I dare saie than the prowdest wight;
And still I hoped to be vp aduaunced,
For my good parts; but still it hath mischaunced.
Now therefore that no lenger hope I see,
But froward fortune still to follow mee,
And losels lifted high, where I did looke,
I meane to turne the next leafe of the booke.

(59–68)

I want to make two points about these passages. The first is that, at least at the beginning of the poem, the complaints of the Fox and the Ape are presented not unsympathetically. The second point, following from this recognition, is that their subsequent commitment to a life of rapaciousness is figured as an extension into action of justifiable complaints about their lack of career advancement. The word *complaint*, derived from the Latin *planctus*, is related to *plaintiff*, an etymology which suggests one version of complaint as a form of recrimination, legal or otherwise. In this case, the treachery of the Fox and Ape is a retributive act, their spoils a way "to finde due remedie" (57) against a system grown disfunctional in its distribution of favor and reward.

The possibility of an "ironic coding" in *Mother Hubberds Tale* of Spenser and Ralegh's 1590 trip to the English court has been suggested by Jonathan Crewe in his extraordinary reading of *Complaints*.[45] Whether or not the poet intended such a parallel to be drawn, I follow Crewe's lead in situating the poem within the context of this "middle" period in Spenser's career. Such positioning stands in contrast, of course, to the longstanding practice (dating back to Edwin Greenlaw's influential essays of the 1900s and 1910s) of reading *Mother Hubberds Tale* as an index only to Spenser's *early* court dealings and particularly to his standing in relation to the Leicester and Burghley factions.[46] For, although some version of the poem possibly circulated in manuscript around 1579–1580 (in Greenlaw's view as a protest and warning concerning the proffered match of Queen Elizabeth and the French Catholic Duc d'Alençon), and although Spenser himself claims in his preface to the poem that it was "long sithens composed in the raw conceipt of my youth" (p. 495), *Mother Hubberds Tale* did not appear in print until the 1591 *Complaints*. Let us consider then what it means for the poem – whether recycled, rewritten, or even newly penned – to be published at this date. For if we take the poem as occasional and instrumental, as both "new" and "old" historicisms would have us regard all texts, we must also recognize that the poem is not bound to a static or even necessarily stable context. Contexts shift as texts are recycled, revised, reprinted. As Crewe puts it in short: "*Mother Hubberd* could not mean or have meant in 1591 what it could have meant *ca.* 1580."[47]

The question I want to address in view of potential new investments and encodings in the 1591 *Mother Hubberds Tale* is what it means for this poem to be published *after* the appearance of the first installment of *The Faerie Queene*. Indeed, that question needs to be opened up to a consideration of the entire *Complaints* volume, a text which resists assimilation to overly streamlined accounts of Spenser's Virgilian laureateship and is consequently often ignored or minimized in those accounts. What kind of career gesture, then, is being staged – midway (as it happened) through Spenser's epic in honor of the Elizabethan regime – in the publication of this manifestly non-laureate tome, which bluntly critiques court values, exposes the shortcomings of the system of court patronage and advancement as it exists under the sway of Lord Treasurer Burghley, and confidently predicts the eventual ruin of the powerful?

The preface to *Complaints* seems written to dodge just such questions. There William Ponsonby, who had been responsible for "setting foorth" the first three books of *The Faerie Queene* just the year before, now assumes full responsibility for compiling (purportedly without Spenser's approval or knowledge) the nine "smale Poemes" that make up the book:

Since my late setting foorth of the *Faerie Queene*, finding that it hath found a fauorable passage amongst you; I haue sithence endeuoured by all good meanes (for the better encrease and accomplishment of your delights,) to get into my handes such smale Poemes of the same Authors; as I heard were disperst abroad in sundrie hands, and not easie to bee come by, by himselfe; some of them hauing bene diuerslie imbeziled and purloyned from him, since his departure ouer Sea. Of the which I haue by good meanes gathered togeather these few parcels present, which I haue caused to bee imprinted altogeather, for that they al seeme to containe like matter of argument in them: being all complaints and meditations of the worlds vanitie, verie graue and profitable. ("The Printer to the *Gentle Reader*," p. 470)

Such disavowals of authorial involvement and investment in publication are, it is well known, quite conventional in Elizabethan literary texts. Here the disclaimer, along with Ponsonby's insistence on a generalizable moral ("the *worlds* vanitie") that discourages particularized applications, seems primarily to be a screen erected (unsuccessfully as it turns out) against the possibility of censorship. Indeed, the portrait of the enterprising publisher scurrying around in pursuit of Spenser's purloined texts and dealing with assorted embezzlers and literary pirates sounds fanciful, and few have doubted at least Spenser's complicity in (if not direction of) the volume's publication.[48] More than an impromptu attempt to cash in on the recent success of *The Faerie Queene*, as Ponsonby alleges, *Complaints* appears to be a fully authorized Spenserian retrospective – the only one published during the poet's lifetime.[49]

Spenser's auto-anthologization contains some recent compositions
(*The Ruines of Time*, for instance, must have been written after Walsingham's death in April, 1590), but the impulse of the volume is thoroughly
retrogressive. We have already noted Spenser's own assignment, whether
ingenuous or not, of *Mother Hubberds Tale* to "the raw conceipt of my
youth." These terms are echoed in *Virgils Gnat*, "Long since dedicated"
to the Earl of Leicester (p. 486), though likewise here published for the
first time. Spenser's impulse to recycle extends even further back to the
inclusion of such juvenalia as the *Visions of Bellay* and the *Visions of
Petrarch*. They were "formerly translated" (p. 525) and are now reprised
from the 1569 *Theatre for Worldlings*, which predates by a full decade *The
Shepheardes Calender* as Spenser's actual literary debut and suggests for
his poetic career yet another road not taken (at least at that time).

The retrogressiveness of this anthology is also apparent from another
perspective in its engagement with an assortment of "archaic" poetic
forms, including beast fable, fabliau, estates satire, dream vision, and of
course complaint. A minor medieval genre – or better, *mode* – the
complaint underwent something of a revival towards the end of the
sixteenth century.[50] Spenser had a part in this revival, and from the
beginning complaint played a determinative role in the articulation of his
career and his ambitions. That career is begun "officially" with the
plaintive "Januarye" eclogue of *The Shepheardes Calender* and its broken
pipes. It is concluded with the railing complaint of Dame Mutabilitie – a
complaint seemingly silenced by the *de facto* verdict of Jove against her,
only to be reprised in the final stanzas of the "Mutabilitie Cantos" by the
poet's own uneasy validation of the goddess's allegations:

> When I bethinke me on that speech whyleare,
>   Of *Mutability*, and well it way:
>   Me seemes, that though she all vnworthy were
>   Of the Heav'ns Rule; yet very sooth to say,
>   In all things else she beares the greatest sway.
>   Which makes me loath this state of life so tickle,
>   And loue of things so vaine to cast away;
>   Whose flowring pride, so fading and so fickle,
> Short *Time* shall soon cut down with his consuming sickle.
>
> (7.8.1)

These expressions of vanity, fickleness, and the devouring appetite of time
are recognizable as a return to the concerns of the generically titled
Complaints volume, in which Spenser gives the complaint form its fullest
exposition.[51] Drawing upon a variety of medieval and Henrician sources,
Spenser makes complaint something of a master form there, weaving into
his book of complaints strands of satire, homily, and elegy; pastoral

locales and epic topoi (the latter most fabulously in the Homeric descent of Mercury in *Mother Hubberds Tale*); and the stern morals of *de casibus* tragedy and *contemptus mundi* philosophy. For poetic models, Spenser turns here to an array of plaintive predecessors including Petrarch, Boccaccio, du Bellay, Langland, Lydgate, Skelton, Wyatt, and especially Chaucer, who had engaged the form of complaint in such works as *Anelida and Arcite*, *The Complaint of Venus*, and *The Complaint of Chaucer to his Purse*, as well as significant portions of *The Legend of Good Women*.

I do not mean to suggest here that the "revived" medievalism of *Complaints* represents an absolute departure in Spenser's poetics. The seminal model of Chaucer, as we have seen, always figured powerfully in Spenser's verse and the shaping of his career. Likewise, both *The Shepheardes Calender* and *The Faerie Queene* regularly touch upon complaint and satire in their generic range. Moreover, there is latent in *The Faerie Queene* an alternative etiology of Spenser's epic, which, running counter to the notion of it as a Virgilian imitation, offers the poem as a sustained effort to finish the unfinished "Tale of Sir Thopas," with Prince Arthur in the role of the Thopas figure. Chaucer's romance, abandoned at the insistence of the other pilgrims, features what is probably the first appearance in English literature of the Faery Queen, and to that extent it foretells Spenser's own romance epic. The medievalism of *Complaints* thus represents less a fundamental change of direction than a strategic foregrounding of "the medieval Spenser" that has been part of the career all along.

At the same time, I see the volume as staging an ostensible public deflection away from Spenser's epic itinerary, as well as much of what that itinerary implies in terms of his role as a poet, his relations to courtly society, and his position towards political power in general. Set aside is the 1590 *Faerie Queene*'s announced agenda of recording and preserving the noble deeds of knights and ladies, not to mention the enshrinement of Elizabeth as the new Augustus. In *The Teares of the Muses*, Spenser now declares, "I have nothing noble to sing" (108). In place of these imperial designs, the poet's abiding concern in his *Complaints* seems to be predicting and documenting the downfall and eventual erasure from cultural memory of the once high and mighty, "Forgotten quite as they were neuer borne" (*The Ruines of Time*, 182). Ironically, despite this shift in matter and style, one concern that remains constant in many of the *Complaints* is Spenser's continued occupation of the role of amanuensis. He is still taking down women's words; but instead of recording the queen's praises as he does in *The Faerie Queene*, Spenser is now taking dictation from a ghost in *The Ruines of Time*, "recording in my troubled brain" (481) the complaints of the deposed Verlame. Similarly, in *The Teares of the Muses* we find him transcribing the "secret causes" (50) of an unhappy troop of muses.

Underpinning many of the poems gathered in *Complaints* is the medieval philosophical commonplace that everything on earth "in th'end to nought shall fade" (*Ruines of Rome*, 280). This sobering lesson is typified, and consequently generalized, in the desolation of ancient cities like Verulamium or Rome. But in *The Ruines of Time* Spenser comes close to naming names and applying this hardly savory moral to the fortunes of contemporary English powerbrokers as well. Presumably even less palatable to the powers that be, his *Visions of the Worlds Vanitie* provides a dozen cautionary exempla about how the small and seemingly powerless are able to upstage or even injure their "betters." A tiny worm fells a mighty cedar; a wasp wounds and incapacitates a lion; a small fish stalls an entire ship; a goose saves Rome from invasion – and all the while the poet keeps reminding us "not to despise, / What euer thing seemes small in common eyes" (*Visions*, 69–70).[52]

By publishing these corrosive poems between installments of his epic, and hence interrupting in midcourse his path along the *rota Virgilii*, Spenser is also staging an implicit challenge to the example of Virgil as the normative model for the poetic career.[53] Taking the place of Virgil, the successful imperial poet (placed by Puttenham rather dubiously among the "cunning Princepleasers")[54] is Chaucer, who is reasserted in *Complaints* as Spenser's major literary propagator. Although in actuality a successful court poet himself, Chaucer had been associated in *The Shepheardes Calender* with the low style and a penchant for personal complaint: "Well couth he wayle hys Woes," Spenser writes of him in the "June" eclogue (85). The strategic reprioritization of Chaucer here in *Complaints* goes hand in hand with Spenser's critical detachment from the court and its values, along with a return to the poetics of lowliness, seemingly set aside in the exchange of pastoral pipes for epic trumpets.

My claims about the restaging of Spenser's career that is enacted by the publication of *Complaints* can be further anchored by returning to *Mother Hubberds Tale*. That poem begins with a rough versed and, after the proems of the 1590 *Faerie Queene*, politically loaded refusal of assistance from any muse: "No Muses aide me needes heretoo to call; /Base is the style, and matter meane withall" (43–44). Overlaying beast fable with a fierce estates satire, this poem is, as many have noted, Spenser's most Chaucerian performance.[55] In addition to its "low" style, *Mother Hubberd* features self-consciously archaic locutions, an astrological *incipit*, and a characteristically Chaucerian sleepless narrator, whose insomnia is

relieved only by the round of storytelling provided by his concerned
friends:

> They sought my troubled sense how to deceaue
> With talke that might vnquiet fancies reaue
> And sitting all in seates about me round,
> With pleasaunt tales (fit for that idle stound)
> They cast in course to waste the wearie howres:
> Some tolde of Ladies, and their Paramoures;
> Some of braue Knights, and their renowned Squires;
> Some of Faeries and their strange attires;
> And some of Giaunts hard to be beleeued.
> That the delight thereof me much releeued.
>
> (23–32)

Mother Hubberd's frame evokes the serial taletelling structure of the
Canterbury Tales, and perhaps also that of Boccaccio's *Decameron* (for
Spenser's poem is likewise set in a time of "plague, pestilence, and death"
[8]). At the same time, however, the principals of the other tales told in the
narrator's bedchamber – ladies, knights, faeries, giants – also foretell
(recall?) the epic matter of *The Faerie Queene*, the poem whose production has been forestalled by the publication of *Complaints* and will
continue to be forestalled on through the 1595 volume containing the
Amoretti and the *Epithalamion* Spenser writes in celebration of his own
marriage.

The "faery" tales of knights and ladies are set aside in *Mother Hubberds
Tale* for the recounting of the satiric adventures of the Fox and Ape, who
begin their pilgrimage disguised as yeoman and soldier – roles selected
from a suitably Chaucerian repertoire that also includes pilgrim and
limitour among its options (see lines 85–86). As the Fox and Ape rise
through the various estates, examples of negligence and corruption are
uncovered at every level of society. What's more striking is that Spenser's
satiric method refuses to provide – unlike, say, Pope's, or even Chaucer's
in the *General Prologue* – a few exemplary models as a contrast to show up
the corrupt ones. There is no honest parson in *Mother Hubberds Tale*, for
instance, to balance the tale's portrait of the unscrupulous priest who
provides detailed instructions on the dissimulative "arte" of winning
benefices. In fact, while the Fox and the Ape may be the poem's chief
culprits, no one they encounter in its tour of abuses entirely
eludes the wide net of *Mother Hubberd*'s satire. Included in its all-fronts
indictment is the royal court that so readily receives the imposters and
provides a platform for their rapid ascendancy, as well as the sleeping
lion/monarch, whose administrative neglect opens the door for his sovereignty to be impersonated and usurped in the first place. The poem even

casts doubt on the so-called "honest" shepherd (259), who responds empathetically, though foolishly, to the complaints of the Fox and the Ape.[56] The point is that there seems to be no position of absolute innocence available in the poem. Even the model courtier, who can appear in the iron age world of *Mother Hubberd* only as a massively idealized abstraction and not as an actual character in its narrative, does not seem very far from the Machiavellian Fox in being himself "practiz'd well in policie" (783).

Satirists, Puttenham tells us in *The Arte*, are "spiers out of all ... secret faults."[57] And as a satirist, Spenser, rather than keeping secrets – a practice out of which he had forged his careers as secretary and poet – systematically uncovers in *Mother Hubberd* what might be better left covered, even if already widely known. Spenser's practice of exposure is conducted at a level aimed beyond the satirical, however, when the Fox and the Ape set their sights on the court. For in charting their rise to positions of prominence and wealth, *Mother Hubberd* becomes a virtual "how-to" manual for achieving a place at a competitive and corrupt court – a kind of demonic *Il Cortegiano* – as it provides instruction on dress, manners, wit, and all the necessary accomplishments. Pedagogic pronouncements such as "This is the way, for one that is vnlern'd / Liuing to get, and not be discern'd" (535–536; cf. 513–514) preface every movement of the Fox and the Ape up the rungs of the social ladder. Even as Spenser satirizes each estate, in other words, he gives away the secrets of the trade.

Not surprisingly, one of the trade "secrets" for success at court is itself the ability to discover and deploy the secrets of others. In his essay "Of Simulation and Dissimulation," Francis Bacon counsels that "an habit of secrecy is both political and moral."[58] By this advice Bacon is recommending the safeguarding of one's own enterprises with a strategic cover of secrecy; but he also means that a well-disseminated reputation for closeness often results in a privileged access to the secrets of others:

But if a man be thought secret, it inviteth discovery [i.e., disclosures], as the more close air sucketh in the more open ... so secret men come to the knowledge of many things in that kind. In few words, mysteries are due to secrecy.

In this Baconian physics of secrecy, one is more likely to earn a privileged access to the secrets of others when he maintains the appearance (whether actual or not) of keeping his own. Thus, in accounting for the Fox and the Ape's social and economic dominance at court, Mother Hubberd explains that the Fox was "school'd by kinde in all the skill / Of close conueyance" (855–856) and

vsd' oft to beguile
Poore suters, that in Court did haunt some while:
For he would learne their busines secretly,
And then informe his Master hastely,
That he by meanes might cast them to preuent,
And beg the sute, the which the other ment.

(877–882)

Similarly, the model courtier, who we have already noted is well practiced in "policie," would be himself no stranger to these arts of "close conveyaunce." Like a kind of ambassador/spy (which, we might recall, is just what Philip Sidney was during his 1577 continental tour), the courtier attempts to uncover the secret

enterdeale of Princes strange,
To marke th'intent of Counsells, and the change
Of states, and eke of priuate men somewhile,
Supplanted by fine falsehood and faire guile;
Of all the which he gathereth, what is fit
T'enrich the storehouse of his powerfull wit.

(785–790)

Mother Hubberds Tale itself daringly participates in such covert "policie" by prying, under the cover of fable, into the internal affairs of the Elizabethan court. The passage, for example, beginning at line 1151 in which the Fox is seen to prefer his own cubs for important administrative offices invites application as an attack on Burghley's controversial efforts to promote his son Robert Cecil to the Privy Council – efforts which succeeded in 1591. The appearance of granting access to court secrets is even more pronounced when the poem turns to the always volatile question of who is currently "in" at court and who is "out": "But tell vs (said the Ape) we doo you pray, / Who now in Court doth beare the greatest sway[?]" (615–616). Although this is an inquiry that would have had a different answer in 1591 than it might have had in 1579, the potentially scandalous gesture of retailing inner court gossip was no doubt of abiding force. For, as the poem goes on to reveal, the status of a favored "Liege" has been put in jeopardy by his acquisition of a "late chayne" (628) – an unapproved marriage? This new bond is deemed "vnmeete" by the lion/monarch because it competes, the poem intimates, with her own claim on that liege, whom she has similarly (and punningly) attempted to "Enchaste with chaine and a circulet of golde" (624).

To a greater extent than any other poem in Spenser's canon, *Mother Hubberds Tale* has been received as a *roman à clef* – a fact to which the dozen pages of the *Variorum* devoted to the endeavor of deciphering its allusions amply testify. The gossipy passage we have been examining about the liege and the lion, for instance, has been variously applied to Leicester, Ralegh, and Essex, all one-time favorites of the queen who contracted secret marriages, and with those secret marriages Elizabeth's jealous displeasure. The iterability of a satire (and here I am referring to the poem as a whole) that can be seen to target so many prominent courtiers points to, as Crewe notes, a flip side to the satiric decorum which declines to name names.[59] For by not naming names just about anyone in the appropriate circumstances – Leicester, Burghley, Simier, Alençon, Essex, Robert Cecil, Ralegh, even the queen – becomes a candidate for identification and stands to have his or her "secret faults" spied out. Furthermore, by establishing the exploitative careers of the Fox and the Ape as constitutive models of what counts as success within the terms of Elizabethan court politics, *Mother Hubberd* threatens to implicate every-one who has ever achieved a measure of success there. To be successful at court, the poem insinuates, is to be like the Fox and the Ape. Even Mercury, eventually sent by Jove to impose order in the animal kingdom and depose the "impostors," too closely resembles them to secure the impression at the end of the poem that the court has been wholly purged of what they represent.[60] For like the Fox and the Ape, Mercury is characterized by his "cunning theeueries" (1287), by his skill at altering his shape (1266; 1289–1290), and of course – being the god of secrecy, Hermes – by his ability to pry "into each secrete part" (1303).

Spenser's systemic indictment of the court was not without con-sequences. It appears from a number of roughly contemporary sources that the poem not only was controversial, but also occasioned, as Thomas Middleton puts it in his own satiric *Black Book* (1604), the "calling in" of *Complaints* for *Mother Hubberd*'s "selling her working bottle-ale to book-binders, and spurting the froth upon courtiers' noses."[61] Judging from the testimony of Middleton and others, the suppression of the volume had nothing to do with the by-then long resolved Alençon crisis, a point that further argues for a recontextualization of *Mother Hubberds Tale* in terms of Spenser's career as it stood in the early 1590s. Nor does it seem from these reports that his troubles with the authorities arose from any notion that, in identifying the shortcomings and abuses of the court, Spenser was disclosing something that was previously unknown. More likely, the official disfavor that met the poem stemmed from the fact that he was disclosing at all – that he was seen to be an arrogant malcontent, far out of line in assuming the role of a satiric "secret agent" uncovering in print what was better left, if not unknown, at least unsaid. (This same "molish" posture of having uncovered scandalous information about the court from the "inside" is again assumed by the poet in *Colin Clouts Come Home Againe*.) The notion that Spenser had stepped out of line in *Mother*

Hubberds Tale is likewise indicated by Gabriel Harvey in a letter he published in his *Fowre Letters and Certaine Sonnets* (1592). There Harvey remarks that "Mother Hubberd in the heat of chollar, forgetting the pure sanguine of her sweete Faery Queene, wilfully over-shot her malcontented selfe."[62] The terms of Harvey's unfriendly public jibe (as Thomas Nashe in his *Strange Newes* [1593] no doubt rightly identified it)[63] also call Spenser to task for having taken a wrong turn *generically*. The poet of *The Faerie Queene*, that is, had no business in abandoning his "sweete" epic to spew up the "chollar" of complaint. Similarly, Middleton's account of Mother Hubberd's "selling her working bottle-ale to bookbinders" suggests that with the publication of *Complaints* Spenser was thought to have turned his back on the court to pander to another audience.

The other poem in *Complaints* that has been singled out in accounts of the volume's difficulties with the censors is *The Ruines of Time*:

> *Colin's* gone home, the glorie of his clime,
> The Muses Mirrour, and the Shepheards Saint;
> *Spencer* is ruin'd of our latter time
> The fairest ruine, Faeries foulest want:
> When his *Time-ruines* did our ruine show,
> Which by his ruine we vntimely know;
> *Spencer* therefore thy *Ruines* were cal'd in,
> Too soone to sorrow least we should begin.

These obituary verses come from the pen of John Weever in 1599, and they suggest that, in satirically uncovering "our ruine," Spenser's "*Time-ruines*" itself ruined the poet.[64] Once again, the cardinal offense as it is figured here resides in Spenser's turn from *The Faerie Queene* ("Faeries foulest want") to the matter of *Complaints* (which "did our ruine show"), in the deflection of his task as an imperial epic poet towards the satirist's exposure of abuses.

As the opening poem in the collection, *The Ruines of Time* foretells the structure of the entire volume and embodies many of its querulous concerns. It begins with a highly formalized complaint voiced by the figure of a woman (another gesture that follows a Chaucerian precedent), and it concludes with two sets of pageant-like visions in sonnet form. The first vision illustrates time's ruinous power over the accomplishments of civilization, while the second exemplifies in the apotheosis of Philip Sidney the memorializing power of the poet to preserve what would otherwise be ravaged by time. The appearance of Mercury in the final vision, forecasting his role in *Mother Hubberds Tale*, ends the poem.

In the prefatory dedication of the poem to Sidney's sister, the Countess of Pembroke, Spenser declares *The Ruines of Time* to be an atonement for his truancy from the task of "renowming" the "noble race" of his first patrons (p. 471). At the center of the poem is an extended necrology of the Dudley and Bedford families, a virtual "political party" upon which all of Spenser's early hopes for advancement had been hung. But Sidney had died in 1586, followed by Leicester in 1588, Leicester's brother Ambrose, the Earl of Warwick, in 1589, and Walsingham in 1590. True to the volume's title, Spenser's memorialization slides from obituary towards complaint. Indeed, his elegies for Leicester, Sidney, and Walsingham can be seen to do double duty as hardly concealed elegies for unrealized versions of Spenser's own career and his hopes for preferment which had died along with these powerful patrons. As the poet complains in the dedication, with Sidney's death his own "hope of anie further fruit was cut off" (p. 471). Beyond a personal loss, however, Spenser is also pointing to a significant alteration in the political landscape of Elizabethan England. For the death of Leicester allowed Burghley to tighten further the reins he held over the Privy Council: "He now is gone, the whiles the Foxe is crept / Into the hole, the which the Badger swept" (216–217). Burghley was always perceived as an adversary by Spenser (the fulsome dedicatory sonnet appended at the last minute to the 1590 *Faerie Queene* notwithstanding), and these lines presage the gloomy prospects for poets – "Not honored nor cared for of anie" (*The Teares of the Muses*, 225) – that are the subject of this next poem in *Complaints*. As Richard Schell has remarked cogently of Spenser's position in the early 1590s, "Old friends and patrons were simply *not there* ... New circles of power provided less hope: Spenser was not so near to their centers, and he knew he never would be."[65]

But if on the one hand *The Ruines of Time* re-enacts Spenser's career-long inability to set himself above factional differences in order to claim the position of a national poet, on the other it reveals his developing ambivalence about the whole process of hiring himself out for patronage. In a poem that is putatively intended to eulogize the departed and console the survivors, Spenser's repeated announcement in *The Ruines of Time* of the inglorious circumstances of Leicester's death, for instance, has a rather unsettling effect:

> I saw him die, I saw him die, as one
> Of the meane people, and brought forth on beare.
> I saw him die, and no man left to mone
> His doleful fate, that late him loued deare.
> . . .
> He now is dead, and all is with him dead,
> . . .
> He now is dead, and all his glorie gone.
>
> (190–193; 211; 218)

It is difficult to name the sentiment underwriting these insistent, unflattering declarations. Is it a feeling of loss, coupled with an attempt to awaken militant action among the "survivors" in the Leicester party? Or is it something approaching satisfaction? Moreover, in the preface and throughout the body of the poem Spenser perhaps too proudly shows off his truancy from the obligation of honoring his departed benefactors. Considered from this perspective, what the poem seems ultimately to enact is Spenser's *refusal* to elegize, his refusal to perform one of the tasks of a patronized poet:

> Ne doth his *Colin*, carelesse *Colin Cloute*,
> Care now his idle bagpipe vp to raise,
> Ne tell his sorrow to the listning rout
> Of shepherd groomes, which wont his songs to praise.

(225–228)

Nor does it help matters that the only sort of memorializing forthcoming for Leicester is put in the mouth of the dubious figure of Verlame, who in *The Ruines of Time* is associated, in addition to her other religious and political encodings, with papism and the Whore of Babylon.

Spenser's ambivalence about "marketing" his poetic abilities as a kind of hired hand, available for the procurement of those who would patronize him, is likewise signalled in the prefatory letter of the publisher that I have already discussed:

I haue sithence endeuoured by all good meanes ... to get into my handes such smale Poemes of the same Authors; as I heard were disperst abroad in sundrie hands, and not easie to bee come by, by himselfe; some of them hauing bene diuerslie imbeziled and purloyned from him, since his departure ouer Sea. (p. 470)

The anxiety expressed in this passage is partly the Orphean anxiety of scattered limbs, a response of poets in this period more regularly associated with the recent practice of anthologization, which presented variously authored small lyric poems in piecemeal miscellanies. But the central concern ventriloquized here on behalf of the poet is the embezzlement and piracy of his poems, the sense that the poems have been "disperst abroad in sundrie hands" while he is himself exiled overseas. In the attempt to reassemble Spenser's poetic corpus, the first claim in print to his ownership of his poems, as well as, ironically, to poems that are chiefly imitations – copies – of du Bellay and Petrarch, is made on behalf of Spenser. I read these aggressive gestures of authorial possession and literary property – of the desire to "get into my handes" what had been "by himselfe" formerly "disperst abroad in sundrie hands" – moreover as a revisionary career move made against what we have seen to be the disseminative "many handedness" of *The Shepheardes Calender* and its production. It is also made against the fully elaborated secretarial poetics of the 1590 *Faerie Queene*, in which Spenser writes under the screening conceit of merely taking dictation at the hand of Elizabeth, his queen and his muse.

And what does it mean for a poet/secretary to assert his own hand? To reclaim what he has penned as belonging to himself? To insist upon ownership and autonomy? What these issues underscore is Spenser's thoroughgoing renegotiation in *Complaints* of both his loss of important patrons and his own discrediting of the operations of preferment established at court into a new statement of poetic self-reliance. *Complaints*, that is, inaugurates the turn towards the personal, the "self-centered," which, though complicated by the questions above, would more overtly inform the rest of Spenser's career.

4   Secret sights, private parts: the 1596 *Faerie Queene*

"Tell me your secrets." I say not a word, for this is under my control.
Epictetus, *Discourses* (cited in Sissela Bok, *Secrets*)

I have been arguing that the legibility of Spenser's career is to a significant extent an aftereffect of repositioning through publication. The appearance of *The Shepheardes Calender* in 1579 as the inaugural poem of that career, for instance, places Spenser within a Virgilian trajectory that characteristically begins in pastoral apprenticeship. Strictly speaking, however, the literary career of "the new Poete" (as he is termed throughout the *Calender*) began some ten years previously with the appearance of his English translations of van der Noot's *Theatre for Worldlings* – a debut which, had it been allotted by Spenser the inaugural position in his canon, would suggest both an alternative poetic lineage and a potentially different (satiric) direction for his career. Similarly, by its positioning of more recent elegaic compositions on the decline of the Leicester/Sidney circle alongside recycled satires and *contemptus mundi* poems (including a reedition of the *Theatre*) written earlier in his career, *Complaints* stages a strategic retreat from Spenser's Virgilian itinerary, as well as from any uncritical perspective on Elizabeth's court as the radiant center of moral and cultural values.[1]

The poet's self-declared distance from the court and its milieu – a distance to be measured, he insists in *Colin Clouts Come Home Againe*, as far as his own Irish estate in Kilcolman is from Westminster Palace – is no doubt related as much to his personal frustration at failing to achieve the status and promotion he sought there when he returned with Ralegh in 1590–1591, as to any finer moral sensibilities on his part about the perceived decline of the court under Burghley's purview. Nonetheless, Spenser's abnegation of Elizabeth's court in *Complaints* does raise questions about what it means for him then to return to the task of writing *The Faerie Queene*, to resume his imperial epic begun in honor of the queen and her court. For that matter, after the publication of this anti-courtly, censured volume, on what grounds, and with what notion of his role as a poet, does Spenser resume his literary career at all? Is the suspension in

Complaints of his grand laureate enterprise, as well as that volume's pronounced ambivalence about Spenser's own secretarial poetics – ambivalence about such practices as taking dictation from a royal muse, writing as a kind of hired hand, and serving as the repository for secrets – simply a detour? Or does the appearance of *Complaints* mark the re-routing of Spenser's poetic career in some more abiding sense?

Colin Cloute's Irish estate

Judging from *Colin Clouts Come Home Againe*, the answer to these questions appears to be that Spenser's career is over, dead-ended after the disappointing trip to court and the poet's forced return "back ... to this barrein soyle" (656) of Ireland, where he believes himself to be "quite forgot" (183). Despite Colin's apparent disavowal in this poem of "Grandams fable stale" (102) (a "penitent" glance back at his own resentful *Mother Hubberds Tale*?), as well as his renewed pledge that Cynthia's "name *recorded* I will leaue for euer" (631; emphasis added), the shepherd's panegyrics never quite find their measure. Instead, his flights of royal encomium are continually stalled, "broke[n] ... asunder" (352), by the interruptions of his by turns wide-eyed and skeptical audience of rustics.[2] While they are suitably impressed with Colin's account of the queen's dazzling majesty, their inquiries about such matters as her "vsage hard" (166) of the Shepherd of the Ocean (the poem's pastoral mask for Ralegh, who had been sent to the Tower when Elizabeth discovered his secret marriage to one of her closely guarded maids of honor), the socio-economic status of poets at her court (Spenser implies that they are all similarly "meanly waged" [382] and under-appreciated), and the reason why Colin felt constrained to abandon his place in Cynthia's presence, tarnish the luster of the praise he offers the queen and her court.

Particularly troubling is Alexis' assertion that in praising Cynthia, Colin "doest thy selfe vpraise" (355), a suggestion of opportunistic flattery that impugns both the role of the court poet and the object of his courtship. Alexis extends his critique of courtly poetry by skeptically questioning why the queen would attend to Colin's poetry at all: "what needeth shee / ... To heare thee sing, a simple silly Elfe?" (368, 371) – a question that for the first time in Spenser's verse goes unanswered. Thus, when Colin and the other shepherds rise at the end of his song and the onset of night, even this conventional pastoral conclusion feels unsettlingly terminal:

> So hauing ended, he from ground did rise,
> And after him vprose eke all the rest:

All loth to part, but that the glooming skies
Warnd them to draw their bleating flocks to rest.

(952–955)

The sense of an ending in this, Spenser's most sustained career "auto-biography," is compounded by the inclusion in the same volume of several elegies (including Spenser's own *Astrophel*) for Philip Sidney, another famous Elizabethan poet/courtier whose career had been untimely cut short. In this context, *Colin Clouts Come Home Againe* thus has the appearance of an elegy, composed in disappointed retirement, for Spenser's own poetic career.

Read from another perspective, however, the poem evinces that same poetic career, which looks as though it were finished and already elegized, starting anew. In the form of an expansive pastoral eclogue, Spenser revives the genre, style ("piping low"), and appellations (Hobbinol, Rosalind, Cuddie, Colin Cloute himself, and so on) of his inaugural poem *The Shepheardes Calender* in order to reinaugurate his poetic career, to begin again with redirected ambitions and a new center. For the return to pastoral in this poem reverses the impetus of the *Calender*, in which the apprenticing poet is repeatedly breaking his pipes, always already looking beyond pastoral both to a loftier genre and to courtly prominence. In *Colin Clout*, on the other hand, the direction is back: back to the fields, "back to my sheep to tourne" (672), back to beginnings – back to Ireland.

But this is a return with a difference. While the setting of *The Shepheardes Calender* – its fields, streams, high and low places – is essentially a lexicon of generic pastoral topoi, the second of Spenser's two pastoral "beginnings" is markedly Irish in its topography. The lays the poet "record[s]" (97) in *Colin Clout* are of specifically Irish mountains, valleys, and streams, including "my riuer *Bregogs*" (92), a stream which flowed through the 3,000 acres allotted to Spenser in 1589 as part of the Munster Plantation scheme.[3] Nicholas Canny has placed Spenser within the emerging ranks of a professional class of English colonist-bureaucrats in Ireland, and this is precisely how Spenser appears in the calendars of Tudor state papers from 1590 onwards: as planter and minor landed gentry; as colonial "servitor of the realm," not courtly poet and would-be courtier.[4] Most of the biographical records we have of Spenser from this period – the deeding to him of Kilcolman Castle in 1590; the longstanding dispute with Lord Roche, who accused Spenser both of having "wasted 6 ploughlands of his Lordship's lands" and of having intended to dispossess him of "his ancient inheritance"; his purchase of lands in County Cork at substantial cost as a provision for his son; the pleas for assistance he carried back to England in 1598 as Thomas Norris' secretary after the

Munster rebellion – show Spenser fully entrenched in what Julia Reinhard Lupton has usefully termed "Home-Making in Ireland."[5] And as if
to correlate this endeavor with his separation from Elizabeth's court,
Spenser in his dedication to Ralegh conspicuously addresses *Colin Clouts
Come Home Againe* "*From my house of* Kilcolman" (p. 536). This
inscription makes it clear that the "Home" of the poem's title is now an
Irish, not an English, one.

Spenser's position in Ireland is thus cast as a basis of security as much
as a kind of self-declared exile.[6] Similarly, Spenser recasts his relative lack
of success at court as self-remove above the fray, implying by the second
half of *Colin Clout* that he now can find poetic inspiration only at a
distance from Elizabeth's court. Irish pastoral thus figures as another
place to go, another space in which to write poetry. And within the
expressly Irish bucolic of *Colin Clout*, the poet fashions a counter to the
court that has no place for him by exerting a nearly occult centripetal
force to establish himself as the poem's center:

> The shepheards boy (best knowen by that name)
> That after *Tityrus* first sung his lay,
> Laies of sweet loue, without rebuke or blame,
> Sate (as his custome was) vpon a day,
> Charming his oaten pipe vnto his peres,
> The shepheard swaines that did about him play:
> Who all the while with greedie listfull eares,
> Did stand astonisht at his curious skill,
> Like hartlesse deare, dismayd with thunders sound.
> At last when as he piped had his fill,
> He rested him: and sitting then around,
> One of those groomes (a iolly groome was he,
> As euer piped on an oaten reed,
> And lou'd this shepheard dearest in degree,
> Hight *Hobbinol*) gan thus to him areed.
>
> (1–15)

In *The Shepheardes Calender*, Colin is only an intermittent presence,
being absented from the eclogues more often than he is present. But in
Colin Clout, Colin, so to speak, himself *holds court*, surrounded by a
captive audience of shepherds who hang on his every word. The narcis-
sism of this scenario is epitomized in Spenser's titling the poem after his
own poetic persona, and not, as in *The Faerie Queene*, after his monarch.
She is instead to be progressively decentered over the course of *Colin
Clout*, as well as the poems that come after it, from her position as the
cynosure of Spenser's poetic world.

Along related lines, much has been made of the fact that by the end of
the poem Colin's royal mistress, Cynthia, has been displaced by his

personal one, Rosalind; that while the poem commences with praise of his queen (40–49), it concludes with an encomium in honor of his shepherd girl (931–951).[7] It should be noted, however, that this opposition is partially undone in *Amoretti* 74 ("Most happy letters fram'd by skilfull trade"), which elides the poet's praise of monarch and mistress under the same name, while adding his mother to the company of these "graces" to form a trinity of "Elizabeths." Wherever the poet turns, there is "Elizabeth," the queen – who represents herself as the "mother" of her subjects, and at the same time invites (or compels) their amorous courtship – routing through herself the oedipal linkage of mother and beloved.[8]

But *Colin Clouts Come Home Againe* also effects another, differently gendered, displacement of Elizabeth on the level of what might be termed the poet's "Imaginary." In vanishing from the final major section of the poem, Cynthia is not only replaced by Rosalind as the object of the poet's courtship; she is also supplanted, in a displacement with potentially wider ramifications, as his sovereign:

> Well may it seeme by this thy deep insight,
> That of that God the Priest thou shouldest bee:
> So well thou wot'st the mysterie of his might,
> As if his godhead thou didst present see.
>
> (831–834)

Because of his abilities to see into the "mysteries" of love, into its "secret sence" (886), Colin is now to be reinvested as Cupid's priest and poet. At stake here is an implicit shift in the poet's allegiance from the virgin queen to the amorous *male* god of love – a father/king who maintains his own court (894), and who is credited, in an account that displaces the principle of female generative power, as the exclusive genitor of the entire world: "For by his power the world was made of yore, / And all that therein wondrous doth appear" (841–842).

Spenser's repositioning of himself as an exiled spokesman of love thus allows him to present himself as possessing an authority independent of his place (or lack of place) at the virgin queen's court.[9] Likewise, just as Colin once had been – in a trope for poetic inspiration which I have associated with the secretarial practice of receiving dictation – "fild with furious insolence" (622) by Cynthia so that he could "record" her praises, in the second part of *Colin Clout* he finds an alternative source in Cupid's "celestiall rage / Of loue," which dictates to him "these oracles so sage" (823, 825). Taken together, the dual displacement of Cynthia by Rosalind as Colin's mistress and by Cupid as his sovereign suggests that the turn towards love as the "new" subject of Spenser's verse ("new" for this turn also revives the erotic concerns of *The Shepheardes Calender*) has less to do with any nascent bourgeois valorization of the private sphere of romantic love and more to do with his effort to secure "another place," an alternative space for poetic production, at once secluded and public. As early as the *Calender* Spenser had been asking, "O pierlesse Poesye, where is then thy place?" ("October," 79). Here that question is answered in a place that is at last truly "pierlesse" – alone, secluded, *nearly* hidden away in the frontiers of Ireland. For that place remains public insofar as it is still inscribed within a highly visible literary career: "[W]ho knowes not *Colin Clout?*" the poet will ask on Mount Acidale at the end of *The Faerie Queene*, calling attention to his public fame even at the poem's most exclusionary private moment – a new version of the Spenserian open secret?

As a "love poet," Spenser writes in lyric genres he had not taken up before: *Amoretti and Epithalamion* (1595), *Fowre Hymnes* (1596), and *Prothalamion* (1596). Spenser's *Epithalamion*, another poem in an overtly Irish setting, is particularly germane in the realignment of his poetic career as we have been examining it. Recalling the impulse ventriloquized through Ponsonby at the beginning of *Complaints* to repossess his poetic texts, to get them back "into my handes" (p. 471), Spenser skirts convention by composing this marriage hymn for himself, and not for some aristocratic patron – nor even, as these lines suggest, for his own bride:

> Helpe me mine owne loues prayses to resound,
> Ne let the same of any be enuide,
> So Orpheus did for his owne bride,
> *So I vnto my selfe alone will sing,*
> The woods shall to me answer and my Eccho ring.
>
> (14–18; emphasis added)

The naming of Orpheus here admits several unsettling possibilities into this nuptial scene, not least of which is the implication that epithalamion is on the verge of metamorphosing into elegy. Related to this threat, the poet's claim to be patterning himself after Orpheus repoints the marriage hymn in the direction of the autoerotic, if not the homoerotic. Accordingly, there is in the *Epithalamion* an enormous expenditure of energy in ritually dismissing everyone from menacing "hob Goblins" (343) and threatening forest animals, to the wedding guests gathered for what is normally the highly public occasion of matrimony. This "exorcism" is performed in order to secure the bridal chamber as a private, even secret space, "Conceald through couert night" (363). Indeed, the bride herself seems to have been absented from the scene, while the much anticipated moment of the bedding is diffused into the form "an hundred little winged loues," miniature Cupids, who

Like diuers fethered doues,
Shall fly and flutter round about your bed,
And in the secrete darke, that none reproues,
Their prety stealthes shal worke, and snares shal spread
To filch away sweet snatches of delight,
Conceald through couert night.

(357–363)

The difficulty of maintaining this "secrete darke" – this place of poetic procreativity where male "amoretti" ("Ye sonnes of Venus" [364]) "filch" private snatches of pleasure, and where "Now none doth hinder you, that say or sing" (370) – is demonstrated in the next stanza. There Spenser reports that no sooner has the private domain of his bedroom been secured than it is infiltrated by the spying figure of the moon:

Who is the same, which at my window peepes?
Or whose is that faire face, that shines so bright,
Is it not Cinthia, she that neuer sleepes,
But walkes about high heuen al the night?
O fayrest goddesse, do thou not enuy
My loue with me to spy.

(372–377)

The panoptical Elizabeth ("she that neuer sleepes") "peepes" in at the window and destroys the poet's protective and productive cover of night. Despite (or because of) this royal intrusion, the poem attempts to mitigate any threat that Cynthia might represent as a rival cultural producer by relegating her to a role that approximates midwifery – "sith of wemens labours thou hast charge" (383) – and hence depriving her of the possession of any generative powers on her own behalf.[10]

In an important essay on "Spenser's Late Pastorals," Paul Alpers usefully directs us to see *Epithalamion*, along with the poet's other attenuated lyrical performances from this period, as representing an "alternative body of major poetry to Spenser's epic endeavors."[11] Alternatively constructed, I would add to Alpers' account, from the vantage of gender as well as genre, as Spenser's late poetry shifts from epic written in honor of a virgin female monarch to lyric composed in the service of an amorous male divinity. But it is also essential to recognize that the significance of such matters as Spenser's shift of allegiance to the god of love, the general turning in his poetry towards the self-centered and the self-occluded – a personal reserve, and his construction of a "private" Irish estate, is not confined to his late lyric poetry. These modulations also have important ramifications for his epic poetry, for Books 4–6 of *The Faerie Queene*, which first appeared in the 1596 reedition of the poem. Moreover, to the extent that such consequences involve Spenser's reappraisal of his cultural function as a poet, the seeming permanence of his post in a hostile colony, and his renegotiated relation to his monarch and her court (which, though distanced, is not – could not be – wholly severed), they are inescapably political consequences. This is a point that needs to be maintained against prevailing accounts of Spenser's late poetry in general, and discussions of Book 6 of *The Faerie Queene* in particular, as constituting his "detached" withdrawal to a purely "contemplative," apolitical pastoral domain.[12] Hence it is to the second and, as it turns out, final installment of Spenser's epic and its quest to secure this paradoxically secret and still public place for his poetry that we will now turn.

Unlocking the "enlocked" sovereign breast

One of the most striking signposts to the altered poetics of the 1596 *Faerie Queene* is the ebbing in Books 4–6 of devotion to Elizabeth's cult of the perpetual virgin queen. This cult Spenser's own poetry helped codify, first in the "Aprill" eclogue of *The Shepheardes Calender*, and later in his making the figure of the powerful, inscrutable chaste female so integral to the first three books of *The Faerie Queene* in her various (dis)guises as Gloriana, Una, Belphoebe, and Britomart. Chastity, the dominant, female-defined virtue of Book 3, is succeeded in Book 4, however, by the virtue of friendship, a social relation historically structured around resemblance and regarded from Aristotle's *Nicomachean Ethics* and Cicero's *De Amicitia* to Bacon's "Of Friendship" as an exclusively male domain. Montaigne, for instance, disqualifies out of hand the likelihood of friendship across gender; the erotically volatile quality of male–female relations (his word for it is "scorching") precludes the "constant and settled warmth, all gentleness and smoothness" that characterizes the idealized friendly male bonds of his paean.[13] (Left unexplored is the possibility of female same-sex friendship.)

In Book 4 of *The Faerie Queene* Spenser follows suit in asserting the superiority of male friendship over all other bonds (9.1–3), although he does provide a few examples of friendships between women. Nonetheless, such bonds are regularly in the service of instigating more highly-valued male ties – as in the case of the "true friendship and affection sweet" of Canacee and Cambina (3.50.9), which serves as a linchpin in the reconciliation of the battling rivals Cambel and Triamond. Related to the valorization of the masculine in Book 4 is Spenser's much remarked upon rewriting of the conclusion of Book 3 in the 1596 edition of the poem, a revision which takes back the original ending's heterosexual coupling of the lovers Amoret and Scudamour. In the recasting of the 1596 edition, their coming together is not so much deferred as undone, and what might be seen as being offered in place of their blissful hermaphroditic union is Scudamour's riding out of the narrative of Book 4 in the friendly company of a group of other male knights. Similarly, the array of chaste females in Book 3 that Spenser's eighteenth-century commentator John Upton found so thrilling gives way in the next book to pervasive bands of male friends and brothers which have found their own admirers: the brothers "-Mond," Cambel and Triamond, Placidas and Amyas, Paridell and Blandamour, the allegorical brethren Love and Hate, as well as a roll call of famous male friendships that includes David and Jonathan, Hercules and Hylas, among others (10.27).

As we might expect, the thematic "masculinization" of the poem – its gestures toward gender separation and the privileging of the male – bears structurally on the position occupied by Queen Elizabeth in Book 4, the single book in *The Faerie Queene* where she is addressed only indirectly and in the third person. From the "Aprill" eclogue through the first installment of his epic, Spenser, we have seen, envisions the queen as the muse dictating the epideictic verses he records as her poet/secretary. Fittingly for Book 4's Legend of Friendship, however, the poet now turns to a male "muse" – Cupid himself, in line with the new poetics of *Colin Clouts Come Home Againe* – for divine assistance:

> Which that she may the better deigne to heare,
>   Do thou dred infant, *Venus* dearling doue,
>   From her high spirit chase imperious feare,
>   And vse of awfull Maiestie remoue:
>   In sted thereof with drops of melting loue,
>   Deawd with ambrosiall kisses, by thee gotten
>   From they sweete smyling mother from aboue,
>   Sprinckle her heart, and haughtie courage soften,
> That she may hearke to loue, and read this lesson often.
>
> (4 pro. 5)

Neglecting to invoke Elizabeth as his muse, Spenser also breaks with the precedent of *The Faerie Queene*'s earlier books in which she is addressed as the perfect embodiment of each titular virtue. Instead, despite naming her "the Queene of loue" (pro. 4.9), Spenser rather high-handedly insinuates that the queen herself needs to be schooled, needs to be disciplined – "her ... haughtie courage soften" – by love, personified in the stanza above as a mollifying, but specifically masculine force.

In passages such as this one, we can glimpse some of the disaffection with Elizabeth's rule that surfaced during its final years. Near the end of that reign, the French ambassador Sieur de Maisse observes in his *Journal* (1597) that "her government is fairly pleasing to the people, who show that they love her, but it is little pleasing to the great men and nobles; and if by chance she should die, it is certain that the English would never again submit to the rule of a woman."[14] Likewise, what is expressed in the proem to Book 4 is a not-so-veiled wish to see the queen herself subjugated ("vse of awfull Maiestie remoue"), and perhaps also a hint of the mounting frustration, noted by de Maisse and others, of her male court subjects at the array of limitations – governmental, militaristic, amorous (hence all those famous secret Elizabethan marriages contracted without the queen's approval or knowledge) – imposed on them in a political domain headed for nearly fifty years by an unsubordinated woman. Such grievances no doubt had their part in the 1601 rebellion of Essex, who is reported to have spoken too openly of Elizabeth as a crabbed old woman jealously attempting to handicap the rising of his career to political and cultural preeminence.[15]

Spenser's allocation of the essentially new role of pupil to Elizabeth in Book 4 entails a new office for the poet as well. Instead of bidding to serve as her secretary, we find him now looking to be the queen's tutor; looking, in a sense, to dictate to her – if, that is, she can be made to listen to him. For gaining audience, gaining access to the queen through texts and letters, emerges as the central concern of this proem.

The path to her, however, is set with obstacles. Significantly, in the oblique address to sovereign authority that opens the proem, Spenser conceives of that authority as residing in, not the *corpus mysticum* of the virgin queen, but rather "The rugged forhead" of a male administrator, of Lord Treasurer and former Principal Secretary Burghley, who "Welds kingdomes causes, and affaires of state" (st. 1.1–2). In discussing the elevation of the secretariat under the Tudors in Chapter 2, I observed that the chief route of access to monarch traveled directly through this office – a matter Spenser, as a career secretary himself, would certainly have well understood. Yet it is precisely this path he now refuses to take. Having been offered a defensive dedicatory sonnet in the 1590 edition of *The Faerie Queene*, Burghley is now first made to misread Spenser solely as a producer of erotic poems:

> The rugged forhead that with graue foresight
>   Welds kingdomes causes, and affaires of state,
>   My looser rimes (I wote) doth sharply wite,
>   For praising loue, as I haue done of late,
>   And magnifying louers deare debate;
>   By which fraile youth is oft to follie led,
>   Through false allurement of that pleasing baite,
>   That better were in vertues discipled,
> Then with vaine poemes weeds to haue their fancies fed.
>
> (pro. 1)

Burghley is then written out, along with all those who similarly "ill judge of loue, that cannot loue" (2.1), of the poet's audience altogether: "To such therefore I do not sing at all" (st. 4.1), Spenser maintains, in what Thomas H. Cain has identified as a startling reversal of the Virgilian epic *cano* formula.[16] Having excluded from his fit audience the Lord Treasurer – probably the single most influential man in the kingdom – Spenser effectively relinquishes any claim he had to the position of national laureate. Burghley's "witing" or blaming of the poet's "looser rimes" in the opening lines of the second installment of *The Faerie Queene* moreover predicts the terrain of the succeeding books, which are to be mapped as increasingly inhospitable for poets and their verses.

Bypassing Burghley, Spenser says he instead sings directly to the queen. But if the Lord Treasurer is one impediment who can be neither appeased nor wholly ignored, Queen Elizabeth herself proves to be another. The proem's description of her "chaste breast [where] all bountie naturall, / And treasures of true loue enlocked beene" (4.3–4) recalls the muse's scrine in Book 1, the occluded space beyond representation where Gloriana is figuratively situated in the 1590 *Faerie Queene*. That hidden treasury was a secret place the poet had taken upon himself to keep sealed – a task of secret-keeping which, I have argued, proves to be in part constitutive of the poem itself.

The possibility, however, of a different perspective in Book 4 on such royal inaccessibility is presaged by the proximity between this reference to Elizabeth's "enlocked" breast and the proem's denunciation two stanzas before of the "frosen hearts" of those who shut out love's "kindly flame" (2.2). A sealed, scrine-like heart thus no longer appears to be a good thing in the reconceived poetics of the 1596 *Faerie Queene*. The queen's body is consequently refigured here as a site of resistance that needs to be made pliable and teachable, her "enlocked" breast a secret cabinet that now stands to be *unlocked*. We have already noticed how, in order that the lessons of his instructive poem might find their royal target, Spenser calls on Cupid to "soften," "remove," "melt," weaken, to dissolve with "ambrosiall kisses," whatever blocks access to this royal virago's heart. That includes the barrier of her own "awfull Maiestie," which she is to let fall aside at the god's penetrative touch. The strange insistence on softening or mollifying the queen – that is, making her a woman (Renaissance dictionaries derive *mulier* from *molli*, softness) – accords with what I noted earlier as the drive in the later books of *The Faerie Queene* towards gender separation and male privilege. Tantamount to ordering her to marry (a belated gesture in the 1590s when Elizabeth was in her sixties), Cupid's mollification of the queen is in effect an attempt to take away the phallus she herself claimed for own her body politic. This point will be seen more plainly in turning now to Book 5.

One possibility for parlaying the condition of exile into one of (relative) empowerment is to see the distance of exile as opening up a space for saying what cannot be said elsewhere, nearer to the centers of power. Shakespeare's *As You Like It* offers a case in point. The usurping Duke Frederick enacts a ban on fools at court, which mimes the expansion of censorship laws in England at this time. Given this prohibition, the satiric voice of Jaques, who is "ambitious for a motley coat," finds its range only in the reclusive woods of Arden – a station Jaques refuses to abandon at the end of the play.[17] Exile thus construed is enabling. Similarly, I have been suggesting that Spenser, writing from what may at last have looked like a permanent Irish civil service "exile," weaves into the panegyric of the second half of *The Faerie Queene* subtle, but discernible, threads of royal admonishment, if not criticism – strands that were not so pronounced a part of the epic's fabric when it was once conceived as the poet's means back to court.

Thus Book 5, for all the complex ways in which it derives its authority from reproducing ("recording") the discourses of sovereign power, continues the task of educating the queen, of providing her with "so diuine a read" (5. pro. 11.7).[18] Moreover, the book deepens the undercurrent of disquietude about unchecked female rule that we first saw expressed in the proem to Book 4. Titled the "Legend of ... Justice," the organization of gender roles are thus included within Book 5's agenda. The notion that sexual hierarchy is an integral aspect of justice is most vigorously expressed in Britomart's bloody overthrow of Radigund's amazonarchy. Having set matters right and dispatched this Amazon queen, Britomart in turn subordinates herself to a chastised Artegall, whom she first reproves for his shameful submission to the rule of a woman. A woman who rules is out of place, Spenser insists – that is, in the necessary Elizabethan exemption, "Vnlesse the heauens them lift to lawfull soueraintie" (5.25.9). Given this qualification, I suggest that we must look past the book's suppression of Radigund and her "monstrous regiment of women" to another episode for what is Book 5's most pertinent exemplum of justice for "state of present time" (pro. 1.1). The one I have in mind is canto 10's allegorization of the trial and execution of Mary Queen of Scots:

> When they had seene and heard her [Mercilla's] doome a rights
> Against *Duessa*, damned by them all;
> But by her tempred without griefe or gall,
> Till strong constraint did her thereto enforce.
> And yet euen then ruing her wilfull fall,

With more then needfull naturall remorse,
And yeelding the last honour to her wretched corse.

(10.4.3–9)

Justice is enacted in this scene in the capital sentence executed against the female arch-villainess Duessa, who here stands for Mary. But it is arguably also exemplified in Queen Mercilla's act of checking her own pronouncedly feminine vacillations towards leniency, and instead wisely deferring to the "strong constraint" of her male ministers and councilors, who advise the swift dispatching of a dangerous traitor and heretic.[19]

Book 5's abiding attention to the proper (en)gendering of justice is established as early as its proem:

Most sacred vertue she of all the rest,
    Resembling God in his imperiall might;
    Whose soueraine powre is herein most exprest,
    That both to good and bad he dealeth right,
    And all his workes with Iustice hath bedight.
    That powre he also doth to Princes lend,
    And makes them like himselfe in glorious sight,
    To sit in his owne seate, his cause to end,
And rule his people right, as he doth recommend.

(st. 10)

Although he does not wholly deviate from the iconographic traditions that have typically personified justice in female form, Spenser adds an element of hermaphrodism to the picture. He does so by asserting here that the goddess Justice is empowered only in her resemblance to a superior (male) God and "his imperiall might." This means, paradoxically, that Justice is justice – is herself – only to the extent that she resembles what she isn't – that is, a male personification – and only inasmuch as she has what she hasn't – that is, a phallus. Similarly, in the final lines of the proem, a male knight is chosen to embody the "great justice" that the poet claims is incarnate in Queen Elizabeth: "The instrument whereof loe here thy *Artegall*" (st. 11.9). Artegall is, in other words, Elizabeth's tool.

This gender sliding mirrors the queen's own claims about her monarchal hermaphrodism. In a now much-cited speech given at Tilbury in 1588 while she surveyed the troops she was dispatching against the Spanish Armada, Elizabeth disclosed: "I know I have the body of a weak and feeble woman, but I have the heart and stomach of a king, and a king of England, too."[20] A number of her subjects evidently concurred. Writing to John Harington after the queen's death in 1603, Principal Secretary Robert Cecil said that his mistress was "more than a man, and, in troth, sometyme less than a woman."[21] As Montrose points out in "Shaping

Fantasies," Queen Elizabeth was thus a cultural anomaly – a woman who ruled men, a queen endowed with male parts – a status that made her fascinating, powerful, and dangerous.[22]

In the proem to Book 5, however, Spenser moves toward a potential undoing of Elizabeth's empowering claims of sexual anomalousness at the same time as he bodies them forth. For in the now departed golden age nostalgically depicted in stanza 10 (designated the age of Saturn, not Astraea) "soueraine powre" clearly resided in male hands. As the stanza continues, it becomes apparent that even then Justice herself had no force as an active principle in the affairs of the world. Rather, all her dealings had been properly ceded to a superior male divinity. It was and continues to be *he* who "dealeth right" to good and bad; *he* who "lends" power to princes. This abnegation of feminine figures of power continues throughout the book, and at the threshold of Isis Church, where Spenser once again offers a personification of justice, that virtue finally becomes reincarnate in male form as the god Osiris.[23]

As Roy Strong and others have noted, the symbolism of Elizabeth's state portraits casts England as once again enjoying a golden age under the long, relatively stable rule of the queen.[24] At odds with this notion, the account of the "state of present time" put forth in the proem asserts that the world is "runne quite out of square" (st. 1.7). Prefacing a book deeply concerned with gender hierarchies, could the proem be implying that part of the problem is that a female monarch "doest highest sit / In seate of iudgment, in th'Almighties stead" (st. 11.1–2)?

Apparently no longer bidding for place at court, Spenser is no court panegyrist in the 1596 books of *The Faerie Queene*. In language more acclimated to satire than to imperial epic, he places his nation in the midst of a stone age, not a golden one:

> For from the golden age, that first was named,
>   It's now at earst become a stonie one;
>   And men themselues, the which at first were framed
> Of earthly mould, and form'd of flesh and bone,
> Are now transformed into hardest stone:
> Such as behind their backs (so backward bred)
> Were throwne by *Pyrrha* and *Deucalione*:
> And if then those may any worse be red,
> They into that ere long will be degendered.

(st. 2)

Once again, the political is framed in Book 5 in terms of the sexual. Interestingly, however, the current stone age is characterized not so much by decay and barrenness as it is by unnatural kinds of generation. Degeneration, in other words, involves "de-gendering" or sterility –

perhaps even the erasure of gender; but it is also related to perverse forms of engendering. In the stone age world of Book 5, fertility only resides in stones, and they are responsible for engendering people of "hardest stone," rather than flesh and bone. The stanza's description of this process of aberrant propagation – "behind their backs (so backward bred)" – indicates human devolution, a sort of downward breeding. At the same time, the figure suggests unauthorized sexual positions and copulating from behind.

This intimation of bestial coupling points towards the "vncouth sight" in the Church of Isis later in Book 5 when Britomart fantasizes herself "enwombed grew" with the "game" of a crocodile and giving birth to a lion (7.16.5–9). The proem's depiction of unnatural forms of reproduction and generation might also be an oblique allusion to the matter of succession – the succession of James I being an unnatural kind of procreation inasmuch as he takes the place of the "natural" heir the queen's own body never produced. Although deemed by Elizabeth a mystery of state not open for her subjects to discuss or look into, consideration of the highly-charged issue of succession would not be out of place in Book 5, the book of *The Faerie Queene* most overtly solicitous of the "affaires of common wele" (9.36.3). Included in its purview, along with the relations between Elizabeth and the Stuarts, are questions of English foreign policy and the nation's role in European political affairs as a Protestant power. Book 5 is similarly concerned with the subjugation of Ireland, its hero Artegall's principal quest being the relief of Irena's "afflicted plight" (1.4.3).

The opening pages of Jonathan Goldberg's *James I and the Politics of Literature* provide a subtle discussion of the rhetorical politics of Book 5, of the ways in which the poet uses the enactment of justice to play out (and uncover?) the enabling contradictions by which absolutist power represents and sustains itself. To this account, however, I would add several points. The first is that Spenser's thinly veiled allegorization of a number of controversial contemporary events – among them, the trial of Mary, English intervention in the Low Countries, and the Irish commission of his former employer, Lord Grey – are recognizably out of sorts with royal propaganda. Elizabeth, for instance, attempted to seal off any discussion of religion from Mary's trial and thus ensure that the prosecution instead focused its accusations on the charge of treason – this despite the insistence of Leicester and others of like mind on the prisoner's heresy and her perceived central position in an international Catholic conspiracy. Spenser's treatment of the trial accords on the whole with the official view of the event, though his affinity with the puritan position is registered in the inclusion of a charge of "lewd *Impietie*" in the case against

Duessa (9.48.9), whose very name carries with its Popish associations from Book 1.

In another source of political frustration to Leicester and his circle, Elizabeth, who had habitually sought to sidestep any kind of commitment to a radical foreign policy, proved reluctant to intervene in the Netherlands and aid the Dutch in their efforts to throw off the rule of Philip II.[25] She disapproved of the militancy of Dutch Protestantism and flinched at the thought of lending support to a religiously motivated rebellion against another monarch. At last in 1585, when the rebels' cause was desperate and Antwerp ready to fall, she capitulated to the urgings of Leicester, permitting him to lead a military expedition to the Netherlands. Though greeted by the Dutch with pageants hailing him in eschatological terms as the nation's savior, Leicester's campaign was (hardly surprisingly given the circumstances) less than a triumph – a judgment emphatically propounded in Camden's "authorized" account of the earl's endeavours. Spenser's allegorical treatment of the same event in cantos 10–11, on the other hand, approaches the spirit of the apocalyptically inflected Dutch pageants. More than flattering the memory of his former patron, Spenser's depiction of Arthur's conquest of the tyrant Geryoneo, his cleansing the church of its false idol, and his restoration of Lady Belge's throne, essentially casts England as the international champion of reformed religion, a role the queen herself never fully embraced. Perhaps even more importantly, as David Norbrook points out in his invaluable consideration of Book 5's engagement with a more militant strain of Protestant politics, Spenser's refiguring in 1596 of Leicester's dubious martial achievement as an event of nearly cosmic significance also serves as an endorsement of the Earl of Essex's current lobbying for renewed military action in the Netherlands.[26] In Norbrook's terms, Book 5 thus "amounts to a sustained defence of the Leicester-Essex foreign policy, looking back over the past ten or fifteen years and looking forward to possible future victories."[27] And as a further indication of his allegiance to the increasingly controversial Essex, Spenser heralds the earl in *Prothalamion* as a hero deserving of his own epic, and hence implicitly a potential rival to the queen.[28] Spenser never wrote that poem – Books 7–12 of *The Faerie Queene*? – but the earl apparently rewarded Spenser's good intentions by picking up the bill for the poet's funeral in 1599.

On yet another battle front, in addition to Book 5's unsanctioned espousal of a more zealous interventionist policy in foreign affairs, Spenser questions Lord Grey's removal under censure from Ireland. Artegall's exorbitantly violent and, if we credit the poem's account against history, successful efforts to fulfill his quest and subdue Ireland are interrupted "ere he could reforme it thoroughly" by his ill-timed recall to the Faery Queen's court (12.27.1). The implication at the end of Book 5 is that Ireland remains unsubjugated because the queen and her ministers are not taking the necessary steps – steps that Grey was apparently willing to take – to defeat the rebellion. Beyond the loyalty of this secretary to his former employer, we should not underestimate in his defense of Grey Spenser's own stake in the effective colonization and administration of Ireland. It was there that this son of a clothworker acquired a castle and an estate.

Beneath the luster of royal celebration in the 1596 *The Faerie Queene* is, then, as Norbrook concludes, a view of Elizabeth's administration of Ireland that is critical enough to court censorship.[29] That was, in fact, the fate of Spenser's other "view" of the Irish problem, the contemporaneous *A View of the Present State of Ireland*, which he entered for publication in 1598, but did not live to see in print. (It wasn't published until 1633, and even then some passages did not make it past the censors.) An even more forthright defense of Grey and his extreme measures (and thus a critique of Elizabeth's vacillating policies), *A View* is nonetheless of a piece with Book 5, and the same thematics of reformation, replanting, and cutting off (pruning *and* decapitation) traverse both texts. Thus, while Book 5 authorizes itself (in Goldberg's chiastic formulation) by "giving voice to the language of sovereignty, taking on a sovereign voice of power,"[30] the book's perspective on several crucial political issues suggests doubts about whether the very sovereignty the poet celebrates is consistently expressed in the sovereign and a number of her more conservative policies. Not at all looking to subvert absolutist power, Spenser, on the contrary, appears to be championing a more vehement expression of it.

Moreover, it is important to note that grafted onto Book 5's representation of justice (and hence of sovereign power) is an iconography of Egyptian hermeticism, "the most secret and arcane lore in all magic philosophy," Angus Fletcher reports in *The Prophetic Moment*.[31] We have already noted that Britomart's bizarre dream, given to her to resolve the conflicting interests of justice and equity, is set in the temple of Isis, where an aura of high occultism, flames "kindled priuily" (7.14.6), and mysterious oracles prevails. Along with its hermetic trappings, the temple is at the same time a place in which all that is hidden is laid bare: "Say on ... the secret of your hart," the high priest instructs Britomart (st. 19.6). Britomart responds by disclosing her troubling dream, though she unsuccessfully attempts to conceal both the truth of her gender (she is still in disguise as a male knight) and her secret love for Artegall:

> Magnificke Virgin, that in queint disguise
>   Of British armes doest maske thy royall blood,
>   So to pursue a perillous emprize,

How couldst thou weene, through that disguized hood,
To hide thy state from being vnderstood?
Can from th'immortall Gods ought hidden bee?
They doe thy linage, and thy Lordly brood;
They doe thy sire, lamenting sore for thee;
They doe thy loue, forlorne in womens thraldome see.

(st. 21)

Britomart's entrance to Isis Church is prefaced by a stanza alluding to
the mysterious process by which God "to Princes hearts ... doth reueale"
the skill to rule "Common weale" (st. 1.8–9). By overlaying sovereign
power with the language of darkest mystery, the poem grants that power
the highest mythic authority. But then it immediately ushers us into the
temple and takes us behind the veil where all secrets are to be penetrated.
The effect of this uncovering is the impression that in Book 5 we are not
only witnessing the inscription of the *arcana imperii*, the secrets of rule,
but also being permitted to look into them. It is as though the call in Book
4's proem to unlock the "enlocked" sovereign breast is answered by this
scene in the temple, where all of royal maid Britomart's secrets are
exposed, where her empowering male disguise is seen through, and where
her female body is penetrated and made to give birth. After this, Britomart is not long for the poem.

The uneasiness provoked by the insights (I use this term literally)
offered in Book 5 is evident in an enduring strain of humanist critical
opinion on this least-loved book (as C. S. Lewis deems it) of *The Faerie
Queene*. That view faults the Legend of Justice as much for its lack of
decorous concealment – for its too transparent allegory, for being too
easily seen through – as for its politics and its unremitting brutality. Kate
M. Warren, writing in 1898, denigrates Book 5 in just such terms:

The allegorical matter ... is, on the whole, quite easy to follow. It is chiefly
historical, and the historical meaning, in its main outline, stands clearly forth.
Much of the narrative in this Book will bear nothing beyond an interpretation by
history ... In the greater part of the poem there is no double allegory, and where
any other meaning does appear it is often of the simplest.[32]

H. S. V. Jones concurs in his *Spenser Handbook*. Discussing cantos 8–10,
he complains: "no allegory could be more transparent than this."[33] More
recently, in his compendiously annotated edition of *The Faerie Queene*,
A. C. Hamilton points to the preponderance of "painfully obvious"
topical allusions to "events in Elizabethan history."[34]

What all these accounts lament is Book 5's collapse of allegory into
referent, its apparent inability to achieve the necessary transport for
allegory. The "darke conceit" evidently isn't dark enough in Book 5. At
least not dark enough to veil the relation between a poetics and its

politics. Or between Spenser's career as a poet and his bureaucratic career as an instrument of a reprehensible English policy in Ireland, first as secretary and righthand man to the ruthless Lord Grey and then as a civil servant in a colonial administration. (This reminder of Spenser's professional life provides another context, incidentally, in which to hear Fletcher's provocative description of Artegall's own righthand man, Talus, as the "mechanism of bureaucratized justice.")[35] Thus, rather than reading Book 5 as the least poetic book of *The Faerie Queene*, I see it as instancing another powerful ligature between Spenser's two careers, a juncture where the concerns of the poet touch those of the bureaucrat in the effort to shape an ideal commonwealth. At the same time, however, it emerges that Spenser is not the state instrument he here claims to be. Inasmuch as he is rewriting history in Book 5 with a political agenda that is not exactly Elizabeth's (so that in actuality the book's allegory is anything but transparent), he is dictating to the queen even as he claims to be taking her dictation.

Secrecy and privacy

Spenser's relation to the secret – a form which we have seen sometimes to conceal a referent and sometimes not – is poised between two equally theatrical impulses to preserve the secret as undisclosed and to divulge it. Neither operation is itself secret: Spenser's texts never keep the secret of knowing or of having secrets. This one secret is not secreted, is everywhere displayed, whether the "content" of any particular secret is revealed or not. There are moments, however, in Spenser's writings and careerist negotiations in which he seems to veer sharply towards one or the other of these impulses. The secretly-authored, secretly-annotated *Shepheardes Calender* is his most occulted text – a secretarial cabinet of secrets, few of which are ever opened. In it, secrecy is an implosive form. We are drawn into it by E.K.'s constant intimations of what is "secreted" within; but once inside we cannot exit the endless work of decipherment. There seems to be no outside – no place outside the secret, that is – to this text, published in a form that ensures its ultimate indecipherability.[36] Similarly, in Spenser's hands epic (romance) becomes a discourse of secret-keeping in the 1590 *Faerie Queene*, where every narrative has its origin in an "euerlasting scryne" that continues to be "hidden still" (1 pro. 2.3–4). On the other – and in another – hand, Spenser's 1591 *Complaints* deploys satire and taletelling (in both senses of the term) as means for exposing what is concealed, or at least not openly spoken – "secrets" about the court and how one gains place there.

But even within these texts, the desire to withold the secret and the desire to disclose it are often set side by side, if not wholly intertwined. The coincidence of these seemingly contrary impulses is particularly marked in the poems we have been examining from the 1595–1596 period of Spenser's career – as in Book 4's proem where the poet first imagines and reveres the queen's body as an unassailable locked cabinet of virtue, and then in the next stanza seeks to pry it open and penetrate it. It is the case again in Book 5 where, as we have seen, absolutist power is enhanced and mystified with tropes of hermetic lore, and then given its fullest allegorical exposition (and exposure) in a temple conceived as a space where all that is hidden comes to be made known. In these instances, the secret is constituted as a field in which the operations of concealment and disclosure, veiling and revealing, are made to compete and collude in the exercise of knowledge and power.

A similar deployment of the secret carries over into Book 6 and the career of its hero, Calidore, the knight of courtesy. Unlike the poem's other heroes, who are all accompanied by squires or guides, Calidore insists that the special (secret?) nature of his quest requires that he "issue forth in waies vntryde" (1.6.4). He is so stealthy, in fact, that the narrative loses track of him for a full six cantos. When Calidore finally does resurface in canto 9, he appears in disguise and in a secluded pastoral retreat. This movement of retreat – and often outright retirement – is repeated in a number of career narratives throughout Book 6 as a pattern of withdrawal to a variety of hiding places.[37] Thus, in the final book of Spenser's epic, we come across a knight turned hermit, having forsaken "this worlds vnquiet waies" for a cell "In which he liu'd alone'.' (6.4.7–9). Likewise, we meet Meliboee, once a successful courtier and now become a shepherd, who has quitted the "vainenesse" of "roiall court" and "backe return[ed] to my sheep againe" (9.24.6–9; 25.7). Even further sequestered from public life, the young Tristram "conceale[s]" himself "amongst the woodie Gods to dwell" (2.26.2–3), while the Salvage Man, dubbed "Nature's nobleman *over against* the courtly reality" by Richard Neuse, abides "Farre in the forrest by a hollow glade," where "foot of liuing creature neuer trode" (4.13.5,8).[38] Like *Colin Clouts Come Home Againe* and much of Spenser's late poetry, these figures pose alternatives to life at court. But even among the characters in Book 6 who retain their ties to the social life of courts and castles, there are those, like Calidore himself, who seek to create private spaces outside its boundaries. Hence Calepine and Serena are discovered "In couert shade ... / To solace ... in delight" (3.20.3–4), just as in the canto before Priscilla and Aladine are found "in shadow ... /Ioying together in vnblam'd delight" (2.43.2–3).

It is in such private places, "free from all gealous spyes," that the titular virtue of the Book 6 may be expressed, there where the lovers "did shew all louely courtesyes" (2.16.6,9). In this way, Spenser links courtesy to privacy, which is a shading of secrecy, and here figured as immunity from unwanted access by others, from being *seen*.[39] Yet the central irony of the book is that Calidore, its exemplar of courtesy, is just as likely to violate the fragile pockets of privacy fostered in the book as is his nemesis the Blatant Beast, who turns up at one point in a monastery, pawing through cloistered "cels and secrets neare" (12.24.4).

Calidore informs Prince Arthur at the beginning of the book that his assigned quest is to contain this monster and the threat to privacy it represents: Calidore's is a kind of damage control mission. At times, however, it isn't clear who is following after whom. In the same passage, Calidore admits that he does not know where to begin looking for the Blatant Beast: "Yet know I not or how, or in what place / To find him out, yet still I forward trace" (1.7.4–5). It is significant, then, that the Blatant Beast makes its initial appearnce in the Legend of Courtesy only after Calidore himself has first intruded upon Serena and Calepine's secret lovemaking in the glade. The Blatant Beast is soon to follow – as though it were the knight's originary violation of a private space that has created an opening for the monster's disruptive entrance into the narrative.

When the Blatant Beast attempts to carry off Serena in its jaws, Calidore follows, and both disappear from the narrative. After the pair reemerge together many cantos later, we learn that Calidore has chased the Blatant Beast throughout the whole of Faery Land:

> So sharply he the Monster did pursew,
>   That day nor night he suffered him to rest,
>   Ne rested he himselfe but natures dew,
>   For dread of daunger, not to be redrest,
>   If he for slouth forslackt so famous quest.
>   Him first from court he to the citties coursed,
>   And from the citties to the townes him prest,
>   And from the townes into the countrie *forsed*,
> And from the country back to priuate farmes he scorsed.
>
> (9.3; emphasis added)

In "forcing" the monster from town to country, is Calidore expelling the Blatant Beast, or simply propelling him into new territories? Indeed, a few stanzas later we learn from some shepherds that Calidore, in driving the monster into their fields, has introduced a menace the likes of which this idyllic world had never seen before:

> They answer'd him, that no such beast they saw,
>   Nor any wicked feend, that mote offend
>   Their happie flockes, nor daunger to them draw:

5 "Quo tendis?" from Claude Paradin, *Symbola Heroica* (1583), p. 115. Spenser's Blatant Beast, associated with gossip and public scandal, is an enemy to secrecy. Similarly, Paradin's menacing emblem makes rumor a penetrative force.

> But if that such there were (as none they kend)
> They prayd high God him farre from them to send.

(st. 6.1–5)

Calidore and the Blatant Beast thus appear to be nearly inseparable: where there is one, the other is sure to follow.[40] And rather than containing the monster, Calidore appears to be disseminating its destructive energies in every corner of Faery Land.

Beast and knight are also linked through their corresponding association with mouths and tongues – that is, with the linguistic. The *member virilis* of the Blatant Beast is of course its many stinging tongues, which multiply from a hundred to a thousand over the course of Calidore's pursuit (see Plate 5). But in a book where what is spoken is a weapon and "Words sharply wound" (7.49.9), the poet also makes a point of showing how Calidore, like his adversary, employs his own tongue – capable of producing both "gracious speech" (1.2.6) and "threatfull words" (3.36.2) – in order to achieve his ends. The knight's reliance on the efficacy of the word is highlighted by a pun near the end of the book when Calidore brandishes "a sword of better say" (11.47.5) to vanquish the brigands that hold Pastorella captive.[41] In place of enchanted weaponry like Arthur's diamond shield, for instance, or Britomart's ashen spear, the "magic" instrument of courtesy is linguistic, and its knight is accordingly described as one "Whose euery deed and word, that he did say, / Was like enchantment, that through both the eyes, / And both the eares did steale the hart away" (2.3.2–4).

This account of Calidore's linguistic prowess and his Acrasia-like power to steal away hearts has overtones of, if not sorcery, at least a potential capacity for deception. Despite having a reputation for a love of "simple truth and stedfast honesty" (1.3.9), Calidore's courtesy takes on this other form – the one closer to deception and enchantment (two more sinister cousins of secrecy) – when he agrees to escort the runaway Priscilla back to her father's castle and there to vouch for her blameless conduct:

> Sir *Calidore* his faith thereto did plight,
>   It to performe: so after little stay,
>   That she her selfe had to the iourney dight,
>   He passed forth with her in faire array,
>   Fearlesse, who ought did thinke, or ought did say,
>   Sith his owne thought he knew most cleare from wite.
> So as they past together on their way,
>   He gan deuize this counter-cast of slight,
> To giue faire colour to that Ladies cause in sight.
>
> (3.16)

As the last lines suggest, Calidore must contrive "white lies" in order to preserve the reputation of Priscilla – who had been discovered enjoying "franke loues" (2.16.6) with a man other than the noble peer her father has arranged for her to marry – as "Most perfect pure, and guiltlesse innocent / Of blame" (3.18.3–4). In Calidore's hyperbolic report of her unimpeachable innocency, claiming that she was abducted by a discourteous knight (whose head he luridly produces to corroborate his account), he is saying what everyone at court wants to hear and believe, as evidenced by the "thousand thankes" his testimony receives from both father and daughter (st. 19). Courtesy in this instance thus entails the maintenance of certain secrets, polite fictions upon which civil society depends – fictions which are known to be groundless. (This is perhaps one reason why Spenser situates the Acidalean dance of courtesy on "hollow ground" [10.10.4].) Calidore conducts himself as a model of courteous behavior inasmuch as he safeguards the secret of the compromising circumstances in which he really found Priscilla, and thereby defuses a potential scandal with a few smooth-tongued lies.

In contrast, the Blatant Beast leaves its victims "spotted with reproch, or secrete shame" (6.12.9). Its myriad tongues associate the monster both with the masses, the *vox populi*, and with scandal, public defamation, and perhaps even with the wounding, sharp-tongued satire then in vogue in the writings of Thomas Nashe, John Donne, John Marston, and Joseph Hall:

> And therein were a thousand tongs empight,
> Of sundry kindes, and sundry quality,
> Some were of dogs, that barked day and night,
> And some of cats, that wrawling still did cry,
> And some of Beares, that groynd continually,
> And some of Tygres, that did seeme to gren,
> And snar at all, that euer passed by:
> But most of them were tongues of mortall men,
> Which spake reprochfully, not caring where nor when.
>
> And them amongst were mingled here and there,
> The tongues of Serpents with three forked stings,
> That spat out poyson and gore bloudy gere
> At all, that came within his rauenings,
> And spake licentious words, and hateful things
> Of good and bad alike, of low and hie;
> Ne Kesars spared he a whit, nor Kings,
> But either blotted them with infamie,
> Or bit them with his banefull teeth of iniury.
>
> (12.27–28)

Whereas Calidore resorts to falsehood in order to preserve certain secrets upon which he has stumbled, the threat to courtesy represented by the Blatant Beast involves *publicity*, and his bite, we hear in Book 5, imprints a "marke" "that long ... was to be read" (12.39.9). More specifically, the Blatant Beast is a threat to courtesy chiefly because its intrusions into privacy have the effect – and this is what finally distinguishes them from Calidore's similarly invasive habit for showing up where he is not wanted – of cheapening secrets, of turning them into gossip and malicious tongue wagging.

In the Priscilla episode of canto 3, we witness Calidore's uncanny immunity to public censure – "Sith his owne thought he knew *most cleare from wite*" (3.16.6; emphasis added) – as almost a willed obliviousness or blank idiocy. At the same time, the pun on *wite* (an archaic word meaning blame) and *white* ("most cleare," innocent, unmarkable by the "imprinting" bite of the Blatant Beast) points in the direction of an inner, more hermetic conception of courtesy.[42] For there is also in Book 6 an alternative construction of this same virtue as an occult, inward attribute that discloses no unproblematic external sign of its existence. This other kind of courtesy exists in tension with, and marks Spenser's ambivalence about, the "showy" sort of courtesy usually exhibited by Calidore. His career is (to use the poem's own term) "menaged" much of the time as a sort of personal public relations campaign, and in that capacity enacts the theatrical strategies of social performance advanced in other Renaissance courtesy manuals.[43] But in the proem we hear of a courtesy that seems to have little to do with Calidore, being "in a siluer bowre hidden . . . / From view of men" (pro. 3.3–4), and subsisting "not in outward shows, but [by] inward thoughts defynd" (pro. 5.9). *Redefined* in these terms, courtesy recedes from the realm of public conduct in the direction of a secret, interior condition. And insofar as it does so, this alternative construction of courtesy begins to be associated, in a way no other virtue represented in *The Faerie Queene* is, with the private, even occluded conditions of modern subjectivity, of a "truer," secret inner self that exists behind the veil of outward appearances.

Over against the "courteous guize" (9.35.6), the theatrical courtesy of Calidore, Book 6 releases few clues about this other, more secretive sort of courtesy. (The implied pedagogical premise of Book 6 seems to be: if you know, you know; if you don't, you never will.) And of those few clues, many turn out to be misleading. "Of court it seemes, men Courtesie doe call," begins canto 1. But this commonsense, etymological derivation ultimately proves misleading to the extent that the epiphany of courtesy – the scene C. S. Lewis describes as the book's allegorical core – is staged as a private fantasy of the poet, sequestered in pastoral retirement on Mount Acidale and far from the Faery Queen's court. There Colin Cloute, whose reappearance at the end of *The Faerie Queene* neatly frames Spenser's career, plays for the Graces and "an hundred naked maidens lilly white" (10.11.8). This set piece, which Harry Berger aptly terms "a digression from a digression," has nothing directly to do with the narrative line of Book 6.[44] Nor does it seem to have much to do with the quest of Calidore apart from representing yet another of his disruptive forays into someone else's privacy. Moreover, even though Calidore is named the legend's exemplar of courtesy, he is excluded from this vision, which immediately vanishes when he discloses himself from his hiding place "in the couert of the wood" (10.11.4). Paradoxically, this secret sight is a sight that is (literally) stripped of all the trappings of concealment: the maidens "naked are," Colin explains, "that without guile / Or false dissemblaunce all them plaine may see, / Simple and true from couert malice free" (st. 24.3–5). Is this fantasy of female nakedness – of a "naked" secret (whatever that may be) – to be connected with the desire expressed in Books 4 and 5 to penetrate the veils that occlude Elizabeth in the 1590 *Faerie Queene*, the desire to penetrate the queen herself?

The canto in which this epiphany occurs begins with a reminder of

Calidore's truancy from "vow and high beheast, / Which by the Faery Queene was on him layd" (10.1.3–4). Colin Cloute, too, is once again discovered playing truant from his own courtly task as a public panegyrist of Queen Elizabeth:

> Sunne of the world, great glory of the sky,
>   That all the earth doest lighten with thy rayes,
>   Great *Gloriana*, greatest Maiesty,
>   Pardon thy shepheard, mongst so many layes,
>   As he hath sung of thee in all his dayes,
>   To make one minime of thy poore handmayd,
>   And vnderneath thy feete to place her prayse,
>   That when thy glory shall be farre displayd
> To future age of her this mention may be made.
>
> (st. 28)

Significantly, the final book of *The Faerie Queene* is the only one in the entire epic that lacks a suitable allegorical representative for Elizabeth in its fiction. Colin's vision of rings within rings of perfectly choreographed dancers – set forth as a celebration of social order and hierarchy: "They teach vs, how to each degree and kynde / We should our selues demeane, to low, to hie" (st. 23.7–8) – is of course exactly the instance in which we would expect to find the queen radiantly figured as the epicenter of this order. This is especially so since the scene of intricate concentricity atop Acidale appears to be the full-bodied realization of the compliment the poet pays the queen in Book 6's proem: "Right so from you all goodly vertues well / Into the rest, which round about you ring" (pro. 7.6–7). But the central position Elizabeth occupies in the proem, as well as her role as the "fourth grace" in the "Aprill" eclogue (which is reprised and recast in this episode), is assigned in canto 10 to another female figure, a "countrey lasse":

> And in the middest of those same three [Graces], was placed
>   Another Damzell, as a precious gemme,
>   Amidst a ring most richly well enchaced,
> That with her goodly presence all the rest much graced.
>
> (st. 12.6–9)

Others have noted the glaring omission in Book 6, apart from a few stanzas in the proem, of royal encomium.[45] And, as we have seen, even the praise that is offered there is reattributed elsewhere on Acidale. Apart from the problematically situated "Mutabilitie Cantos" (which, if anything, are directed to the diminishment of the cult of a monarch whose motto was "*semper eadem*"), we have little way of knowing for sure in which direction Spenser would have carried further installments of his epic had he lived long enough (and indeed been willing) to go on producing them. There are, however, enough suggestions in the 1596 books to indicate that the epic's direction now leads away from the Faery Queen herself – at least in her former capacity as the privileged "secret" of the poem.

It is often assumed that the "countrey lasse" who has displaced Elizabeth as the focal point of the dance on Acidale is a figuration of the poet's own "real-life" beloved, whom he had also celebrated in his other great work of poetic truancy, the 1595 volume of *Amoretti and Epithalamion*.[46] Such an identification would first need to be qualified, however, with the recognition that this "countrey lasse" is never thus explicitly identified; the text reveals only that she is the source of an inspiration that keeps Colin Cloute piping "as neuer none" (st. 15.9). Secondly, we need to bear in mind that this mysterious, muse-like figure is not present on Acidale in the way that Colin and Calidore are. Instead, she exists within the text, as David L. Miller points out, only *in propria idea*.[47] That is, this figure exists only as an imaginative conjuration in an intensely private, autoerotic fantasy of enfolded desire and poetic production. Even the outsider Calidore is said – in an insistently, redundantly, solipsistic figure for a scene of spying on the fantasy of someone else – to have "euen he him selfe his eyes enuyde" (st. 11.7) at the sight of her. It is, furthermore, the desire to project this apparition beyond the visionary to some other ontological order – figured in Calidore's need to know "Whether it were the traine of beauties Queene, / Or Nymphes, or Faeries, or enchaunted show, / With which his eyes mote haue deluded beene" (st. 17.5–7) – that causes the apparition to be lost. The poet's maiden it seems is no longer imaginable except as imagined.

Given these caveats, I too want to associate the "countrey lasse" of Colin's ecstatic vision with the figure of the poet's beloved, and specifically with the shepherdess Rosalind, who becomes increasingly fantasmatic as a recurring figure in Spenser's pastoral fictions. That is, the "countrey lasse" on Acidale "is" Rosalind inasmuch as that name names the secret inspiration – the inspiration of the secret – which Spenser's text always keeps hidden in plain sight:

> Such were those Goddesses, which ye did see;
>> But the fourth Mayd, which there amidst them traced,
>> Who can aread, what creature mote she bee,
>> Whether a creature, or a goddesse graced
>> With heauenly gifts from heuen first enraced?
>> But what so sure she was, she worthy was,
>> To be the fourth with those three other placed:
>> Yet was she certes but a countrey lasse,
> Yet she all other countrey lasses farre did passe.

(st. 25)

In Chapter 3, I called attention to E.K.'s directions in *The Shepheardes Calender* for reading the character of Rosalind as a literal character – a linguistic figure, an anagram whose name, he intimates, "being wel ordered, will bewray the very name of hys loue and mistress, whom by that name he coloureth" (p. 423). Similarly, the now unnamed (unnameable) female figure who inspires Colin Cloute in private in Book 6 is represented as a hermetic text: "Who can aread, what creature mote she bee[?]" That figure, we are told here, is an imperceptible "tracing," a kind of hieroglyph that even the poem itself cannot decipher: "Whether a creature, or a goddesse"; one who is like a country lass, but finally unlike; a poor handmaid who takes the place of her queen; a perpetual source of inspiration that vanishes out of sight. What she is, in other words, is (the) secret.

Although what is ultimately privileged in *The Faerie Queene*, as in all of Spenser's writing, is what is secret, it would be an over-simplification to link the poetic project in Book 6 solely to the reclusive Colin Cloute and his final vision of a poetry too intensely private to bear the presence of an audience. For just as Colin's private site of inspiration on Mount Acidale recalls the poet/narrator's "secret comfort" in the proem as he is guided into the muses' hidden store of "learnings threasures" (another scrine) atop Mount Parnassus (pro. 2.1–3), so too does the ceaseless footing, tracing, and traveling/travailing of Calidore's highly public quest resemble the discursive activities of the same poet/narrator.[48] What we find in Book 6 is a divided or doubled poetic persona, incorporating both the questing knight of the open, serendipitous romance world of the poem, and the retired shepherd of its closed, occluded pastoral domain:

> Ne may this homely verse, of many the meanest,
> Hope to escape his venomous despite,
> More then my former writs, all were they clearest
> From blamefull blot, and free from all that wite,
> With which some wicked tongues did it backbite,
> And bring into a mighty Peres displeasure,
> That neuer so deserued to endite.
> Therefore do you my rimes keep better measure,
> And seeke to please, that now is counted wisemens threasure.
>
> (12.41)

This final stanza of the last completed book of *The Faerie Queene* reveals the poet attempting to elude the Blatant Beast by modeling himself both after the pattern of Calidore, who is similarly engaged in seeking "To please the best" (1.3.7), but also after the reclusive Colin Cloute in his espousal of "cleare writ" – of a poetics of withholding, concealment, and even disappearance.

In Book 6, then, Spenser has cleared out enormous space for his poetry in dispersing the poetic function in several places at once: in an originary, hidden "noursery / Of vertue" in the proem (st. 3.1–2); in Colin Cloute's private pastoral fantasy; in the go-between, romance position of Calidore, who belongs neither to the court nor to the pastoral but is able to negotiate both; and perhaps even in the Blatant Beast, the monstrous embodiment of satire and exposure unleashed by Spenser himself in *Complaints*, only to dog the poet throughout the final installment of his epic. It is through and across these shiftingly delineated spaces of publicity and privacy, of visibility and opacity, of disclosure and secrecy, that the verses of this doubly employed poet/secretary, this taletelling holder of secrets, keep their measure.

Notes

Introduction

1 Richard Mulcaster, *Positions*, ed. Robert Herbert Quick (London: Longmans, Green, and Co., 1888), p. 269. Emphasis is added.

2 Thomas Nashe, "A Generall Censure," from *The Anatomie of Absurditie*, in *Elizabethan Critical Essays*, 2 vols., ed. G. Gregory Smith (Oxford: Oxford University Press, 1904, rpt. 1959), 1:328.

3 George Chapman, "A Free and Offenceles Justification of *Andromeda Liberata*," in *The Poems of George Chapman*, ed. Phyllis Brooks Bartlett (New York: Russell and Russell, 1962), p. 327.

4 Philip Sidney, *An Apology for Poetry*, ed. Forrest G. Robinson (Indianapolis: Bobbs-Merrill, 1970), p. 88.

5 Edmund Spenser, "A Letter of the Authors," *The Faerie Queene*, in *The Poetical Works of Edmund Spenser*, ed. J. C. Smith and E. De Selincourt (Oxford and New York: Oxford University Press, 1912), p. 407. All further citations of Spenser's works are according to this edition, with references supplied in the text, line numbers for verse and page numbers for prose.

6 Stephen Greenblatt, *Renaissance Self-Fashioning: From More to Shakespeare* (Chicago: University of Chicago Press, 1980), p. 121.

7 Spenser, of course, is not the only Renaissance literary figure to have been employed as a secretary. Elyot, Ascham, Harvey, Lyly, Greville, Wilson, Carew, Cowley, Tuberville, Dyer, Donne, Milton, and Marvell, among others, each held secretaryships of various kinds. But Spenser stands out in this list, I will argue in what follows, inasmuch as the protocols of secretaryship have a shaping effect on the development of his poetics that is not evident to the same degree in these other writers.

8 D. A. Miller, *The Novel and the Police* (Berkeley and Los Angeles: University of California Press, 1988), p. 206.

9 My thinking about these questions has been stimulated by a paper presented by Angus Fletcher on "Allegory and Secrecy" at The Johns Hopkins University in 1989.

10 For a recent example see Douglas Brooks-Davies' *The Mercurian Monarch: Magical Politics from Spenser to Pope* (Manchester: Manchester University Press, 1983). Whereas Brooks-Davies aims to place Spenser's poetics and politics within the esoteric terms of Renaissance hermeticism, Theresa M. Krier, in the other recent major study of Spenserian secrecy, offers a literary historical context for the poet's attention to figurations of concealment. In her

admirable study, *Gazing on Secret Sights: Spenser, Classical Imitation, and the Decorums of Vision* (Ithaca and London: Cornell University Press, 1990), Krier discusses the recurrence of motifs of withdrawal, secrecy, and invisibility in *The Faerie Queene* in terms of Spenser's revisionary treatment of scenes of violated privacy derived from Virgilian and Ovidian sources. Krier is, as I am here, concerned with the question of how one represents secrets while avoiding wholly giving them away. However, whereas she argues that the question of "How to show hiddenness without violating it and turning it into display becomes an ethical issue and ... a representative problem" for Spenser (p. 11), I suggest that display is often precisely the point of Spenser's often flagrant deployment of secrets and secrecy.

1 Professional secrets

1 Richard Helgerson, *Self-Crowned Laureates: Spenser, Jonson, Milton, and the Literary System* (Berkeley and Los Angeles: University of California Press, 1983). See especially pp. 55–66. See also Helgerson's earlier book, *The Elizabethan Prodigals* (Berkeley and Los Angeles: University of California Press, 1976), for an extended study of the literary contemporaries against which, in Helgerson's argument, Spenser had to define himself.

2 Helgerson, *Self-Crowned Laureates*, p. 60. Emphasis is added.

3 Ibid., p. 63.

4 See, in addition to Stephen Greenblatt's pathbreaking *Renaissance Self-Fashioning*, his *Shakespearean Negotiations: The Circulation of Social Energy in Renaissance England* (Berkeley and Los Angeles: University of California Press, 1988). See also Louis Adrian Montrose's now classic essays on pastoral: "'The perfecte paterne of a Poete': The Poetics of Courtship in *The Shepheardes Calender*," *TSLL* 21 (1979): 34–67; "'Eliza, Queene of shepheardes' and the Pastoral of Power," *ELR* 10 (1980): 153–182; and "Of Gentlemen and Shepherds: The Politics of Elizabethan Pastoral Form," *ELH* 50 (1983): 61–94. Finally, see Frank Whigham, *Ambition and Privilege: The Social Tropes of Elizabethan Courtesy Theory* (Berkeley and Los Angeles: University of California Press, 1984).

5 Paul Alpers discusses the history of this Spenserian epithet and its apocryphal assignment to Charles Lamb in an entry on "The Poet's Poet" in *The Spenser Encyclopedia*, general ed. A. C. Hamilton (Toronto and Buffalo: University of Toronto Press, 1990), p. 551.

6 See Helgerson, *Self-Crowned Laureates*, p. 66. He is citing p. 234 of Durling's *The Figure of the Poet in Renaissance Epic* (Cambridge, Mass.: Harvard University Press, 1965), p. 234.

7 This aegis-making declaration appears in the course of Jonson's tributary verses on Shakespeare for the *First Folio* of 1623.

8 The entitling of Spenser as "Englands Arch-Poet" occurs on the title page of the folio edition of his collected works in 1611.

9 The symptomatically unstable economic and social position of the Elizabethan and Jacobean author is ably discussed in Michael Brennan's *Literary Patronage in the English Renaissance: The Pembroke Family* (London: Routledge, 1988), especially pp. 11–18.

10 A disregard of Spenser's secretarial career distorts even Ciaran Brady's otherwise adept and informative account of Spenser's career in Ireland, "Spenser's
Irish Crisis: Humanism and Experience in the 1590s," *Past and Present* 111
(1986): 17–49. In forging a reading that implicates *The Faerie Queene* in the
project of *A View of the Present State of Ireland* and which thus correctly
refuses to unyoke Spenser the poet from "Spenser the prosaic English official
in Ireland" (p. 17), Brady pointedly remarks that "The attempt to distinguish
the poet Spenser from any of his presumed personae in Ireland is ... futile"
(p. 18). Despite his own injunction, Brady in my view unproductively con-
descends to Spenser's secretaryship: "his briefly held post as secretary to Lord
Deputy Grey was merely that of an important personal servant in a great noble
household" (ibid.).

11 Still to be written is an adequate biography of Spenser. The standard biography, Alexander C. Judson's *The Life of Edmund Spenser* for *The Works of
Edmund Spenser: A Variorum Edition*, 11 vols., ed. Edwin Greenlaw, *et al.*
(Baltimore: The Johns Hopkins University Press, 1932–1957), though useful,
offers a blithely romantic and regularly fanciful account of Spenser's life and
career, and especially of his Irish tenure. In addition to Judson, I rely in what
follows in terms of secondary sources on Frederic Ives Carpenter's still
invaluable *A Reference Guide to Edmund Spenser* (Chicago: University of
Chicago Press, 1923). Carpenter usefully gathers and collates references to
Spenser in the *Calendar of State Papers, Ireland*, the *Calendar of Fiants*, and
other public records.

  See also: Edwin Greenlaw, "Spenser and the Earl of Leicester," *PMLA* 25
(1910): 535–561; Percy Long, "Spenser and the Bishop of Rochester," *PMLA*
31 (1916): 713–735; Pauline Henley, *Spenser in Ireland* (Dublin and Cork:
Cork University Press, 1928); Raymond Jenkins, "Spenser and the Clerkship
in Munster," *PMLA* 47 (1932): 109–121; "Spenser with Lord Grey in Ireland,"
PMLA 52 (1937): 338–353 and "Spenser: The Uncertain Years 1584–1589,"
PMLA 53 (1938): 350–362. In lieu of an account from Spenser's own hand,
H. R. Plomer and T. P. Cross, *The Life and Correspondence of Lodowick
Bryskett* (Chicago: University of Chicago Press, 1927) provides pertinent
information about what a civil service career in Ireland in the 1580s and 1590s
entailed. Finally, see Ruth Mohr's entry on Spenser's biography for *The
Spenser Encyclopedia*, pp. 668–671.

12 Phillips' account of Spenser's life can be found in his *Theatrum Poetarum, or a
Compleat Collection of the Poets* (London, 1675). See also Blount's *De Re
Poetica: or, Remarks upon Poetry* (London, 1694). Both sources are repro-
duced in *Edmund Spenser: The Critical Heritage*, ed. R. M. Cummings (New
York: Barnes and Noble, 1971). See pp. 323, 331.

13 The significance of this book and its inscription is noted and briefly discussed
by Israel Gollancz in "Spenseriana," in the *Proceedings of the British
Academy, 1907–1908*: 101–102.

14 Eleanor Rosenberg, in her *Leicester: Patron of Letters* (New York: Columbia
University Press, 1955), p. 329, likewise suggests that Spenser may have
worked as a secretary for the earl. Percy Long, on the other hand, dismisses the
possibility of a secretaryship for Spenser in "Spenser and the Bishop of
Rochester," pointing out that William Aytes served as Leicester's secretary at

the time. However, Aytes' post does not discount the possibility that Spenser could have been similarly employed by the earl. It was not unusual for a figure of Leicester's stature to have several under-secretaries in his employment. In *Servant of the Cecils: The Life of Sir Michael Hickes, 1543–1612* (London: Jonathan Cape, 1977), p. 40, Alan G. R. Smith reports that between 1580 and 1598 Burghley, for instance, had three to four secretarial assistants at any given time. Similarly, we know that Spenser was not the only secretary employed by Lord Grey during his tenure in Ireland.

15 A document giving a complete listing of the duties and authority of this position is reproduced in Plomer and Cross, *The Life and Correspondence of Lodowick Bryskett*, pp. 9–10.

16 The letter recommending Spenser's appointment as sheriff is cited in Henley, *Spenser in Ireland*, p. 154.

17 See Carpenter, *A Reference Guide*, pp. 33–34.

18 Helgerson, *Self-Crowned Laureates*, p. 82.

19 See "A letter from the queen's majesty sent to the bishops through England" (8 May 1577), reprinted in Claire Cross, *The Royal Supremacy in the Elizabethan Church* (London: George Allen and Unwin, 1969), p. 191. For more on the controversy surrounding Grindal and prophesyings, as well as its bearings on Spenser's association with John Young, see Paul E. McLane's learned, but often reductive and too ingenious, study, *Spenser's Shepheardes Calender: A Study in Elizabethan Allegory* (Notre Dame: University of Notre Dame Press, 1961), pp. 140–174. See also Percy Long, "Spenser and the Bishop of Rochester."

20 Harry Berger, Jr. makes a similar point in his deft reading of the "Julye" eclogue in *Revisionary Play: Studies in the Spenserian Dynamics* (Berkeley and Los Angeles: University of California Press, 1988), p. 306.

21 Compare the following passage from Spenser's *Epithalamion*:

> Who is the same, which at my window peepes?
> Or whose is that faire face, that shines so bright,
> Is it not Cinthia, she that neuer sleepes,
> But walkes about high heauen al the night?
> O fayrest goddesse, do thou not enuy
> My love with me to spy.

(372–377)

I discuss this moment of royal panoptical intrusion more fully in Chapter 4 as part of an argument about the intense drive in Spenser's late poetry to establish a variety of private refuges. No sooner does the poet cordon off his bridal chamber as such a space than he finds Cynthia (Elizabeth) peering in at the window. Not even his own bedroom, hidden as it is in the Irish wilds, can provide absolute coverture from the queen's powers of surveillance.

22 Cf. Nancy Jo Hoffman's discussion of "Julye" in *Spenser's Pastorals: The Shepheardes Calender and "Colin Cloute"* (Baltimore: The Johns Hopkins University Press, 1977), pp. 30–34.

23 In one of the "Familiar Letters" Gabriel Harvey does refer to some "nine Englishe *Commoedies*" Spenser had reportedly written (p. 620), though these plays have never been discovered. In Chapter 2, I discuss the references throughout Spenser's published canon that catalog his supposedly "lost"

works. In *Hidden Designs: The Critical Profession and Renaissance Literature* (New York and London: Methuen, 1986), pp. 93–118, Jonathan Crewe suggests that Spenser's theatre (and Spenserian theatricality) is played out on the "paper stage" of his early translation of Jan van der Noot's *A Theatre for Worldlings* (1569).

24 For example, in addition to the model of Virgil, the successfully patronized *court* poet, there was also available the significant counter-model of Ovid, the exiled poet who writes from a place quite outside the court, the putative epicenter of power and influence. The career model of the poet in exile will emerge as a particularly important one for Spenser near the end of his career, as it will be for Milton throughout his entire career. Nor, as I argue in this chapter, should we neglect the significance for Spenser of the Chaucerian literary career – a career marked, particularly in his lyric poetry, by the revisionary rewriting and even "deformation" of Virgilian narratives and positionings.

25 The possibility of a spying mission is suggested by Long in "Spenser and the Bishop of Rochester" (p. 723), as well as by Edwin Greenlaw in "Spenser and the Earl of Leicester" (p. 549).

One of the period's most powerful examples of the interconnections between letters, secretaryship, spying, and secrecy is to be found in the career of Francis Walsingham. Walsingham, who was later appointed Principal Secretary, had turned his own home into a school for forgery and cipher composition and afterwards went on to found a fully operational secret service for Queen Elizabeth. Sidney (and perhaps Spenser too?) may have attended some of Walsingham's classes. See R. A. Haldane's *The Hidden World* (New York: St. Martin's Press, 1976), pp. 60–61.

26 See Malcolm William Wallace, *The Life of Sir Philip Sidney* (Cambridge: Cambridge University Press, 1915), p. 173.

27 These credentials for admission to the Privy Chamber are recorded in Naunton's *Fragmenta Regalia*, ed. John S. Cerovski (Washington: The Folger Shakespeare Library, 1985), p. 41, as cited in Steven W. May, *The Elizabethan Courtier Poets: The Poems and Their Contexts* (Columbia and London: University of Missouri Press, 1991), p. 19. Naunton advances the necessary criteria of "being well known" or "a sworn servant to the Queen" in discussing an episode involving a "very great captain," a protégé of the Earl of Leicester, who was denied admittance to the Privy Chamber on just such grounds.

28 Eve Kosofsky Sedgwick, *Epistemology of the Closet* (Berkeley and Los Angeles: University of California Press, 1990), p. 4. Cf. Michel Foucault, *The History of Sexuality*, Vol. 1, *An Introduction*, trans. Robert Hurley (New York: Vintage Books, 1980), "Silence itself – the things one declines to say, or is forbidden to name, the discretion that is required between different speakers – is less the absolute limit of discourse, the other side from which it is separated by a strict boundary, than an element that functions alongside the things said, with them and in relation to them within over-all strategies ... Silences ... are an integral part of the strategies that underlie and permeate discourses" (p. 27). Spenser, we shall see, is always speaking such silences and secrets.

29 *The Letter-Book of Gabriel Harvey, A.D. 1573–1580*, ed. Edward John Long Scott, published for the Camden Society (Westminster, 1884), p. 101. Emphasis is added.

30 This apt phrase is taken from David L. Miller's excellent discussion of *Virgils Gnat* in "Spenser's Vocation, Spenser's Career," *ELH* 50 (1983): 197–230, at 212.

31 I take the paradoxical notion of the "open secret" from D. A. Miller and his extraordinary discussion of the complicated registers of secrets that function as at once open and closed. See his much-cited and much-admired essay, "Secret Subjects, Open Secrets," in *The Novel and the Police*, pp. 192–220.

32 Harold Stein, *Studies in Spenser's Complaints* (New York: Columbia University Press, 1934), p. 77.

33 See J. E. Neale's *Queen Elizabeth* (London: Jonathan Cape, 1954), pp. 244–246, for the details of these meetings of the Privy Council and the timing of Elizabeth's discovery of Leicester's secret marriage. Milton Waldman similarly places the disclosure of Leicester's marriage late in the summer of 1579 when the matchmaking negotiations reached their climax. See his *Elizabeth and Leicester* (Boston: Houghton Mifflin, 1945).

For a fuller account of the Alençon marriage negotiations, as well as both the part played in them by Simier's disclosure of Leicester's secret marriage and Spenser's treatment of the episode in *The Shepheardes Calender*, see Wallace T. MacCaffrey, *Queen Elizabeth and the Making of Policy, 1572–1588* (Princeton: Princeton University Press, 1981), pp. 243–266. MacCaffrey argues that Elizabeth's overtures of marriage were not at all disingenuous, but that her desire for the match was checked by the Privy Council.

34 So claims Charles Mounts in "Spenser and the Countess of Leicester," *ELH* 19 (1952): 191–202, at 195. Mounts, too, has detected the reference to the countess in the "March" eclogue. He argues plausibly that it is this use of Lettice's name, and not some manuscript version of *Mother Hubberds Tale* (as Greenlaw contends) that served as the "dynamite ... to blow the poet out of Leicester's favor and into Ireland" (p. 196). Where my argument diverges from Mounts' is at his foreclosing gesture of minimizing the naming of Lettice as nothing more than a careless slip on Spenser's part – perhaps a leftover from a much earlier version of the poem. He thus too quickly discounts the real possibility that the eclogue might be staging an intentional, if still misconceived, display of the poet's knowledge of Leicester's "secret."

35 Crewe, *Hidden Designs*, pp. 76–79.

36 Mohr, in *The Spenser Encyclopedia*, p. 670.

37 Henry Plomer, "Edmund Spenser's Handwriting," *Modern Philology* 21 (1923–1924): 201–207. See also Jenkins, "Spenser with Lord Grey in Ireland."

38 Cummings has usefully gathered many of these accounts in his *Critical Heritage* volume on Spenser. See pp. 315–341.

39 In addition to Helgerson's account, see David L. Miller's "Spenser's Vocation, Spenser's Career" for another example of this tendency. Miller does offer something of a differentiation between these terms: *vocation* refers to the "ideal of the poet's cultural role" and *career* to the "rhetorical strategies by which the ideal ... becomes explicit" (pp. 198–199). Both terms, however, are applied exclusively to Spenser's poetic career, as though he pursued no other career.

40 *Epicoene* 2.3.94–96. Cited from the *Complete Plays of Ben Jonson*, 4 vols., ed. G. A. Wilkes (Oxford: Clarendon Press, 1981), Vol. 3.

41 See J. W. Saunders, "The Stigma of Print: A Note on the Social Bases of Tudor Poetry," *Essays in Criticism* 1 (1951): 139–164 for a classic account of the social and economic conditions which shaped literary authorship in Tudor England.

42 I am referring, of course, to Michel Foucault's "What is an Author?" and his seminal discussion of the "author function." The essay appears in *Language, Counter-Memory, Practice*, trans. Sherry Simon and ed. Donald F. Bouchard (Ithaca: Cornell University Press, 1977).

2 The secretary's study: the secret designs of *The Shepheardes Calender*

1 Annabel M. Patterson, "Re-opening the Green Cabinet: Clement Marot and Edmund Spenser," *ELR* 16 (1986): 44–70, at 68–69. Patterson's discussion and mine overlap at points, particularly around the collocation of meanings suggested by the figure of the cabinet: "As a private chamber of the privileged, for reading, writing or keeping one's treasures, we find it in Rabelais' *Gargantua* (1532) ... These green cabinets are recreational; but as a private place for conducting business, especially of state, 'cabinet' could acquire a more tendentious meaning. In Francis Bacon's essay 'Of Counsels' we find a critique of 'the doctrine of Italy, and the practice of France in some Kings' times,' the introduction of 'cabinet councils' for the sake of secrecy, a remedy, Bacon added in 1627, 'worse than the disease.'" (p. 46). But whereas Patterson discusses the "green cabinet" as Spenser's inheritance from Marot, along with a "poetics of [political] accommodation and ... dissent" (p. 62), I am particularly interested in the cabinet as a figure that links Spenser's "vocational" career as a poet with his professional one as a secretary.

2 Ibid., p. 68.

3 Cf. Patterson again: "But the second meaning of the cabinet is, surely, that is 'privie,' a place of secrets. The function of E. K.'s apparatus is not only to present the English *Eclogue-book* and its producers as 'the equal to the learned of other nations' (p. 418), but also to reveal *by failing to reveal* the mysteries of the text" (ibid., p. 69).

4 Spenser's careerist negotiations in *The Shepheardes Calender* vis à vis the form of pastoral – as well as his erotic positionings and the ways in which those positionings overlap with the careerist ones – is also the subject of Jonathan Goldberg's "Colin to Hobbinol: Spenser's Familiar Letters," in *Displacing Homophobia: Gay Male Perspectives in Literature and Culture*, ed. Ronald R. Butters, John M. Clum, and Michael Moon (Durham, N.C.: Duke University Press, 1989), pp. 107–126.

5 Angel Day, *The English Secretary* (London, 1599), Pt. 2, pp. 102–103. Day's book is available in facsimile, introduction by Robert O. Evans (Gainesville: Scholars' Facsimiles and Reprints, 1967). The first edition of *The English Secretorie* (London, 1586) is also available in a facsimile edition (Menston: Scolar Press, 1967). All further references are supplied in the text and, unless otherwise indicated, are to the 1599 edition.

6 Here I am referring to Thomas Gainsford's letterwriter, *The Secretaries Studie* (London, 1616).

7 At least thirteen editions of *The English Secretary* can be counted between its
   initial publication in 1586 and 1639. For more on the publication history of
   Day's letterwriter, see Kathering Gee Hornbeak, "The Complete Letter-
   Writer in English, 1568–1800," in *Smith College Studies in Modern Languages*
   15 (1934), i–xii, 1–150, especially p. 28 and pp. 129–131. Jean Robertson, *The
   Art of Letter Writing: An Essay on Handbooks Published in England during the
   Sixteenth and Seventeenth Centuries* (London: University Press of Liverpool,
   1942) provides a helpful bibliography of "Secretaries" and letterwriters on
   pp. 67–80. For more on early modern letterwriters in general, see Louis B.
   Wright, *Middle-Class Culture in Elizabethan England* (Ithaca: Cornell University Press, 1935), pp. 135–146. See also Janet Altman, "The Letter Book as
   a Cultural Institution, 1539–1789: Toward a Cultural History of Published
   Correspondence in France," *Yale French Studies* 71 (1986): 17–62.
8 In the first edition of his manual, however, Day does acknowledge his indebt-
   edness to Erasmus (specifically to *De ratione conscribendis epistolas liber*) and
   to other rhetoricians for the organizational and theoretical components of his
   letterwriter. Significantly, the acknowledgment of foreign influences drops out
   of the later editions of *The English Secretary* – a deletion I attribute to Day's
   aspirations towards "authorship'" and the creation of an English poetics of
   letterwriting.
9 The third section of Fulwood's manual does move away, it should be noted,
   from its numerous Ciceronian models to include more workaday examples,
   such as "The answere of one Marchant to an other."
10 Raymond Williams historicizes the slippery terms "literature" and "literary"
   in his *Keywords* (New York: Oxford University Press, 1985), pp. 183–188. On
   the constitutive relations between Renaissance letterwriters, letters, and literature see Claudio Guillén's valuable essay, "Notes Toward the Study of the
   Renaissance Letter," in *Renaissance Genres: Essays on Theory, History, and
   Interpretation*, Harvard English Studies 14, ed. Barbara Keifer Lewalski
   (Cambridge, Mass.: Harvard University Press, 1986), pp. 70–101.
11 Michael McCanles offers an insightful consideration of the ways in which *The
   Shepheardes Calender* imitates Renaissance editions of classical texts in *"The
   Shepheardes Calender* as Document and Monument," *SEL* 22 (1982): 5–19.
12 It is necessary, however, to contextualize Day's innovation in terms of the long
   association of letterwriting and rhetoric – an association which produced the
   medieval *ars dictamini*. On this relation, see Robertson's *The Art of Letter
   Writing*, pp. 9–13, as well as Guillén's "Notes Toward the Study of the
   Renaissance Letter."
13 Spenser's commendatory verses are reproduced in the Smith and De Selincourt
   edition on p. 603. George Chapman and Samuel Daniel, along with Day and
   Spenser, also contributed prefatory poems to Jones' *Nennio*.
14 Cf. Evans in the introduction to his edition of *The English Secretary*: "The
   letters themselves provide many of the figures, tropes, and schemes of rhetoric in
   actual use ... but it is the 'Declaration' itself ... that proves most interesting to
   us today" (p. vii). There is no acknowledgment here that Day's book even
   includes a treatise on secretaryship. An important exception to the tendency of
   passing over the last section of Day's manual can be found in Jonathan
   Goldberg's *Writing Matter: From the Hands of the English Renaissance* (Stan-

ford: Stanford University Press, 1990). In his masterful account of the social production of writing and the writing hand in Elizabethan England, Goldberg offers a chapter on secretaries that treats several of the letterwriters and bureaucratic treatises, including Day's, that I read in this chapter. My discussion of this material and the various rhetorical routes of the secretarial – the path from letters and letterwriters to literariness, the alignment of the office with the ideals of courtly service, the fostering of selfhood in a secret-sharing – overlaps at points with Goldberg's account. See pp. 265–272 for his discussion of Day's manual.

15 Day's expertise on the subject is derived, he claims, from having at "one time or other ... (not without some considerate aduerting) eyed the demeanours, issues, and dispositions of sundrie humors, by insight whereinto, and some proofe made of that which my self haue practised in place of seruice" (Pt. 2, p. 101).

16 Many of these later printed "Secretaries," in fact, advertise themselves as *replacements* for real, flesh-and-blood secretaries. John Hill's *The Young Secretary's Guide* (London, ed. of 1699), for instance, opens with the claim: "I dare presage it will stand those in much Stead who want those larger Endowments, when in so many Cases, relating to Business and Important Affairs, they may find Forms and Precedents ready drawn up to their Hands, and save themselves the Charge, if not (as in Country Towns and Villages it often happens) the tedious, fruitles search of a Secretary or Scrivner, that is thorowpac'd, as some term it, or well-vers'd in these Matters" (A3ᵛ). In addition to model letters, Hill's manual also reproduces bills, bonds, bills of sale, a table of interest, and the like.

17 Cf. Fulwood's *Enimie of Idlenesse*:

> When louing letter trots betwene,
> and mynde to mynde declares,
> It blabbeth not ablaze the hid
> and secrete of our mynde,
> To any one, saue vnto him
> to whom we have assignde.

                                                        (edition of 1568, Aiiiʳ)

18 As Jonathan Goldberg notes, Day's secretary shares many points of resemblance with Castiglione's courtier: "The 'being' of the secretary is fetched from all the requirements of humanistic, courtly gentleness and civilization; it extends from proper birth through high rhetorical education to include even a well-formed body and face" (*Writing Matter*, pp. 265–266).

The incipient courtliness of the Renaissance discourse on secretaryship can also be remarked in setting Day's *English Secretary* (which includes, it will be remembered, a rhetorical handbook) alongside Puttenham's *Arte of English Poesie*, now widely read as much as an encoded manual of political courtship as it is read as a poetics. Puttenham declares that it is "for Courtiers for whose instruction this trauaile is taken" (p. 170) and, like both Castiglione and Day, his instruction is centrally concerned with secrets and "close conveyance." In the section of *The Arte* concerned with rhetorical ornament, Puttenham establishes the pattern of the model poet (and by implication the model courtier) in terms of "the discreet vsing of his figures" (p. 150). What then

follows is a lexicon of figures and tropes, nearly all of which are made by
Puttenham to turn on the operations of secrecy and dissimulation: thus the
figure of metonymy (the "Misnamer" in Puttenham's Englishing) is the "secret
conceyt ... of wrong naming" (p. 191); emphasis (the "Renforcer") is that
which is "secretly implyed" (p. 194); enigma (the "Riddle") involves dissem-
bling "vnder couert and darke speaches" (p. 198); charientismus (the "Priuy
nippe") "fight[s] vnder the banner of dissimulation" (p. 201); periphrasis (the
"Figure of ambrage") works "by reason of a secret intent not appearing by the
words" (p. 203); synecdoche (the "Figure of quick conceite") is known for the
"darknes and duplicitie of his sence" (p. 205); and so on. The "Courtly figure
Allegoria" (p. 196) is for Puttenham the master figure of all these others
because, as the "Figure of the false semblant" (p. 197), its designs are the
darkest, the most occult. Puttenham renames a number of his tropes after
clichéd court "types" (e.g., hyperbole becomes "the Ouerreacher," sententia
"the Sage sayer," etc.). As a handbook for courtiers, Puttenham's grammar of
secrecy, masking, disguise, and their various shadings is thus also available as
a guidebook of courtly maneuverings, which so often depend, as Castiglione
shows, on strategies of dissimulation.

19 Robert Cecil, "The State and Dignity of a Secretary of State's Place, with the
Care and Peril Thereof," in *The Harleian Miscellany* 5 (1810): 166–168, at 167.
20 This story is told in Florence M. Grier Evans, *The Principal Secretary of the
State: A Survey of the Office from 1558–1689* (Manchester: Manchester University Press, 1923), and in two books by G. R. Elton: *The Tudor Revolution in
Government* (Cambridge: Cambridge University Press, 1959) and *The Tudor
Constitution* (Cambridge: Cambridge University Press, 1982). But see *Revolution Reassessed: Revisions in the History of Tudor Government and Administration*, ed. Christopher Coleman and David Starkey (Oxford: Clarendon
Press, 1986). The essays collected in this volume call into question Elton's
narrative of bureaucratic "revolution" and the virtuoso role of Thomas
Cromwell in administrative reform. See also Goldberg, *Writing Matter*,
pp. 257–266.
   Conyers Read provides extended accounts of the careers of the two most
powerful Elizabethan secretaries in his *Mr. Secretary Walsingham and the
Policy of Queen Elizabeth*, 3 vols., (Oxford: Clarendon Press, 1925) and *Mr.
Secretary Cecil and Queen Elizabeth* (New York: Alfred A. Knopf, 1955).
21 R. A. Haldane discusses Walsingham's role in the formation of an Elizabethan
"secret service" in *The Hidden World*, pp. 59–65. Walsingham's far-flung
network of agents is reported to have provided him with intelligence from
thirteen towns in France, seven in the Low Countries, five in Italy, five in
Spain, nine in Germany, and even three more in Turkey. He also maintained
spies in every quarter of England. The latter provisions accorded with the
Principal Secretary's commission as guardian of peace in the realm. On this
role, see also Evans, *The Principal Secretary of State*, pp. 286–287.
22 Cf. Benigno Sánchez-Eppler's interesting discussion of a related sixteenth-
century Spanish secretarial manual, "The Pen That Wields the Voice That
Wills: Secretaries and Letter Writing in Antonio de Torquemada's *Manual De
Escribientes*," in *Neophilologus* 70 (1986): 528–538.
23 I do not mean to imply that the monarch is to be thought the secretary's dupe,

or that he would necessarily be unaware of the possibility that the secretary might be advancing his own agenda by means of subtle rhetorical shadings in the letters he composed at the monarch's behest. When Cardinal Wolsey was offended by one of the letters he received from Richard Pace, Principal Secretary to Henry VIII, for instance, Pace replied that he had originally composed the letter differently. But, he continues, the king would not approve it, "and commanded me to bring your said letter into his privy chamber, with pen and ink, and there he would declare unto me what I should write ... He ... commanded me to write and to rehearse as liked him, and not further to meddle with that answer, so that I herein nothing did but obeyed the king's commandment" (*Letters and Papers* III, No. 1713, Pace to Wolsey, October 29, 1521, cited in Evans, *The Principal Secretary*, pp. 24–26). Henry, according to Evans, usually took care in his correspondence with Wolsey to deal himself with matters requiring the utmost secrecy. He wrote to Wolsey in [?] July 1518: "I have received your letters, to which (because they ask long writing) I have made answer by my secretary; two things there be which be so secret that they cause me at this time to write to you myself." This assertion is remarkable in view of Henry's well-known aversion to writing and attending to bureaucratic matters. See Elton, *The Tudor Revolution*, pp. 66–69.

Though probably a regular enough occurrence, any such concealment from one's secretary would be, as we shall see, practically unthinkable in the account of secretaryship advanced by Angel Day.

24 Evans, *The Principal Secretary of State*, p. 6.

25 "Nicholas Faunt's Discourse Touching the Office of Principal Secretary of Estate, &c. 1592," ed. Charles Hughes, *EHR* 20 (1905): 499–508, at 499–500.

26 Cecil, "The State and Dignity," p. 166.

27 The wide scope and unspecified prerogatives that come with the secretary's office, however, also entail the very real possibility that the secretary could give offence by seeming to overstep his official authority, by seeming to take too much into his own hands. This is something, according to Evans, that secretaries were doing all the time, but were punished for only when they made a mistake. Such was the case with Secretary of State William Davison who, as the scapegoat in the execution of Mary, was charged with "misprision and contempt" in his secretarial role as go-between for the queen and her other ministers. Davison was punished with loss of office, a heavy fine, and imprisonment. His political career never recovered.

28 Evans, *The Principal Secretary of State*, p. 3.

29 Cecil, "The State and Dignity," pp. 166–167.

30 Ibid., p. 167.

31 Faunt, "Discourse Touching the Office of Principal Secretary," p. 501; Cecil, "The State and Dignity," p. 167.

32 What was enacted symbolically in Elizabeth's court may have been actualized in the relations between Mary Queen of Scots and her secretary David Rizzio. Having obviously displaced the queen's husband in terms of counsel and political authority, Rizzio was widely thought to have concurrently taken the husband's place in the royal bed as well. Rumors persisted well into the reign of James I that the king himself was the son of his mother's secretary. I am indebted to Stephen Orgel for this point.

33 "The Fabulous Bush and Baker Boys," Maureen Dowd and Thomas L. Friedman, *New York Times Magazine*, 6 May 1990, sec. 6, pp. 34ff. I am grateful to
Charles Tonetti for directing my attention to this article.

34 Ibid., p. 58.

35 Ibid., p. 36.

36 Ibid., pp. 36, 67.

37 Ibid., p. 36.

38 Ibid. In *Epistemology of the Closet*, Eve Kosofsky Sedgwick argues powerfully
against the notion that the "apparent floating-free from its gay origins of that
phrase 'coming out of the closet' in recent usage might suggest that the trope of
the closet is so close to the heart of some modern preoccupations that it could
be, or has been, evacuated of its historical gay specificity" (p. 72). In the case
of the Dowd and Friedman piece in the *New York Times Magazine*, the
flamboyance of its claims of intimacy between men ("out of the closet," the
secretary in the First Lady's berth, even an accompanying photograph
showing the President helping Baker shed his rain pants on a Bermuda golf
course) seems to be proffered in the face of any possible imputation of an
erotics to this particular friendship or to the office of secretary as structured.
The relation is figured as so normative, these "good ol' boys" so much like us,
that such terms can be used with impunity. The lubricity of this move, of
course, elides the whole question of how much the relations between the
President and his secretary are structured in terms that have survived from an
early modern discourse on secretaryship (as well as one on male friendship)
and its attendant erotics.

39 Alan Bray, "Homosexuality and the Signs of Male Friendship in Elizabethan
England," *History Workshop Journal* 29 (1990): 1–19. Interestingly, several of
Bray's examples of friendship and clientage in this essay concern secre-
taries.

40 Alan Bray's earlier work, *Homosexuality in Renaissance England* (London:
Gay Men's Press, 1982) remains the best account we have of the wider social
significations of sodomy. See especially pp. 13–32. Bray writes: "Homosexuality was not part of [Richard] Hooker's law of nature [in *Of the Laws of
Ecclesiastical Polity*]. It was not part of the chain of being, or the harmony of
the created world ... It was not part of the Kingdom of Heaven or its
counterpart in the Kingdom of Hell (although that could unwittingly release
it). It was none of these things because it was not conceived of as part of the
created order at all; it was part of its dissolution. And as such it was not a
sexuality in its own right, but existed as a potential for confusion and disorder
in one undivided sexuality" (p. 25).

Bruce R. Smith, in *Homosexual Desire in Shakespeare's England: A Cultural
Poetics* (Chicago: University of Chicago Press, 1991), pp. 42–53, takes issue,
however, with the prevailing notion in Bray's account, as well as in those of
other historians of sexual behavior in early modern Europe, that sixteenth-
century legal discourse concerning homosexuality was framed essentially as a
reiteration of thirteenth-century proscriptions. Smith offers a more variegated
account of that legal discourse in Renaissance England, showing that the
juridical history of homosexuality in this period is not simply a question of the
greater or lesser severity with which the laws against sodomy were enforced,

but also a matter of the transfer of sodomy from legal category to legal category. Smith's account thus tracks "a shift in ideology, a progression from religious to political to personal ways of thinking about sodomy" (p. 53).

41 *Health to the Gentlemanly Profession of Seruingmen* (London, 1598), cited in Bray, "Homosexuality and the Signs of Male Friendship," p. 10.

42 Bray, "Homosexuality and the Signs of Male Friendship,"pp. 14–15.

43 Cf. Goldberg, *Writing Matter*, p. 248:"Secretaries were not only able to forge their master's hands – they were permitted and even expected to do so, as Paul Saenger notes in a comment on the role of royal secretaries in early modern France, where the assumption that the royal hand would autograph certain state missives was met when Louis XI empowered his secretaries to imitate his hand in order to speed the flow of letters ('Silent Reading,' 406n). Sir Hilary Jenkinson claims that the same was true in England, where it is not uncommon to find letters signed by secretaries in a different hand from the one in which they wrote the body of the letter ('Elizabethan Handwriting,' 31)."

44 Jacques Derrida, *The Post Card: From Socrates to Freud and Beyond*, trans. Alan Bass, (Chicago: University of Chicago Press, 1987), p. 3.

45 Ibid., p. 9.

46 Ibid., p. 20.

47 Ibid., p. 12.

48 Ibid., p. 19.

49 Elias Canetti, *Crowds and Power* (New York: Viking Press, 1966), pp. 290–296.

50 John Milton, *Samson Agonistes*, line 394. All references to Milton's poetry are to *John Milton: The Complete Poems and Major Prose*, ed. Merritt Y. Hughes (New York: Macmillan Publishing Company, rpt. 1989).

51 *The Complete Essays of Montaigne*, trans. Donald M. Frame (Stanford: Stanford University Press, 1965), p. 136.

52 Faunt, "Discourse Touching the Office of Principal Secretary," p. 500.

53 Ibid., p. 501.

54 Ibid., p. 500.

55 Ibid., p. 503.

56 Cited in Evans, *The Principal Secretary of State*, p. 47. Cf. the following from Naunton's account of Walsingham in *Fragmenta Regalia*: "I must confess that I have read many of his letters (for they were common) sent to my Lord of Leicester and of Burghley out to France, containing many fine passages and secrets, yet if I might have been beholding to his ciphers (whereof they are full) they would have told pretty tales of the times" (p. 61).

57 Robert Beale, "A Treatise of the Office of a Councellor and Principall Secretarie to her Ma[jes]tie," printed in Conyers Read's *Mr. Secretary Walsingham*, pp. 423–443. This citation is from p. 428.

58 Cited in Evans, *The Principal Secretary of State*, p. 2. The post-Burckhardian literature on Renaissance subject formation is substantial. For an extended meditation on the developing private conditions of early modern subjectivity, and its relations to various forms of subjugation, see Francis Barker, *The Tremulous Private Body: Essays on Subjection* (London: Methuen, 1984). In contrast to Barker's thoroughly subjugated, premodern surface subject is Stephen Greenblatt's virtuosically self-fashioning subject. Unlike Barker's

subject, which seems to be all surface inscription, Greenblatt's *Renaissance Self-Fashioning* posits an occluded interiority, which may be empty (as in the case of More), or may be a negation (as in the case of Spenser), or may even be an inner theatre (as in the case of Marlowe).

On the relations in the late sixteenth century between secrecy and the self – "the ushering in [of] the 'modern' idea of self at a distance from public expression" – as well as on the Elizabethan court's fetishization of secrecy, see Patricia Fumerton's fascinating "'Secret' Arts: Elizabethan Miniatures and Sonnets," in *Representing the English Renaissance*, ed. Stephen Greenblatt (Berkeley and Los Angeles: University of California Press, 1988), pp. 93–133. Anne Ferry sets up her readings of Renaissance sonnets and interiority by historicizing the language of self, privacy, and secrecy in *The "Inward" Language: Sonnets of Wyatt, Sidney, Shakespeare, Donne* (Chicago: University of Chicago Press, 1983). See also *Passions of the Renaissance*, ed. Roger Chartier and trans. Arthur Goldhammer, Vol. 3 of *A History of Private Life*, general eds. Philippe Aries and Georges Duby (Cambridge, Mass. and London: The Belknap Press of Harvard University Press, 1989). Finally, see Bruce R. Smith, *Homosexual Desire in Shakespeare's England*, chapter seven, "The Secret Sharer." Smith reads Shakespeare's sonnets as a narrative which fosters a secret inwardness in the service of originating a specifically homosexual subjectivity.

59 My discussion of Spenserian dispersal has been informed by Jonathan Goldberg's reading of *The Shepheardes Calender* in *Voice Terminal Echo: Postmodernism and English Renaissance Texts* (New York and London: Methuen, 1986), pp. 38–67. See also his "Colin to Hobbinol," p. 115: "the secret of authorship [in the *Calender*] is maintained through a disappearing act in disseminative naming."

60 Cf. Goldberg, "Colin to Hobbinol," p. 116.

61 George Puttenham, *The Arte of English Poesie*, A Facsimile Reproduction, introduction by Baxter Hathaway (Kent, Ohio: Kent State University Press, 1970), p. 53.

62 William Webbe, *A Discourse of English Poesie*, in G. Gregory Smith, *Elizabethan Critical Essays*, 1:262.

63 I take the term "empty secret" from Eve Kosofsky Sedgwick, *Epistemology of the Closet*, pp. 163–167.

64 Georg Simmel, "The Role of the Secret in Social Life," in *The Sociology of Georg Simmel*, trans. and ed. Kurt H. Wolff (Glencoe, Ill: The Free Press, 1950), p. 335.

65 Ibid., p. 338. Interestingly, Francis Bacon anticipates Simmel's observations in "Of Simulation and Dissimulation," his own investigation of the aims and structures of concealment. There Bacon theorizes an aesthetics of secrecy in terms similar to Simmel's: "Besides (to say truth) nakedness is uncomely, as well in mind as body; and it addeth no small reverence to men's manners and actions, if they be not altogether open." See *Essays*, ed. John Pitcher (New York: Penguin Books, 1987), pp. 76–78, at p. 77.

66 Simmel, *The Sociology of Georg Simmel*, p. 337.

67 J. W. Saunders, "The Stigma of Print," p. 144.

68 "A Discourse of Civill Life," (1606) in *The Works of Lodowick Bryskett*, ed.

J. H. P. Pafford (London: Gregg International Publishers, 1972), p. 26. The context of Bryskett's remarks, which provide a frame for "Civill Life," is his recollection of a small gathering of friends, Spenser among them, at his house in Ireland. Bryskett reports that he had asked Spenser to expound on "Morall Philosophie." Spenser, of course, decorously declines, thus opening up the space for Bryskett to present his own translation of the *Dialogues* of Giovanni Battista Giraldi (Cinthio). Before Spenser leaves off, however, he does take the opportunity to advertise his as yet unpublished *Faerie Queene*, which will "represent all the moral vertues, assigning to euery vertue, a Knight to be patron and defender of the same" (p. 26).

69 Muriel Bradbrook, "No Room at the Top: Spenser's Pursuit of Fame," in *Elizabethan Poetry*, Stratford-upon-Avon Studies 2 (London: St. Martin's Press, 1960), pp. 91–109, at p. 99.

70 See Saunders, "The Stigma of Print," p. 158. See also Michael Brennan, *Literary Patronage in the English Renaissance*, pp. 1–4; 11–12.

71 Cf. Simon Shepherd's volume, *Spenser*, in the Harvester New Readings series (Atlantic Highlands, N.J.: Humanities Press International, 1989), p. 68: "It is clear from EK's notes to 'Januarye' that homosexual desire is being spoken of ... Despite the disclaimer, he gives a Platonic definition to 'paederastice' as a love of souls ... He hastily forbids anyone to think that he defends 'execrable and horrible sinnes of forbidden and unlawful fleshinesse' (pp. 422–23). This repeats the strategy in Scudamour's narrative, where physical homosex was denied while homoerotic bondings were suggested. Needless to say, EK's lead has been followed by modern commentators."

72 Goldberg, "Colin to Hobbinol," p. 119.

73 Ibid.

74 *Paradise Lost* 9:21–23.

75 See Cain's introduction to the "October" eclogue in the already indispensable *Yale Edition of the Shorter Poems of Edmund Spenser*, ed. William A. Oram, *et al.* (New Haven: Yale University Press, 1989), p. 168.

76 This is not to say, despite Marx's denunciation of Spenser in his *Ethnological Notebooks* as "Elizabeth's Arse-Kissing poet" (cited in Shepherd, *Spenser*, p. 3), that the queen's poet/secretary disinterestedly "transcribed" in his poetry exactly what she would have in reality dictated. We already know from our consideration of various Renaissance treatments of secretaryship that the hierarchical and power relations between master and secretary are not always wholly stabilized, and that drafting letters allowed the secretary some latitude for attempting to advance his own agenda in certain circumstances.

In the "Aprill" eclogue, Spenser "records" Elizabeth's image, but it is the image of her as a seemingly perpetual virgin queen. In the 1570s, as David Norbrook points out in *Poetry and Politics in the English Renaissance* (London: Routledge and Kegan Paul, 1984), the cult of Elizabeth as maiden goddess was a relatively new phenomenon, with the "Aprill" eclogue itself being a seminal work in "creating" the image of the virgin queen (see pp. 83–89). But while Spenser was celebrating her as another Diana, we know that Elizabeth herself was considering a match with a French Catholic duke. Such a marriage, however, would exclude the queen from her position as the epicenter of the chaste pastoral world of virgins that Spenser's blazon establishes around her. She is "Eliza," the fourth Grace and "Queene of shepheardes all," only so long as she remains a virgin: "Let none come there, but that Virgins bene" (129).

In short, if Spenser can have a hand (that is, a secretary's hand) in scripting the royal image, he can by the same token attempt to contour that image towards a particular end. My argument is that the empowering of the secretary exemplified in Day's, Cecil's, and Faunt's texts empowers Spenser *as a poet*, so that he is not just taking dictation, but dictating to E.K., to Hobbinol, and even to the queen. Thus, although he professes his subservience, he is in fact demonstrating a measure of power, however circumscribed by his relatively marginal social and occupational position. For a compelling argument (though one that is chiefly confined to the representational practices of poetry) on the ways in which the Elizabethan ruler and ruled are reciprocally constituted, see Louis Adrian Montrose's "The Elizabethan Subject and the Spenserian Text," in *Literary Theory/Renaissance Texts*, ed. Patricia Parker and David Quint (Baltimore: The Johns Hopkins University Press, 1986): "In Spenser's text, the refashioning of an Elizabethan subject as a laureate poet is dialectically related to the refashioning of the queen as the author's subject" (p. 323).

77 Puttenham, *The Arte of English Poesie*, p. 32.
78 Cf. Patterson, "Re-Opening the Green Cabinet," p. 69.

3 "In sundrie hands": the 1590 *Faerie Queene* and Spenser's *Complaints*

1 On this problematic see Jacques Derrida's disquisition on the unsayable, "How to Avoid Speaking: Denials," trans. Ken Frieden, in *Languages of the Unsayable: The Play of Negativity in Literature and Literary Theory*, ed. Sanford Budick and Wolfgang Iser (New York: Columbia University Press, 1989), pp. 3–70, especially p. 25. See also, in a very different register, D. A. Miller, *The Novel and the Police*, pp. 194–195.

2 Bradbrook, "No Room at the Top," p. 103.

3 I am adapting this point from Crewe's *Hidden Designs*, p. 55: "In a strongly autonomizing but by no means irrevocable gesture, Spenser proclaims himself, in the wake of the 1590 *Faerie Queene*, no longer the nameless 'Immerito' of *The Shepheardes Calender*, but also not the incorporated Elizabethan court poet, and he aggressively repossesses his early work as his own property, also now claiming title to hitherto anonymous or unpublished imitations of Petrarch, du Bellay and many others."

4 For an adept and elegant consideration of similar career concerns and positionings, see John D. Bernard's *Ceremonies of Innocence: Pastoralism in the Poetry of Edmund Spenser* (Cambridge: Cambridge University Press, 1989), pp. 106–134. Bernard offers the valuable insight that pastoral is Spenser's career-long "mode" for examining his relations to the court and to political power in general. I do want to take issue, however, with Bernard's assertion that Spenser's later poetry (beginning with what we both recognize as the pivotal *Complaints* volume) articulates a "conception of a more personal, detached, and contemplative pastoral whose sources transcend the political

community altogether" (p. 107). No doubt in his post-1590 poetry Spenser launches a critique – and in Book 6 of *The Faerie Queene* perhaps even a disavowal – of the court as the epicenter of cultural values. But the 1596 *Faerie Queene* is too deeply embroiled with what it calls "affaires of common wele" (5.9.36.3) to transcend the political. Thus the "detachment" that I see enacted at the end of Spenser's career is not an absolute rejection of the "political community" for some kind of transcendental poetics of contemplation, but rather, as I discuss in Chapter 4, Spenser's inescapably politicized construction of a kind of imaginary "counter-court" with himself established at its center.

5 Among the accounts of Book 1's proem that have been most influential for my reading of it are: Thomas H. Cain, *Praise in "The Faerie Queene"* (Lincoln: University of Nebraska Press, 1978), pp. 37–57; Jonathan Goldberg, *Endlesse Worke: Spenser and the Structures of Discourse* (Baltimore: The Johns Hopkins University Press, 1980), pp. 12–24; A. Leigh Deneef, *Spenser and the Motives of Metaphor* (Durham, N.C.: Duke University Press, 1982), pp. 91–141; and Elizabeth J. Bellamy, "The Vocative and the Vocational: The Unreadability of Elizabeth in *The Faerie Queene*," *ELH* 54 (1987): 1–30.

6 See Goldberg, *Endlesse Worke*, p. 13.

7 Cf. Crewe, *Hidden Designs*, p. 93: "An actor, for example, apparently unmasks in the pseudo-Virgilian proem to *The Faerie Queene*, Book I ... but who is the actor and why the unmasking? The *Muse* rather than the author unmasks or gets unmasked, and who is she, this inspiring pseudo-shepherdess? Is the masque now over, or is it just entering a new phase, with the players changing costumes? What is the relation of Spenser ('I ... the man') to this theatricality?"

8 Judith H. Anderson, "'Myn auctour': Spenser's Enabling Fiction and Eumnestes' 'immortall scrine,'" in *Unfolded Tales: Essays on Renaissance Romance*, ed. George M. Logan and Gordon Teskey (Ithaca: Cornell University Press, 1989), pp. 16–31, at 17. Spenser's presentation of a sacred scrine as the source or storehouse of his poem is also discussed, though with less emphasis on the scrine as a kind of secret reserve, by Cain in *Praise in "The Faerie Queene,"* p. 49, and by Goldberg in *Endlesse Worke*, pp. 17, 19.

9 Robert Estienne, *Dictionariolum Puerorum Tribus Linguis Latina, Anglica, and Gallica*, facsimile reproduction published in *The English Experience* series, No. 351 (Amsterdam and New York: Da Capo Press, 1971), s.v. *scrinium*.

10 I take this point from David Lee Miller's rich discussion of Arthur's role in the poem in *The Poem's Two Bodies: The Poetics of the 1590 "Faerie Queene"* (Princeton: Princeton University Press, 1988), pp. 134–140.

11 Ibid., p. 138.

12 See *Amoretti* 33: "Great wrong I doe, I can it not deny, / to that most sacred Empresse my dear dred, / not finishing her Queene of faery, / that mote enlarge her liuing prayses dead."

13 Cf. Anderson, "'Myn auctor,'" p. 18.

14 I have adapted this point from Goldberg's *Endlesse Worke*, p. 23, and from Cain's *Praise in "The Faerie Queene,"* p. 48. My concern here is to rearticulate their seminal observations about Spenser's assignment of authorial control to Elizabeth in terms of what I have been calling his secretarial poetics and its attendant conceit that *The Faerie Queene* is produced as "dictation" Spenser has taken at the hand of the queen.

15 Deneef, *Spenser and the Motives of Metaphor*, p. 104.
16 Goldberg, *Endlesse Worke*, p. 124.
17 See Orest Ranum, "The Refuges of Intimacy" in *A History of Private Life*, Vol. 3, *Passions of the Renaissance*, pp. 206–263. Ranum reports that the closet or cabinet of Nicolas Fouquet, who oversaw Louis XIV's finances, was constructed as itself a mirror, being entirely lined with looking glasses. Similarly, Louis XIV's great cabinet at Versailles was mirror-lined (see p. 228). In the course of his essay Ranum also reproduces a number of images of women who have retreated to private chambers in order to gaze at themselves in mirrors.
18 Anne Ferry, *The "Inward" Language*, p. 50. For a taxonomic (but not much more than that) account of mirrors in sixteenth-century English literature, see Herbert Graves, *The Mutable Glass: Mirror-imagery in Titles and Texts of the Middle Ages and the English Renaissance*, trans. Gordon Collier (Cambridge: Cambridge University Press, 1982).
19 Puttenham, *The Arte of English Poesie*, p. 70.
20 Ibid., p. 32.
21 Ibid., p. 35.
22 Montrose, "The Elizabethan Subject," p. 325.
23 This pun on the two kinds of containing/"pen-ning" takes on a more ghastly quality when it recurs in the concluding cantos of Book 3. There Scudamour's complaint, "Why then is *Busirane* with wicked hand / Suffred, these seuen monethes day in secret den / My Lady and my loue so cruelly to pen?" (11.10.7–9), is refigured in the discovery of Busirane using the "liuing bloud" dripping from Amoret's pierced heart to "pen" his occult love enchantments (12.31).
24 Montrose, "The Elizabethan Subject," p. 324.
25 Ibid.
26 Cited in *The Works of Edmund Spenser: A Variorum Edition*, at 3:310.
27 See 3.4.26. I do not mean to imply by these examples, however, that the other versions of chastity offered in Book 3 are that much less problematic. Florimell's arresting virginal beauty, for instance, rarely has the effect of inspiring the kind of awe that might safeguard her; instead, it seems to transform every male who beholds her – including those like Arthur who are otherwise "honorable" – into a potential rapist. Britomart likewise offers a disruptive model of virginity inasmuch as her transvestism, like the crossdressing heroines in Shakespeare's comedies, makes her equally available as an object of desire for both sexes.
28 Montrose, "The Elizabethan Subject," pp. 323–324.
29 Bellamy, "The Vocative and the Vocational," p. 3.
30 Ibid., p. 1.
31 See Jacques Derrida, "The Double Session," in *Dissemination*, trans. Barbara Johnson (Chicago: University of Chicago Press, 1981), pp. 173–285, especially pp. 252–260.
32 See J. E. Neale, *Elizabeth I and Her Parliaments, 1559–1581* (London: Jonathan Cape, 1965), p. 49. On Elizabeth's negotiations of power vis à vis her gender and her virginity, see Louis Adrian Montrose, "'Shaping Fantasies': Figurations of Gender and Power in Elizabethan Culture," in *Representing the*

English Renaissance, ed. Stephen Greenblatt (Berkeley and Los Angeles: University of California Press, 1988), pp. 31–64, especially pp. 45–55. See also Philippa Berry, *Of Chastity and Power: Elizabethan Literature and the Unmarried Queen* (London and New York: Routledge, 1989).

33 Montrose discusses Spenser's self-censoring impulses in *The Faerie Queene* in his "The Elizabethan Subject," p. 328.

34 Goldberg, "Colin to Hobbinol," p. 115.

35 Jean Starobinski, *Words Upon Words: The Anagrams of Ferdinand de Saussure*, trans. Olivia Emmet (New Haven: Yale University Press, 1979). According to Starobinski, Saussure filled ninety-nine notebooks with reflection and research on anagrams and other kinds of logograms. Saussure comes close to making the claim that these cryptographic forms are a fundamental basis of poetic composition – a regulator of poetic production, rather than merely a kind of clever rhetorical ornament (pp. 17, 103, 129). Given the linguistic primacy Sussure assigns to the anagrammatic, I find his passing notation of the fact that *hupographein* (the Greek term for "hypogram" – another kind of anagram) also designates the kind of reproductive writing a secretary performs interesting in view of the role Puttenham assigns to secretaries as coiners of proper speech: "*Politien*, this word also is receiued from the Frenchmen, but at this day vsuall in Court, and with all good Secretaries" (*The Arte of English Poesie*, pp. 158–159).

36 Putttenham, *The Arte of English Poesie*, p. 123. Cf. Crewe, *Hidden Designs*, pp. 170–171 on what he terms the "playful 'undoing' of the queen's name."

37 Given that several extant copies of the poem contain only ten sonnets, it has been deduced that these dedications were added to *The Faerie Queene* in two batches. The remaining seven – including, most notably, the one to Lord Burghley – would then have been appended just before printing was completed. See the account offered by Judson in his *Variorum* biography of Spenser, 11:142–143.

38 Jane Tylus, "Spenser, Virgil, and the Politics of Poetic Labor," *ELH* 55 (1986): 53–77, at 54.

39 For a related discussion of the relations between Red Crosse, the rustics of *The Shepheardes Calender*, and Immeritô, see Bernard, *Ceremonies of Innocence*, pp. 79–81; 91–92.

40 See, for example, the account offered by Thomas Fuller in *The History of the Worthies of England* (London, 1662): "There passeth a story commonly told and believed, that *Spencer* presenting his Poems to Queen *Elizabeth*: She highly affected therewith, commanded the Lord *Cecil* Her Treasurer to give him an hundred pound; and when the Treasurer (a good Steward of the Queens money) alledged that sum was too much, then *give him* (quoth the Queen) *what is reason*; to which the Lord consented, but was so busied, belike, about matters of higher concernment, that *Spencer* received no reward; Whereupon he presented this petition in a small piece of paper to the Queen in her Progress,

> *I was promis'd on a time,*
> *To have reason for my rhyme;*
> *From that time unto this season,*
> *I receiv'd nor rhyme nor reason.*

Hereupon the Queen gave strict order (not without some check to her Treasurer) for the present payment of the hundred pounds [sic], the first intended upon him." Fuller's account is reproduced in Cummings, *Spenser: The Critical Heritage*, pp. 320–321. While this particular anecdote may very well be apocryphal, Spenser's dissatisfaction with what his poetic endeavors had earned him at Elizabeth's court is evident in nearly every poem of the 1591 *Complaints* volume.

41 See Shepherd, *Spenser*, p. 105. Steven W. May notes that annuities from the crown averaged on the short side of twenty pounds. Even so, he reports, Lord Henry Seymour, sewer to the queen, for example, gained an annuity of three hundred pounds, while the countess of Kildare's amounted to seven hundred pounds. See May's *The Elizabethan Courtier Poets*, p. 29. For a detailed consideration of Spenser's annuity, see Herbert Berry and E. K. Timings, "Spenser's Pension," *Review of English Studies* 11 (1960): 254–259.

42 On this unprecedented social flux, see Lawrence Stone, *The Crisis of the Aristocracy: 1558–1641* (Oxford: Oxford University Press, 1967), abridged edn., pp. 21–28.

43 This point is discussed by William A. Oram in his informative introduction to *Mother Hubberds Tale* for the *Yale Edition of the Shorter Poems*, p. 330.

44 It is true that the Fox and the Ape are described at the onset of the poem as "craftie and unhappie witted" (49), but the moral valences of these terms are not necessarily as one-directional and censorious as the *Yale Edition*'s gloss of "apt to cause trouble" might suggest.

45 Crewe, *Hidden Designs*, p. 56.

46 See, for example, Greenlaw's "Spenser and the Earl of Leicester," *PMLA* 25 (1910): 535–561; "*The Shepheardes Calender*," *PMLA* 26 (1911): 419–451; and "*The Shepheardes Calender* II," *SP* 11 (1913): 3–25.

47 Crewe, *Hidden Designs*, p. 55. Crewe continues: "The immediate point, however, is that if the 1580 'Mother Hubberd' is encoded with anti-French and anti-Catholic meanings, other codings or contextual investments, whether intentional or merely accruing to the poem in time, must be inferred in the 1591 'Mother Hubberd'" (p. 56).

48 Cf. Ronald Bond's introductory remarks on *Complaints* in the *Yale Edition of the Shorter Poems*: "Spenser's direct involvement [in the publication of *Complaints*] emerges in the careful disposition of the material into sections with discrete title pages and separate dedications, and in the various minor textual changes he seems to have authorized in some of the copies printed in 1591" (p. 217). In *Ceremonies of Innocence*, Bernard takes a different path to arrive a similar conclusion concerning the poet's role in the publication of *Complaints*. Unlike Bond, who discerns a careful ordering to the volume which evidences authorial involvement, Bernard adduces Spenser's hand in the book's "seemingly [but only seemingly] shapeless composition" which "conceals a retrospective bias closely related to that of *Colin Cloute*" (p. 107).

Jean R. Brink, in "Who Fashioned Edmund Spenser? The Textual History of *Complaints*," *SP* 87 (1991): 153–168, however, does dispute the prevailing assumption that Spenser directed the publication of *Complaints*. Rightly recognizing the antagonistic force of the volume's anti-court (specifically anti-Burghley) satire, Brink argues that "If Spenser hoped to reap any benefit from having written *The Faerie Queene*, it is extremely doubtful that he would have authorized the publication of *Complaints*" (p. 158). Accordingly, she takes at face value Ponsonby's preface and its claim that the printer published these poems strictly on his own initiative.

I find Brink's contentions valuable in that they work against romanticized notions that Spenser's texts were produced in a "privileged literary world in which major poets, respected by patrons and printers, controlled the publication of their texts" (p. 154). Yet I also find that her account of how *Complaints* made it into print raises more questions than it answers. If *The Faerie Queene* was not a major popular success, as Brink herself points out, why would Ponsonby go through all the trouble he details in order to bring out *Complaints*? Ponsonby says that he does so because *The Faerie Queene* has been so successful. Since this claim is not strictly true, it seems to be that what is being negotiated in the Preface is too shifty to be taken at face value. Moreover, given the volatility of Spenser's satire in *Mother Hubberds Tale* and *The Ruines of Time*, Brink never accounts for why Ponsonby would go out of his way to publish the collection in view of the damage those poems could do to Spenser's chances for reward and advancement. Is Ponsonby out to undermine the poet's standing, or simply unaware of what is going on in these poems? And if Ponsonby's presumption and "unauthorized" publication of *Complaints* did do damage (inadvertent or not) to Spenser's career, why would Spenser return to this printer with the next installment of *The Faerie Queene*?

49 See Bernard, *Ceremonies of Innocence*, p. 113, for a similar point. See also Bond's Introduction to *Complaints* in the *Yale Edition*, p. 218.

50 See Hallett Smith, *Elizabethan Poetry* (Cambridge, Mass.: Harvard University Press, 1964), p. 103.

51 Linda Vecchi notes that Spenser's volume is the only book in *The Short-Title Catalog* to appear under the title "Complaints." See her essay "Spenser's *Complaints*: Is the Whole Equal to the Sum of its Parts?" in *Spenser at Kalamazoo* (1984): 127–138, at 130.

52 Bernard offers the best account I have found of these seldom-discussed poems and the way they figure in Spenser's revisionary appraisal of his career in *Complaints*. See *Ceremonies of Innocence*, pp. 111–113.

53 Significantly, *Virgils Gnat*, the most "Virgilian" – or more precisely, pseudo-Virgilian – poem in the volume does not represent the high "canonical" Virgil; nor has it, as a complaint, found a place in the authorized Virgilian progression of pastoral–georgic–epic.

54 Puttenham, *The Arte of English Poesie*, p. 32.

55 See, for example, Oram's Introduction to *Mother Hubberds Tale* for the *Yale Edition of the Shorter Poems*, p. 329.

56 Cf. Crewe's discussion in *Hidden Designs*, p. 61, of this episode and its implications for the potential insidiousness of any sympathetic response in this poem. Moreover, Crewe points out that it is less a question here of what business a shepherd could ever have with a fox than one of truancy. That is, what kind of shepherd is it that would abandon his flock to the unsupervised care of a total stranger?

57 Puttenham, *The Arte of English Poesie*, p. 46.

58 Bacon, "Of Simulation and Dissimulation," in *Essays*, p. 77.

59 Crewe, *Hidden Designs*, p. 62.
60 Cf. Oram's discussion of this point in the *Yale Edition of the Shorter Poems*, pp. 332–333.
61 Thomas Middleton, *The Black Book*, in *The Works of Thomas Middleton*, 8 vols., ed. A. H. Bullen (London: John C. Nimmo, 1886): 8:31.
62 Gabriel Harvey, *Foure Letters and Certeine Sonnets*, in *The Works of Gabriel Harvey*, 3 vols., ed. Alexander B. Grosart (London: Hazel, Watson, and Viney, 1884): 1:164.
63 Thomas Nashe, *Strange Newes*, in *The Works of Thomas Nashe*, 5 vols., ed. R. B. McKerrow (London: Sidgwick and Johnson, 1904–1910): 1:281–282: "Thou bringst in *Mother Hubbard* for an instance. Go no further, but here confesse thy selfe a flat nodgscombe before all this congregation; for thou hast dealt by thy friend as homely as thou didst by thy father ... Besides, whereas before I thought it made matter of some malitious moralizers against him, and no substance of slaunder in truth; now, when thou (that proclaimest thy selfe the only familiar of his bosome, *and therefore shouldst know his secretes*) giues it out in print that he ouershotte himselfe therein, it cannot chuse but be suspected to be so indeed" (emphasis added).
64 John Weever, *Epigrammes* (London, 1599), sig. G3a, reproduced in facsimile in *John Weever*, ed. E. A. J. Honigmann (Manchester: Manchester University Press, 1987).
65 Richard Schell, Introduction to *The Ruines of Time*, in the *Yale Edition of the Shorter Poems*, p. 227.

4 Secret sights, private parts: the 1596 *Faerie Queene*

1 Spenser's deflection from the path of the Virgilian career is matched in the last decade of his life with a notion of secretaryship and bureaucratic service which is no longer strictly courtly. For Spenser's poetry of the 1595–1596 period can be seen, I suggest, as a further movement away from the secretarial poetics which give shape to *The Shepheardes Calender* and the 1590 *Faerie Queene* – texts which aim for, and measure success by, the gaining of access to the privy chambers of the powerful as secretary, laureate, counselor, and friend. But it is not the case that Spenser ever stops being employed in various secretarial capacities. The letters he carried to England from president Thomas Norris (letters Spenser perhaps took down as dictation) in 1598 during the Munster rebellion show his continuing engagement with secretarial service right up to the time of his death. Yet after the disappointment of his 1590 trip back to court, neither Spenser's poetic efforts nor his service as a secretary seem to be conceived of any longer as a means to gain him that always elusive place at court. Instead, those efforts now appear to be repointed towards advancing his Irish career, and securing his own interests as the "undertaker" of a substantial Irish plantation and colonial administrator against the regularly competing interests of the "Old English" or "Anglo-Irish" – settlers descended from the Norman conquerors of Ireland and thus possessed of English titles, but whose administration of Ireland tended towards the Gaelic and whose religion was Catholic.
2 Bernard offers a related discussion of these interruptions in *Ceremonies of Innocence*, pp. 127–131.

3 See *Calendar of State Papers, Ireland, 1509–1596*, ed. Hans Claude Hamilton, 5 vols. (London: Longman, Green, Longman, and Roberts, 1860–1890), at 4:198.

4 See Nicholas B. Canny, "Edmund Spenser and the Development of an Anglo-Irish Identity," *Yearbook of English Studies* 13 (1983): 1–19. See also Canny's *The Elizabethan Conquest of Ireland: A Pattern Established 1565–76* (New York: Barnes and Noble, 1976).

5 Julia Reinhard Lupton, "Home-Making in Ireland: Virgil's Eclogue I and Book VI of *The Faerie Queene*," *SpStud* 7, ed. Patrick Cullen and Thomas P. Roche, Jr. (New York: AMS Press, 1990), pp. 119–145. See also Carpenter, *A Reference Guide*, pp. 19–22.

6 Another Englishman who made a lifelong bureaucratic career of service in Ireland was Lodowick Bryskett. Although in his letters to Walsingham and others back at court Bryskett regularly complains about being stationed in "this miserable countrey," his intention seems not so much to be to open a way for himself out of Ireland, as to secure a better station there in terms of office and earnings. See Plomer and Cross, eds., *The Life and Correspondence of Lodowick Bryskett*, especially pp. 29–35.

7 Cf. William A. Oram's Introduction to *Colin Cloute* for the *Yale Edition of the Shorter Poems*, p. 523.

8 The empowering convergence of matron, maid, mother, and monarch in Elizabeth's public self-representations – recognizable as an appropriation of the similarly oedipally inflected codes of devotion to the Virgin Mary – is given an exemplary treatment in Montrose's "Shaping Fantasies," especially pp. 75–81. See also Donald Cheney, "Spenser's Fortieth Birthday and Related Fictions," *SpStud* 4, ed. Patrick Cullen and Thomas P. Roche, Jr. (New York: AMS Press, 1984), pp. 3–31, especially pp. 8–9.

9 Bernard makes this point in *Ceremonies of Innocence*, p. 133.

10 I am indebted to Jonathan Crewe for the observation here about Cynthia's figural status in this episode.

11 Paul Alpers, "Spenser's Late Pastorals," *ELH* 56 (1989): 797–817, at 810.

12 See, for instance, Bernard, *Ceremonies of Innocence*, on Spenser's developing pessimism "about poetry's usefulness and his inclination to withdraw from the active world into an inviolate and wholly private contemplative center" (p. 163). Consider also David L. Miller's agenda in "Spenser's Vocation, Spenser's Career": "In what follows I will explore this troubled questioning of his own poetics by following certain related motifs through Spenser's late work: gestures of exclusion that 'purify' the acts and occasions of poetic vision; actual and potential violations of such purity; and signs of withdrawal, finally, from direct engagement in the historical world" (p. 216).

13 "Of Friendship," in *The Complete Essays of Montaigne*, p. 137.

14 André Hurault, Sieur de Maisse, *Journal* (1597), trans. and ed. G. B. Harrison and R. A. Jones (London: Nonesuch Press, 1931), pp. 11–12.

15 See G. R. Elton, *England under the Reign of the Tudors* (London: Methuen and Co., 1974), pp. 469–471. Cf. also the sympathetic account written by Essex's secretary, Sir Henry Wotton, several years after the unhappy event: "He [Essex] had to wrestle with a queen's declining, or rather with her very setting age, which, besides other respects, is commonly even of itself the more

umbratious and apprehensive, as for the most part all horizons are charged with certain vapours towards their evening." Cited in J. B. Black, *The Reign of Elizabeth: 1558–1603*, 2nd edn. (Oxford: Clarendon Press, 1959), p. 441.

16 Cain, *Praise in "The Faerie Queene,"* p. 165.

17 *As You Like It* 2.7.43. The citation is from *The Riverside Shakespeare*, ed. G. Blakemore Evans, *et al.* (Boston: Houghton Mifflin, 1974).

18 Cf. Jonathan Goldberg, *James I and the Politics of Literature: Jonson, Shakespeare, Donne, and Their Contemporaries* (Baltimore: The Johns Hopkins University Press, 1983), p. 3: "From the opening of book V on, Spenser seems to want his reader to believe that his tongue, like Bon/Malfont's, is at the royal command, and that his text is 'privileged' to speak the truths Elizabeth wanted to hear. The 'discourse of so divine a read' (V. pro. 11.7), the text of book V represents – Spenser insists – the reproduction of the queen's justice, her dreadful doom; the hero of the poem, Spenser concludes in the proem to book V, is not his invention but her instrument: 'loe here thy *Artegall*,' he writes (11.9); her hero, not his."

19 My treatment of the poem's squaring off of the queen and her male counselors is not meant to obscure the fact that Mercilla's reluctance to pronounce judgment against Duessa, as well as the (crocodile) tears she sheds at Duessa's capital sentence, likewise serves Elizabeth's interests, inasmuch as she wished to be seen as personally opposed to the trial and execution of her cousin.

20 Cited from Paul Johnson, *Elizabeth I: A Study in Power and Intellect* (London: Weidenfeld and Nicolson, 1974), p. 320. Queen Elizabeth's public poses of double genderedness and the political work those poses accomplish is expertly discussed by Leah S. Marcus in *Puzzling Shakespeare: Local Reading and Its Discontents* (Berkeley and Los Angeles: University of California Press, 1988), pp. 51–66.

21 Sir Robert Cecil, reported in John Harington's *Nugae Antiquae*, 3 vols., ed. Henry Harington (1779; rpt., Georg Olms: Hildesheim, 1968), 2:264.

22 Montrose, "Shaping Fantasies," p. 48.

23 See 5.7.2.1–5:

> Well therefore did the antique world inuent,
> That Iustice was a God of soueraine grace,
> And altars vnto him, and temples lent,
> And heauenly honours in the highest place;
> Calling him great *Osyris*.

24 Roy C. Strong, *Portraits of Queen Elizabeth* (Oxford: Oxford University Press, 1963), p. 41.

25 Here I am heavily indebted to the account of English intervention in the Netherlands, as well as of Spenser's allegorization of it in the Lady Belge episode of Book 5, provided in Norbrook, *Poetry and Politics*, pp. 133–136. Norbrook offers the best discussion I know of Spenser's relation to activist Protestant politics, and particularly his self-alignment with the late 1590s embodiment of that zeal, and the heir apparent of Leicester, the Earl of Essex. Spenser's alignment with Essex also helps account for his increasingly critical perspective on the court, which is seen to be the domain of Essex's regular adversary Lord Burghley.

26 Ibid., p. 136.

27 Ibid., p. 132.
28 Spenser was not the only poet who had his sights on cultivating the favor and patronage of Essex. In a paper presented at the Folger Shakespeare Library in 1991, Alastair Fox reported that in the period 1590–1600, the earl was the recipient of more literary dedications than even the queen herself.
29 See Norbrook, *Poetry and Politics*, p. 143.
30 Goldberg, *James I*, p. 6.
31 Angus Fletcher, *The Prophetic Moment: An Essay on Spenser* (Chicago: University of Chicago Press, 1971), p. 275.
32 Kate M. Warren, ed., *Spenser's "Faerie Queene,"* 6 vols. (London, 1897–1900), cited in A. C. Hamilton, ed., *The Faerie Queene* (Longman: London, 1977), p. 525.
33 H. S. V. Jones, *A Spenser Handbook* (New York: F. S. Crofts and Co., 1947), p. 264.
34 A. C. Hamilton, ed., *The Faerie Queene*, pp. 525–526.
35 In view of my contention throughout this study that the poetic career and the bureaucratic career were never wholly segregated for Spenser, Fletcher's remarks merit citation at length: "Talus cannot act without orders from someone over him, whether his master Artegall, or Britomart, or Prince Arthur. He thus corresponds to any so-called 'instrument of the law,' that is, an order given out by some higher officer of justice to a lower constabulary which then carries it out. Talus also performs the policing function of the law, as Padelford showed, and when he ferrets out criminals, he resembles the police detective whose officious labors are in modern romances of crime undercut and even opposed by the 'private eye.' The robot's relentless and cold rage also suggests the mechanism of bureaucratized justice" (*The Prophetic Moment*, p. 138).
36 Cf. Jean Baudrillard's brief remarks on the secret in *Seduction*, trans. Brian Singer (New York: St. Martin's Press, 1990), pp. 79–80: "The hidden or the repressed has a tendency to manifest itself, whereas the secret does not. It is an initiatory and implosive form: one enters into a secret, but cannot exit. The secret is never revealed, never communicated, never even 'secreted' . . . Whence its strength, the power of an allusive, ritual exchange." While Baudrillard's comments are suggestive, especially in terms of the distinction he posits here between the repressed and the secret, I find that his model does not seem to pay enough attention to *differences* among secrets themselves. Treating all secrets as homologous and parallel, Baudrillard tends to foreclose on the different registers of secrecy that – as we have seen in Spenser's writings – at times can cross each other or even run on distinctively disjunctive paths.
37 The prevailing motif of retreat and retirement in Book 6 is treated in Harry Berger, Jr.'s seminal essay, "A Secret Discipline: *The Faerie Queene*, Book VI," reprinted in *Revisionary Play*, pp. 215–242, especially at pp. 218–219. See also Patricia Parker's insightful discussion of Spenser in *Inescapable Romance: Studies in the Poetics of a Mode* (Princeton: Princeton University Press, 1979), particularly pp. 102–107.
38 Richard Neuse, "Book VI as Conclusion to *The Faerie Queene*," reprinted in *Critical Essays on Spenser from "ELH"* (Baltimore: The Johns Hopkins University Press, 1970), pp. 222–246, at p. 232.

39 Cf. Sissela Bok, *Secrecy: On the Ethics of Concealment and Revelation* (New York: Vintage Books, 1981), pp. 10–14. Bok's account is particularly adept at relating, as well as teasing out the differences between secrecy and privacy: "Privacy and secrecy overlap whenever the efforts at such control rely on hiding. But privacy need not hide; and secrecy hides far more than what is private. A private garden need not be a secret garden; a private life is rarely a secret life. Conversely, secret diplomacy rarely concerns what is private" (p. 11).

40 Kenneth Gross makes a similar point in *Spenserian Poetics: Idolatry, Iconoclasm, and Magic* (Ithaca: Cornell University Press, 1985), p. 231: "For there is a sense in which the transgressive idolatry of the knight and the tenuous, celebratory grace of the shepherd continue not only to attract the sounds or wounds of the Blatant Beast but also to feed on the same ambivalences in desire and language which give that creature life."

41 This pun is noted by Parker in *Inescapable Romance*, p. 110.

42 The wite/wit conjunction also needs to be recognized here, inasmuch as "wit" and blame (satire) go so easily together in Renaissance poetics.

43 For an illuminating account of the theatrical strategies of decorum, duplicity, and deceit in Renaissance courtesy manuals, see Whigham, *Ambition and Privilege*. See also Neuse's acute (and highly critical) discussion of Calidore's "eagerness to maintain the appearance" of courtesy and of his career as an "exercise in 'public relations'" in "Book VI as Conclusion to *The Faerie Queene*," pp. 235–240.

44 Berger, "The Prospect of Imagination," *SEL* 1 (1961): 93–120, at 94.

45 See, for instance, Cain, *Praise in "The Faerie Queene*," p. 155.

46 Cf. Philippa Berry, *Of Chastity and Power*, pp. 153–164: "Once again, female chastity is defined in relation to marriage. Indeed, Spenser's wife Elizabeth has other 'soveraine' attributes formerly identified with Elizabeth the queen ... The scene echoes that in the April eclogue of *The Shepheardes Calender*, written some fifteen years earlier. The difference is, however, that by replacing queen with wife, as the feminine receptacle of numerous virtues, Spenser has the right to enter the circle of graces which also figures the body of his beloved. Now his 'piping' affirms, not his surrender of the powers of the phallus, but rather his phallic control of the female body, as both poet and lover. In this relationship, the male calls the tune."

47 David L. Miller, "Spenser's Vocation, Spenser's Career," p. 219.

48 Cf., for instance, pro. 2.7–9 and 1.6; pro. 1.1 and 1.10.4; pro. 1.2–3 and 12.1–2.

Works cited

Alpers, Paul. "Spenser's Late Pastorals." *ELH* 56 (1989): 797–817.

Altman, Janet. "The Letter Book as a Cultural Institution, 1539–1789: Toward a Cultural History of Published Correspondence in France." *Yale French Studies* 71 (1986): 17–62.

Anderson, Judith H. "'Myn auctor': Spenser's Enabling Fictions and Eumnestes' 'immortal scrine.'" In *Unfolded Tales: Essays on Renaissance Romance*, ed. George M. Logan and Gordon Teskey. Ithaca: Cornell University Press, 1989.

Bacon, Francis. *The Essays.* Ed. John Pitcher. New York: Penguin Books, 1987.

Barker, Francis. *The Tremulous Private Body: Essays on Subjection.* London: Methuen, 1984.

Baudrillard, Jean. *Seduction.* Trans. Brian Singer. New York: St. Martin's Press, 1990.

Beale, Robert. "A Treatise of the Office of a Councellor and Principall Secretarie to her Majestie." In *Mr. Secretary Walsingham*, Conyers Read, q.v.

Bellamy, Elizabeth J. "The Vocative and the Vocational: The Unreadability of Elizabeth in *The Faerie Queene*." *ELH* 54 (1987): 1–30.

Berger, Harry, Jr. "The Prospect of Imagination." *SEL* 1 (1961): 93–120.

Revisionary Play: Studies in the Spenserian Dynamics. Berkeley and Los Angeles: University of California Press, 1988.

Bernard, John D. *Ceremonies of Innocence: Pastoralism in the Poetry of Edmund Spenser.* Cambridge: Cambridge University Press, 1989.

Berry, Herbert and E. K. Timings. "Spenser's Pension." *RES* 11 (1960): 254–259.

Berry, Philippa. *Of Chastity and Power: Elizabethan Literature and the Unmarried Queen.* London: Routledge, 1989.

Black, J. B. *The Reign of Elizabeth: 1558–1603.* 2nd edition. Oxford: The Clarendon Press, 1959.

Blount, Thomas. *The Academie of Eloquence.* London, 1654.

Bok, Sissela. *Secrecy: On the Ethics of Concealment and Revelation.* New York: Vintage Books, 1981.

Bradbrook, Muriel. "No Room at the Top: Spenser's Pursuit of Fame." In *Elizabethan Poetry*, Stratford-upon-Avon Studies 2. London: St. Martin's Press, 1960.

Brady, Ciaran. "Spenser's Irish Crisis: Humanism and Experience in the 1590s." *Past and Present* 111 (1986): 17–49.

Bray, Alan. "Homosexuality and the Signs of Male Friendship in Elizabethan England." *History Workshop Journal* 29 (1990): 1–19.

Homosexuality in Renaissance England. London: Gay Men's Press, 1982.

Brennan, Michael. *Literary Patronage in the English Renaissance: The Pembroke Family*. London: Routledge, 1988.

Brink, Jean R. "Who Fashioned Edmund Spenser? The Textual History of *Complaints*." *SP* 87 (1991): 153–168.

Brooks-Davies, Douglas. *The Mercurian Monarch: Magical Politics from Spenser to Pope*. Manchester: Manchester University Press, 1983.

Bryskett, Lodowick. "A Discourse of Civill Life" (1606). In *The Works of Lodowick Bryskett*, ed. J. H. P. Pafford. London: Gregg International Publishers, 1972.

Cain, Thomas H. *Praise in "The Faerie Queene."* Lincoln, Neb.: University of Nebraska Press, 1978.

Canetti, Elias. *Crowds and Power*. New York: Viking Press, 1966.

Canny, Nicholas B. "Edmund Spenser and the Development of an Anglo-Irish Identity." *Yearbook of English Studies* 13 (1983): 1–19.

   The Elizabethan Conquest of Ireland: A Pattern Established, 1565–1576. New York: Barnes and Noble, 1976.

Carpenter, Frederic Ives. *A Reference Guide to Edmund Spenser*. Chicago: University of Chicago Press, 1923.

Cecil, Robert. "The State and Dignity of a Secretary of State's Place, with the Care and Peril Thereof." *Harleian Miscellany* 5 (1810): 166–168.

Chapman, George. *Andromeda Liberata*. In *The Poems of George Chapman*, ed. Phyllis Brooks Bartlett. New York: Russell and Russell, 1962.

Chartier, Roger, ed. *A History of Private Life*, Vol. 3, *Passions of the Renaissance*. Trans. Arthur Goldhammer. Cambridge, Mass.: Belknap Press, 1989.

Cheney, Donald. "Spenser's Fortieth Birthday and Related Fictions." In *SpStud* 4, ed. Patrick Cullen and Thomas P. Roche, Jr. New York: AMS Press, 1984, pp. 3–31.

Coleman, Christopher and David Starkey, eds. *Revolution Reassessed: Revisions in the History of Tudor Government and Administration*. Oxford: Clarendon Press, 1986.

Conrad, Joseph. *The Heart of Darkness*. Ed. Robert Kimbrough. New York: Norton and Co., 1971.

Crewe, Jonathan. *Hidden Designs: The Critical Profession and Renaissance Literature*. New York and London: Methuen, 1986.

Cross, Claire. *The Royal Supremacy in the Elizabethan Church*. London: George Allen and Unwin, 1969.

Cummings, R. M. *Edmund Spenser: The Critical Heritage*. New York: Barnes and Noble, 1971.

Day, Angel. *Daphnis and Chloe: The Elizabethan Version from Amyot's Translation*. Ed. Joseph Jacobs. London: David Nutt, 1890.

   The English Secretary (1599). Facsimile. Ed. Robert O. Evans. Gainesville: Scholars' Facsimiles and Reprints, 1967.

   The English Secretary. London, 1592.

   The English Secretorie (1586). Facsimile. Menston: Scolar Press, 1967.

Deneef, A. Leigh. *Spenser and the Motives of Metaphor*. Durham N.C.: Duke University Press, 1982.

Derrida, Jacques. *Dissemination*. Trans. Barbara Johnson. Chicago: University of Chicago Press, 1981.

"How to Avoid Speaking: Denials." Trans. Ken Frieden. In *Languages of the Unsayable: The Play of Negativity in Literature and Literary Theory*, ed. Sanford Budick and Wolfgang Iser. New York: Columbia University Press, 1989.

The Post Card: From Socrates to Freud and Beyond. Trans. Alan Bass. Chicago: University of Chicago Press, 1987.

Dowd, Maureen, and Thomas L. Friedman. "The Fabulous Bush and Baker Boys." *New York Times Magazine*, 6 May 1990, pp. 34ff.

Durling, Robert. *The Figure of the Poet in Renaissance Epic*. Cambridge, Mass.: Harvard University Press, 1965.

Elton, G. R. *England Under the Reign of the Tudors*. London: Methuen and Co., 174.

The Tudor Constitution. Cambridge: Cambridge University Press, 1982.

The Tudor Revolution in Government. Cambridge: Cambridge University Press, 1959.

Estienne, Robert. *Dictionariolum Puerorum Tribus Linguis Latina, Anglica, and Gallica* (1552). Facsimile. In *The English Experience*, No. 351. Amsterdam and New York: Da Capo Press, 1971.

Evans, Florence M. Grier. *The Principal Secretary of the State: A Survey of the Office from 1558–1689*. Manchester: Manchester University Press, 1923.

Falkiner, C. L. *Essays Relating to Ireland*. New York: Longman, Green, and Co., 1909.

Faunt, Nicholas. "Nicholas Faunt's Discourse touching the Office of Principal Secretary of Estate, &c." Ed. Charles Hughes. *EHR* 20 (1905): 499–508.

Ferry, Anne. *The "Inward" Language: Sonnets of Wyatt, Sidney, Shakespeare, Donne*. Chicago: University of Chicago Press, 1983.

Fleming, Abraham. *A Panoplie of Epistles, Or, a Looking Glasse for the Unlearned*. London, 1576.

Fletcher, Angus. *The Prophetic Moment: An Essay on Spenser*. Chicago: University of Chicago Press, 1971.

Foucault, Michel. *The History of Sexuality*, Vol. 1, *An Introduction*. Trans. Robert Hurley. New York: Vintage Books, 1980.

"What Is an Author?" Trans. Sherry Simon. In *Language, Counter-Memory, Practice*, ed. Donald F. Bouchard. Ithaca: Cornell University Press, 1977.

Fraunce, Abraham. *The Arcadian Rhetorike*. Ed. Edith Seaton. Oxford: Basil Blackwell, 1950.

Fuller, William. *The History of the Worthies of England*. London, 1662.

Fulwood, William, *The Enimie of Idlenesse*. London, 1568.

The Enemie of Idlenesse. London, 1607.

Fumerton, Patricia. "'Secret' Arts: Elizabethan Miniatures and Sonnets." In *Representing the English Renaissance*, ed. Stephen Greenblatt, q.v.

Gainsford, Thomas. *The Secretaries Studie* (1616). Facsimile. In *The English Experience*, No. 658. Amsterdam: Theatrum Orbis Terrarum, Ltd., 1974.

Goldberg, Jonathan. "Colin to Hobbinol: Spenser's Familiar Letters." In *Displacing Homophobia: Gay Male Perspectives in Literature and Culture*, ed. Ronald R. Butters, John M. Clum, and Michael Moon. Durham, N.C.: Duke University Press, 1989.

Endlesse Worke: Spenser and the Structures of Discourse. Baltimore: The Johns Hopkins University Press, 1980.

James I and the Politics of Literature: Jonson, Shakespeare, Donne, and Their Contemporaries. Baltimore: The Johns Hopkins University Press, 1983.

Voice Terminal Echo: Postmodernism and English Renaissance Texts. New York and London: Methuen, 1986.

Writing Matter: From the Hands of the English Renaissance. Stanford: Stanford University Press, 1990.

Gollancz, Israel. "Spenseriana." *Proceedings of the British Academy 1907–1908*: 101–02.

Graves, Herbert. *The Mutable Glass: Mirror-Imagery in Titles and Texts of the Middle Ages and the English Renaissance.* Trans. Gordon Collier. Cambridge: Cambridge University Press, 1982.

Greenblatt, Stephen, *Renaissance Self-Fashioning: From More to Shakespeare.* Chicago: University of Chicago Press, 1980.

ed., *Representing the English Renaissance.* Berkeley and Los Angeles: University of California Press, 1988.

Shakespearean Negotiations: The Circulation of Social Energy in Renaissance England. Berkeley and Los Angeles: University of California Press, 1988.

Greenlaw, Edwin. "Spenser and the Earl of Leicester." *PMLA* 25 (1910): 535–561.

"*The Shepheardes Calender.*" *PMLA* 26 (1911): 419–451.

"*The Shepheardes Calender* II." *SP* 11 (1913): 3–25.

Gross, Kenneth. *Spenserian Poetics: Idolatry, Iconoclasm, and Magic.* Ithaca: Cornell University Press, 1985.

Guillén, Claudio. "Notes Toward the Study of the Renaissance Letter." In *Renaissance Genres*, ed. Barbara Keifer Lewalski. Cambridge, Mass.: Harvard University Press, 1986.

Haldane, R. A. *The Hidden World.* New York: St. Martin's Press, 1976.

Hamilton, A. C., general editor. *The Spenser Encyclopedia.* Toronto and Buffalo: University of Toronto Press, 1990.

Hamilton, Hans Claude, ed. *Calendar of State Papers, Ireland, 1509–1596.* 5 vols. London: Longman, Green, Longman, and Roberts, 1860–1890.

Harington, John, *Nugae Antiquae.* 3 vols. Ed. Henry Harington (1779). Rpt. Hildesheim: Georg Olms, 1968.

Harvey, Gabriel. *Foure Letters and Certeine Sonnets.* In *The Works of Gabriel Harvey.* 3 vols. Ed. Alexander B. Grosart. London: Hazell, Watson, and Vivey, 1884.

The Letter-Book of Gabriel Harvey, A. D. 1573–1580. Ed. Edward John Long Scott. London: Camden Society, 1884.

Health to the Gentlemanly Profession of Seruingmen. London, 1598.

Helgerson, Richard. *The Elizabethan Prodigals.* Berkeley and Los Angeles: University of California Press, 1976.

Self-Crowned Laureates: Spenser, Jonson, Milton, and the Literary System. Berkeley and Los Angeles: University of California Press, 1983.

Henley, Pauline. *Spenser in Ireland.* Dublin and Cork: Cork University Press, 1928.

Hill, John, *The Young Secretary's Guide.* London, 1699.

Hoffman, Nancy Jo. *Spenser's Pastorals: "The Shepheardes Calender" and "Colin Clout."* Baltimore: The Johns Hopkins University Press, 1977.

Hornbeak, Katherine Gee. "The Complete Letter-Writer in English, 1568–1800." *Smith College Studies in Modern Languages* 15 (1934): i–xii, 1–150.

Hurault, André, Sieur de Maisse. *Journal* (1597). Trans. and ed. G. B. Harrison and R. A. Jones. London: Nonesuch Press, 1931.

Jenkins, Raymond. "Spenser and the Clerkship in Munster." *PMLA* 47 (1932): 109–121.

"Spenser: The Uncertain Years 1584–1589." *PMLA* 53 (1938): 350–362.

"Spenser with Lord Grey." *PMLA* 52 (1937): 338–353.

Jenkinson, Hilary. "Elizabethan Handwriting: A Preliminary Sketch." *The Library*, 4th series, 3 (1922): 1–35.

Johnson, Paul. *Elizabeth I: A Study in Power and Intellect*. London: Weidenfeld and Nicolson, 1974.

Jones, H. S. V. *A Spenser Handbook*. New York: Crofts and Co., 1947.

Jonson, Ben. *Complete Plays of Ben Jonson*. 4 vols. Ed. G. A. Wilkes. Oxford: Clarendon Press, 1981.

Judson, Alexander Corbin. "A Biographical Sketch of John Young, Bishop of Rochester, with Emphasis on his Relations with Edmund Spenser." *Indiana University Studies* 21 (1934): 3–41.

Krier, Theresa M. *Gazing on Secret Sights: Spenser, Classical Imitation, and the Decorums of Vision*. Ithaca and London: Cornell University Press, 1990.

Lewis, C. S. *The Allegory of Love*. Oxford: Oxford University Press, 1936.

English Literature in the Sixteenth Century Excluding Drama. Oxford: Oxford University Press, 1954.

Long, Percy. "Spenser and the Bishop of Rochester." *PMLA* 31 (1916): 713–735.

Lupton, Julia Reinhard. "Home-Making in Ireland: Virgil's Eclogue I and Book VI of *The Faerie Queene*." In *SpStud* 7, ed. Patrick Cullen and Thomas P. Roche, Jr. New York: AMS Press, 1990, pp. 119–145.

MacCaffrey, Wallace T. *Queen Elizabeth and the Making of Policy, 1572–1588*. Princeton: Princeton University Press, 1981.

McCanles, Michael. "*The Shepheardes Calender* as Document and Monument." *SEL* 22 (1982): 5–19.

McLane, Paul E. *Spenser's Shepheardes Calender: A Study in Elizabethan Allegory*. Notre Dame: University of Notre Dame Press, 1961.

Marcus, Leah S. *Puzzling Shakespeare: Local Reading and Its Discontents*. Berkeley and Los Angeles: University of California Press, 1988.

Markham Gervase. *Conceyted Letters, Newly Layde Open*. London, 1618.

May, Steven W. *The Elizabethan Courtier Poets: Their Poems and Their Contexts*. Columbia and London: University of Missouri Press, 1991.

Middleton, Thomas. *The Black Book*. In *The Works of Thomas Middleton*. 8 vols. Ed. A. H. Bullen. London: John C. Nimmo, 1886.

Miller, D. A. *The Novel and the Police*. Berkeley and Los Angeles: University of California Press, 1988.

Miller, David Lee. *The Poem's Two Bodies: The Poetics of the 1590 "Faerie Queene."* Princeton: Princeton University Press, 1988.

"Spenser's Vocation, Spenser's Career." *ELH* 50 (1983): 197–230.

Milton, John. *The Complete Poems and Major Prose*. Ed. Merritt Y. Hughes. New York: Macmillan, Rpt. 1989.

Montaigne. *The Complete Essays of Montaigne*. Trans. and ed. Donald M. Frame. Stanford: Stanford University Press, 1965.

Montrose, Louis Adrian. "Celebration and Insinuation: Sir Philip Sidney and the Motives of Elizabethan Courtship." *Elizabethan Drama* 8 (1977): 3–35.

"'Eliza, Queene of shepheardes,' and the Pastoral of Power." *ELR* 10 (1980): 153–182.

"The Elizabethan Subject and the Spenserian Text." In *Literary Theory/Renaissance Texts*, ed. Patricia Parker and David Quint. Baltimore: The Johns Hopkins University Press, 1985.

"Of Gentlemen and Shepherds: The Politics of Elizabethan Pastoral Form." *ELH* 50 (1983): 415–459.

"'The perfecte paterne of a Poete': The Poetics of Courtship in *The Shepheardes Calender*." *TSLL* 21 (1979): 34–67.

"'Shaping Fantasies': Figurations of Gender and Power in Elizabethan Culture." In *Representing the English Renaissance*, ed. Stephen Greenblatt, q.v.

Mounts, Charles. "Spenser and the Countess of Leicester." *ELH* 19 (1952): 191–202.

Mulcaster, Richard. *Positions*. Ed. Robert Herbert Quick. London: Longman, Green, and Co., 1888.

Nashe, Thomas. *The Anatomie of Absurditie*. In *Elizabethan Critical Essays*, ed. G. Gregory Smith, q.v.

Strange Newes. In *The Works of Thomas Nashe*. 5 vols. Ed. R. B. McKerrow. London: Sidgwick and Johnson, 1904–1910.

Naunton, Robert. *Fragmenta Regalia*. Ed. John S. Cervoski. Washington, D.C.: The Folger Shakespeare Library, 1985.

Neale, J. E. *Elizabeth I and Her Parliaments, 1559–1581*. London: Jonathan Cape, 1965.

Queen Elizabeth. London: Jonathan Cape, 1954.

Neuse, Richard. "Book VI as Conclusion to *The Faerie Queene*." In *Critical Essays on Spenser from "ELH"*. Baltimore: The Johns Hopkins University Press, 1970.

Norbrook, David. *Poetry and Politics in the English Renaissance*. London: Routledge and Kegan Paul, 1984.

Parker, Patricia A. *Inescapable Romance: Studies in a Poetic Mode*. Princeton: Princeton University Press, 1979.

Patterson, Annabel M. "Re-Opening the Green Cabinet: Clement Marot and Edmund Spenser." *ELR* 16 (1986): 44–70.

Plomer, Henry. "Edmund Spenser's Handwriting." *MP* 21 (1923–1924): 201–207.

and T. P. Cross, eds. *The Life and Correspondence of Lodowick Bryskett*. Chicago: University of Chicago Press, 1927.

Puget de la Serre, Jean. *The Secretary in Fashion: or a compendious and refined way of expression in all manner of letters*. Trans. John Massinger. London, 1658.

Puttenham, George. *The Arte of English Poesie* (1589). Facsimile. Ed. Baxter Hathaway. Kent, Ohio: Kent State University Press, 1970.

Ralegh, Walter. *The Works of Sir Walter Ralegh Kt*. 8 vols. No editor. Oxford: Oxford University Press, 1829.

Ranum, Orest. "The Refuges of Intimacy." In *A History of Private Life*, Vol. 3, *Passions of the Renaissance*, Roger Chartier, ed., q.v.

Read, Conyers. *Mr Secretary Cecil and Queen Elizabeth*. New York: Alfred A. Knopf, 1955.

Mr Secretary Walsingham and the Policy of Queen Elizabeth. 3 vols. Oxford: Oxford University Press, 1925.

Robertson, Jean. *The Art of Letter Writing: An Essay on Handbooks Published in England during the Sixteenth and Seventeenth Centuries*. London: University of Liverpool Press, 1942.

Rosenberg, Eleanor. *Leicester: Patron of Letters*. New York: Columbia University Press, 1955.

Saenger, Paul. "Silent Reading: Its Impact on Late Medieval Script and Society." *Viator* 13 (1982): 367–414.

Sánchez-Eppler, Benigno. "The Pen That Wields the Voice That Wills: Secretaries and Letter Writing in Antonio de Torquemada's *Manual De Escribientes*." *Neophilogus* 70 (1986): 528–538.

Sansovino, Francesco. *Del Secretario*. Venice, 1565.

Saunders, J. W. "The Stigma of Print: A Note on the Social Bases of Tudor Poetry." *Essays in Criticism* 1 (1951): 139–164.

Sedgwick, Eve Kosofsky. *Epistemology of the Closet*. Berkeley and Los Angeles: University of California Press, 1990.

Shakespeare, William. *The Riverside Shakespeare*. Ed. G. Blakemore Evans, *et al.* Boston: Houghton Mifflin Co., 1974.

Shepherd, Simon. *Spenser*. Harvester New Readings. Atlantic Highlands, N.J.: Humanities Press International, 1989.

Sidney, Philip. *An Apology for Poetry*. Ed. Forrest G. Robinson. Indianapolis: Bobbs-Merrill, 1970.

Simmel, Georg. *The Sociology of Georg Simmel*. Trans. and ed. Kurt H. Wolff. Glencoe, Ill.: The Free Press, 1950.

Smith, Alan G. R. *Servant of the Cecils: The Life of Sir Michael Hickes, 1543–1612*. London: Jonathan Cape, 1977.

Smith, Bruce R. *Homosexual Desire in Shakespeare's England: A Cultural Poetics*. Chicago: University of Chicago Press, 1991.

Smith, G. Gregory, ed. *Elizabethan Critical Essays*. 2 vols. Oxford: Oxford University Press, 1904, rpt. 1959.

Smith, Hallett. *Elizabethan Poetry*. Cambridge, Mass.: Harvard University Press, 1964.

Spenser, Edmund. *The Faerie Queene*. Ed. A. C. Hamilton. London: Longman Press, 1977.

The Poetical Works of Edmund Spenser. Ed. J. C. Smith and E. De Selincourt. Oxford and New York: Oxford University Press, 1912.

The Works of Edmund Spenser: A Variorum Edition. 11 vols. Ed. Edwin Greenlaw, *et al.* Baltimore: The Johns Hopkins University Press, 1932–1957.

The Yale Edition of the Shorter Poems of Edmund Spenser. Ed. William A. Oram *et al.* New Haven: Yale University Press, 1989.

Starobinski, Jean. *Words upon Words: The Anagrams of Ferdinand de Saussure*. Trans. Olivia Emmet. New Haven: Yale University Press, 1979.

Stein, Harold. *Studies in Spenser's "Complaints."* New York: Columbia University Press, 1934.

Stone, Lawrence. *The Crisis of the Aristocracy: 1558–1641.* Abridged edition. Oxford: Oxford University Press, 1967.

Strong, Roy C. *Portraits of Queen Elizabeth.* Oxford: Oxford University Press, 1963.

Tylus, Jane. "Spenser, Virgil, and the Politics of Poetic Labor." *ELH* 55 (1986): 53–77.

Vecchi, Linda. "Spenser's *Complaints*: Is the Whole Equal to the Sum of Its Parts?" *Spenser at Kalamazoo* (1984): 127–138.

Vickers, Brian, ed. *Shakespeare: The Critical Heritage.* 2 vols. London: Routledge and Kegan Paul, 1974.

Waldman, Milton. *Elizabeth and Leicester.* Boston: Houghton and Mifflin, 1945.

Wallace, Malcolm William. *The Life of Sir Philip Sidney.* Cambridge: Cambridge University Press, 1915.

Webbe, William. *A Discourse of English Poesie.* In *Elizabethan Critical Essays*, G. Gregory Smith ed., q.v.

Weever, John. *Epigrammes.* Facsimile. In *John Weever*, ed. E. A. J. Honigmann. Manchester: Manchester University Press, 1987.

Whigham, Frank. *Ambition and Privilege: The Social Tropes of Elizabethan Courtesy Theory.* Berkeley and Los Angeles: University of California Press, 1984.

Williams, Raymond. *Keywords.* New York: Oxford University Press, 1985.

Wright, Louis B. *Middle-Class Culture in Elizabethan England.* Ithaca: Cornell University Press, 1935.

Index